IT and the Shaping of New Social Order

IT and the Shaping of New Social Order

Exploring Possibilities and Challenges in the Digital Age

Mun Cho Kim

KOREA
UNIVERSITY
PRESS

Korea University Press
145, Anam-ro, Seongbuk-gu, Seoul, 02841 Republic of Korea

ISBN: 978-89-7641-829-6 93330

Printed in Republic of Korea

Preface

This book seeks to examine IT-driven social transformation over the past four decades and gain the insight into the future prospect of "Digital Society." It adapts SST(Social Studies of Technology) framework that presupposes the reciprocal interface between technology and society.

Information society has brought out various spectacular technological and social innovations. Breakthroughs in information processing, storage and transmission have led to the application of IT in all corners of society. We tend to experience social upheaval of such magnitude as to declare that we are entering a new civilization stage. Especially, the convergence of information and communication technologies and the inflow of artificial intelligence amplify the magnitude and scope of social transformation and urges us to develop more extensive and sophisticated perspective for identifying 'the new.'

Numerous research has explored the consequences of digital revolution. Nevertheless, they are predominantly biased towards utopian technological determinism, failing to grasp the core of complex dynamics. We need to investigate the inter-systemic mechanisms that arise from the interactions between technology and society.

Korea is known as one of the leading countries of informatization in the world. Despite abundant analyses on social consequences of information revolution, scant attention has been paid to the underlying mechanisms of information society. What I aim in this volume is to recast current 'informational phenomena' considering more comprehensive theoretical framework centering on the idea of techno-social formation. In this techno-social formation, the dualism of technology and society collapse in the same immanent plane. This collapse of representation is the crucial element that convinces the relevance of SST approaching to ongoing information society.

With the spread of IT-based communication, individuals as well as groups and organizations function as nodes of social network. Even cities and nations are reduced to a sub part of a complex global network. Accordingly, seemingly independent behaviors of a node or element should be connectedly or relationally recognized. Such a composite societal order characterized by heterogeneous, infinite nodes and connections can be captured by the notion of 'heterotopic society,' that may be the contemporaneous version of what Michel Foucault called 'heterotopia' in 1967.

The heterotopic society is expected to move toward a new stage by adopting new technologies that meet emerging societal needs. Seen from SST perspective, the heterotopic society will particularly require advanced technologies that are able to fulfill not only the demand of proliferation, but also additional demands of connectivity, convergence and transgression. Embedded within these new technologies, the society will shift to a higher stage of complexity. The emerging social order stemming from the mutual interactions can be named as 'technosocial formation.'

The whole volume consists of preface, an introductory chapter, five main sections with 2 chapters each and a final concluding chapter. Introductory chapter addresses central dimensions of emerging IT-based society that has risen rapidly to displace the older industrial society. Section I deals with the typical structural problematics raised by the social diffusion of IT. Section II discusses subsequent cultural and religious re-arrangements witnessed in the process of informatization. Section III investigates intrapersonal aspects of self and identity in the digital age. In Section IV, focusing on two key issues of surveillance and risks, present and future society are critically reexamined. In Section V, broader discussions on new media and society are followed. Finally, the prospect of 'Digital Society' is forecasted under the theme of 'convergence civilization' in the closing chapter.

Given the discussion, three main thrusts are expected to come out. First, Information Revolution is not just a technological revolution. It should be regarded as an outcome of the interplay between technology and society. Second, changing social environment such as structural transitions may not be the end of the social informatization. Rather, changes in cultural, mental and institutional aspects are not less important than overt, external ones since they contribute more to activate the interface of technological system and social system. Finally, the information society cannot be taken as an independent civilization unit. Instead, the information society is considered as a precursor of the forthcoming convergence civilization or a civilization of transient category at best, that bridges the industrial civilization and the convergence civilization to come.

This work was supported by the National Research Foundation of Korea Grant funded by the Korean Government(NRF-2017S1A3A2066149). Earlier version of the chapters have appeared as follows: 'Surveillance Technology, Privacy and Social Control,' International Sociology 19(2), (2004): 193-213; 'Online Buddhist Community: An Alternative Religious Organization in the Information Age.' in M. Hojsgaard and M. Warburg (eds), Religion and Cyberspace, (2005), London, Routledge: 138-148; 'Dialectics of Risk, Security and Surveillance in a High-Tech Society,' Society and Theory 19(2), (2011): 373-392. I would like to thank the publishers for permission to reprint here.

I wish to express my sincere appreciation of the help and support I have received throughout writing of this book. In the first place, I owe thanks to my scholarly colleagues, Professor David Lyon, Jong-Kil Kim, Seoung-Ho Ryu, Su-Ho Park, Hye-Soo Lee and Ji-Yeon Jeong and the folks of Social Science Korea Research Project on Convergent Social Integration, who offered valuable inspiration, suggestion, material and criticism during the various stages of its preparation, The staff members of Korea University Press deserve my gratitude for the production of this volume as well. And finally, I am grateful than ever to my family for their love, support and faith.

Contents

Figures and Tables

Figures

Tables

Chapter 1

Introduction

The Rise of New Technological Social Formation

I. Informational Turn Everywhere

A new social formation is emerging with the informational turn, a new great transformation following agricultural and industrial revolution. It is totally different from traditional industrial society that has continued for about two centuries since the first industrial revolution in the late 18th century.

While some scholars initiated to analyze and interpret characteristics of the information society from creative standpoints (Bell, 1973; Masuda, 1980; Lyon, 1988; Webster, 1995; Poster, 1995), Maunel Castells sharpened understanding of the society by examining it from a civilization perspective in his trilogy The Information Age: Economy, Society and Culture (1996-1998).

One of the most conspicuous characteristics of the information society is a shift in the time-space concept, which long remained unchanged from ancient to modern period. Discussing the formation of new time-space concept, Castells stressed the feature of the network society by differentiating what he called 'global economy' from what world system theorists called "world economy.'

> The information economy is global. A global economy is historically new reality, distinct from a world economy. A world economy, that is an economy in which capital accumulation proceeds throughout the world, has existed in the West at least since the sixteenth century, as Fernand Braudel and Immanuel Wallerstein have taught us. A global economy is something different: it is an economy with the capacity to work as a unit in a real time on a planetary scale. While the capitalist mode of production

> is characterized by its relentless expansion, always trying to overcome limits of time and space, it is only in the late twentieth century that the world economy was able to become truly global on the basis of the new infrastructure provided by information and communication technologies. This globality concerns the core processes and elements of the economic system (Castells, 1996: 92-93).

In the global network economy, everything relates to each other both vertically and horizontally. Production procedures, equipment, goods and services are all quickly becoming useless, making long-term ownership more disadvantageous than short-term connectivity. With the rise of the network society, the system of access is replacing that of possession, which has long defined living conditions, dominated political discourse and decided individual statuses. As described by a modified Cartesian 'cogito' dictum "I connect, therefore I exist," the age of access is likely to undergo significant changes in various aspects from economic transactions and political participation to highly private aspects of everyday lives. Here in this society, the gap between connected and not-connected is wider than the chasm between haves and have-nots (Rifkin, 2000).

II. Societal Impacts of IT

While societal impacts of IT can be analyzed in various ways, considering major conceptual aspects of the society which manifest technological influence could serve as the first course of action. Extrovert or centrifugal effects of technology on the society can be analyzed largely in structural, institutional, cultural and mental aspects. More specifically, the structure and mentality can represent macro and micro aspects, and the institution and culture, instrumental and expressive aspects respectively. Also, structure-institution and culture-mentality may represent objective and subjective aspects, and structure-culture and institution-mentality, contextual and textual aspects. Based on such classification scheme, types and characteristics of the IT-based society can be illustrated in (Figure 1-1).

1. Structural Impact: Network Society

Structural impact of IT forms the material basis of network society, where its constitutive elements are closely connected with each other. An individual element such as a point or a node is characterized by where it is placed in a network, rather than by its independent properties (Barabasi, 2002; Van Dijck, 2013). With the spread of new communication media, connectivity tends to determine links between individual elements. As a result, the society is

Figure 1-1 **Societal Impact of IT**

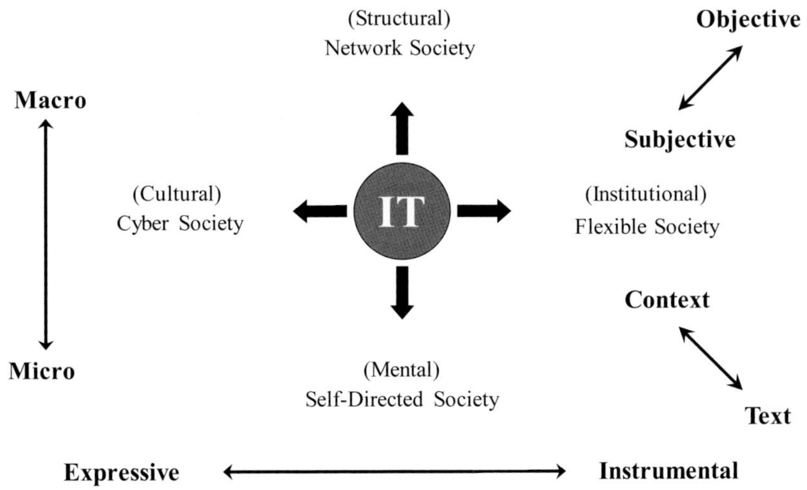

changing from a node-centered society to a link-centered one, so much as a current prevalent buzzword "Link or die."

Elements of the network society are not linked in a fixed manner. Rather, they are loosely connected and exchange repercussions with each other, making the society fluid. Accordingly, their perception of a place to live in radically changes. They perceive it not as the "space of stay", but as the "space of flow", generating nomadic situation where disembeddedness takes place routinely (Harvey, 1989; Castells, 1989).

2. Institutional Impact: Flexible Society

Increasing connectivity does not apply only to structural relations among elements. It also raises interaction density, weakening existing institutional boundaries and facilitating exchanges between institutional spheres. Epitomized by implosion and convergence, such process can help the institutional spheres, which have so far been considered oppositional components, coexist harmoniously (Baudrillard, 1983). It can be recognizable in such compositional words as edutainment, prosumer, faction, culduct, cyborg.

As a result, social heterogeneity rises, creating pluralist and multicultural conditions in which various ideas, norms and values exist together. However, increasing opportunities or choices do not always guarantee positive effects. Sometimes they may aggravate social indeterminacy and weaken social responsibilities or civic morality (Robin and Webster, 1999).

3. Cultural Impact: Cyber Society

In a virtual space where advanced information and communication technology function as a medium, intangible symbols tend to wield their power. Cyber society is formed when such phenomenon spreads even to offline arena and behavior patterns on cyberspace prevail in the entire society (Jones, 1997). This is evidenced by the fact that impression management, putting more value on outward appearance than on substance, or emotional work is more prevalent than ever in the society (Goffman, 1959; Hochschild, 1983).

4. Mental Impact: Self-Directed Society

A self-directed person, in contrast to an other-directed person described by David Riesman, is born in a highly individualized society that requires individuals to plan their lives on their own. This is particularly true in Western industrialized countries which have achieved a certain level of material well-being.

Differentiating this trend from individualization of the 17-18th century modern Western society, Ulrich Beck and Elisabeth Beck-Gernsheim (2002) contend that today's secondary individualization maximizes personal autonomy or spontaneity, making everything, such as marriage, divorce, child-bearing and jobs, something to choose subjectively. Such internal changes tend to lead to identity claims, eventually creating new forms of social conflicts called recognition struggles (Bauman, 2001; Honneth, 2001).

III. Advent of Heterotopic Society

1. IT and Infrastructural Transformation of Society

With the spread of computer-mediated communications, there has been a research boom to figure out the social meanings of IT diffusion. Concerned about a possible loss of communities, many researchers expected an emergence of net communities established through electronic communications media (Rheingold, 1993b; Smith and Kollock, 1999). Nevertheless, they were predominantly biased towards utopian technological determinism, failing to grasp the core of complicated dynamics.

To overcome such limitations, it is necessary to examine, based upon the principles of interpenetration underlying transformations of societal order that come from interactions between technological system and social system (see Münch, 1984). More specifically, consideration should be given to (1) ubiquity and virtuality of the social environment that stem from changing social structure and culture; (2) multiplicity and selectivity of social organizations that are related to social structure and institutions; (3) superficiality and ephemerality of social relations; (4) social psychology characterized by self-identity and self-actualization. Only through considerations of these infrastructural social transformations mentioned above, it would be possible to decipher the nature of new social order.

1) Social Environment: Ubiquity and Virtuality

In a global network era in which both integration and disintegration occur continuously, information can flow anywhere. A digital network not only guarantees interaction between providers and receivers of information but also offers connectivity space that links network users with each other. Such networking is facilitated with the influx of broadband technology which makes it much easier to deal with massive information (Gilder, 2002). Networking individuals formulate a new relationship or establish a virtual network with others. The very logic that IT developments reorganize relations comes from this reinforced networking function.

Meanwhile, reality principle is to be gradually replaced by fantasy principle in a virtual world. Individuals can easily indulge in metamorphic fantasy in such free-associational virtual world. Here, the past, present and future get intertwined with each other, life is cheerful rather than solemn, and it is always fluid without any rigid rules. Therefore, individuals are apt to enjoy as much esoteric imagination or experience as possible (Rifkin, 2000).

In addition, Sherry Turkle (1995) argues that multiple personality is found in the youths who spend much time in a virtual world. Tiny pieces of multiple selves they use to mingle with others in the network of a virtual world often destroy their unitary self-image. Also, in multiple virtual worlds they contact, they play different roles in various situations, making their lives increasingly decentered and thereby reinforcing virtual networking. Therefore, the stable and integrated self-concept of the past is replaced by various competing mutable selves.

Moreover, ubiquity and virtuality of the social environment trigger another problem: intervention of commercialized interests in the process of establishing individual consciousness. Market experts, advertisers or cultural administrators snatch entrance fees at gateways, showing accessibility to new cultural products and experience. Individual mental worlds are linked to the outside and information communication technology that affects every nook and corner of the nervous system with its insatiable commercial interests (Lash and Urry, 1994).

2) Social Organization: Multiplicity and Selectivity

Themes of "multiple selection society" or "paradox of choice" provide a clue to understand a changing organizational aspect of life (Pongs, 1999; Schwartz, 2004). No doubt a new type of society with higher multiplicity and selectivity plays an effective role in enhancing individual freedom or capacity. However, brainwashed into believing that they should make progress, the people may fail to narrow the gap between possible state and real state and end up with the feeling of great frustration. They are highly likely to suffer from anxiety, doubt and pressure as they unsuccessfully struggle to achieve goals or to catch up with others. They are likely to reach the complexity system that are described by Niklas Luhmann (1995[1984]) as "Nothing is more certain than uncertainty."

The rising multiplicity and selectivity of the social system helps them get whatever they want at any time, while raising the prospect of the uncertain future at the same time. Uncertainty of the future mainly comes from ignorance or helplessness and protecting the despairing class may constitute an urgent social agenda to be resolved in the age of high uncertainty. Even more, a weakening traditional familial safety net will worsen such problem, requiring more responsibilities of individual choices or decisions.

3) Social Relations: Superficiality and Ephemerality

Richard Sennett provides, in his book The Corrosion of Character, a keen insight into the weakening social relations in the condition of fierce competition. The main theme of the book is that as the flexibility and risks increase in institutional spheres, dedication to duties, loyalty to the organization and trust between coworkers are all disappearing. Paradoxically, strong solidarity between members is vanishing in a modern organization where teamwork and group culture are emphasized so much (Sennett, 1998).

Organizational flexibility removes the need for interests in and attachment to work and fellow workers. That is because networking is becoming more important than focusing on work itself. This is true of both those who have high work ethic and those who don't. Therefore, flexibility reduces dedication to the organization. When dissatisfied with the job, one would not struggle to remain in the workplace and instead he or she is more likely to quit. That is, adjusting to a new job has become more important than accumulating job experience.

Therefore, a change itself is accepted as valuable, while deferring it is a sign of failure. Also, short-term projects and contracts, flexible work and rising turnover rates remove an opportunity to form an enduring interpersonal association which is essential to cultivating informal trust. As a result, dedication, royalty, responsibility, trust and friendship are all devaluated (Sennett, 1998). It is true that such a sarcastic view on the utopian prospect for virtual communities could trigger many counterarguments. But it is Sennett who offers us a typical socioscape to watch the ephemeral aspect of current social relations.

Meanwhile, superficiality of social relations basically seems to stem from modernization. That is because the modernization process is closely associated with the decline of communal tie and the rise of utilitarian personal interaction. Thus, modernization is the process in which a social system expands itself into the state of high ambiguity.

Calling this loosening link between communal and personal life "de-socialization," Carole Stone (2000) worries about a possible collapse of social bonds and relations. However, superficiality of social relations can sometimes be regarded as a positive indication turning a "closed relationship" into an "open one," rather than as a negative sign of de-socialization (Putnam, 2000).

4) Social Psychology: Self-Identity, Self-Actualization

Individualization in a postmodern society can be defined as a process where historically defined forms of society are disappearing, and traditional rituals, behavioral norms and pragmatic knowledge are losing their social salience. It is considered as active individual efforts to build his(her) own personal biography.

While social relations in a traditional society are not conventionally established by individual autonomous decisions and rather reflected sociality of a community, those in a late modern condition come from fluidity, local communication, multilateral social contacts and autonomous management. In other words, they are a product of not defensive but offensive identity. Individuals can secure a stronger social mastery over their lives, by determinedly cutting chains of the past and overcoming unfair interventions to transform their future actively (Touraine, 1988).

During the late modern individualization process, individuals are required to cultivate and maintain new relations to set up their lives in an active manner. They therefore should expand and renew social contacts and attach high value to them. Explaining the concept of "life politics" aimed at escaping rigid tradition or hierarchical dominance, Antony Giddens (1991) stresses the significance of individual decision-making in the age of high modernity. Because life politics is based on autonomous decision-making that influences self-identity, he argues, self-identity is a result of individual reflection.

2. The Making of New Social Order

In the radically changing environment, autonomous individual decision tends to be despised as outdated, whereas online group-think in an endlessly connected network will emerge as a dominant force. As autonomy is replaced with immediate social interactions, individuals come to live in a complicated interdependent order established by networks of constantly changing relationships (Wellman et. al., 1996).

In fact, people form more various social relations than ever before. In our ever-increasing global net world, individuals function as just one node of a social network, and this is also true of companies and social organizations. Even citizens and nations are reduced to one element of a complicated international cooperation community network. Accordingly, independent behaviors of a disconnected node or element are socially and globally criticized. Such a composite societal order basically characterized by heterogeneous, infinite nodes and connections come down to the notion "heterotopic society,"(Figure 1-2) as originally suggested by M. Foucault (see Faubion, 1999).

Figure 1-2 **Advent of Heterotopic Society**

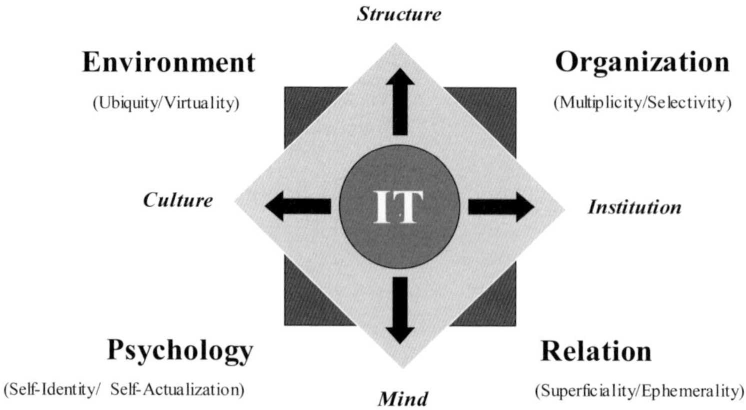

Information communication forms a technological basis that makes it possible to take a cognitive leap from one idea to another, to get a simultaneous grasp of paratactic issues, to have a multilineal conception which presupposes a dramatic trajectory of an event and to develop a holistic thinking that makes seemingly unorganized messages an integrated version. Therefore, the heterotopic society has peculiar properties that go far beyond the epistemological horizon of a lineal world-view. To fully understand these characteristics, an alternative perspective is necessary from which a very complicated social order can be grasped.

IV. Forecasting the Dynamics of Technological Society

1. Dialectic of Technology and Society

When the conceptual layers of the heterotopic society marked by the coexistence of heterogeneous elements are classified into the four categories of ontology, relationship, quality and topology, their properties can be identified as follows (Table 1-1).

Table 1-1 **Nature of Heterotopic Society**

Ontology	Heterogeneity: Coexistence of Different Constituents
Relationship	Hiatus: Intercourse of Heterogeneous Elements
Quality	Hybrid: Emergence of New Synthetic Properties
Topology	Phase Transition: Transformation of the State

The heterotopic society is expected to move toward a new stage by using technology that satisfies its intrinsic desires. Based on a social constructivist view, the heterotopic society will particularly require BT, IT, NT and ST, the advanced technologies that could immediately fulfill not only the demand of proliferation as various elements want to mingle to step forward, but also the demand of connectivity, convergence and transgression as well. Being embedded with these new technologies, the society will move toward a higher stage of complexity. The emerging social order coming from this reciprocal process is the product of dialectic interplay between technological system and social system and can be named as "neo-technosocial formation (Figure 1-3).

Figure 1-3 **Shaping of Neo-Technosocial Formation (NTSF)**

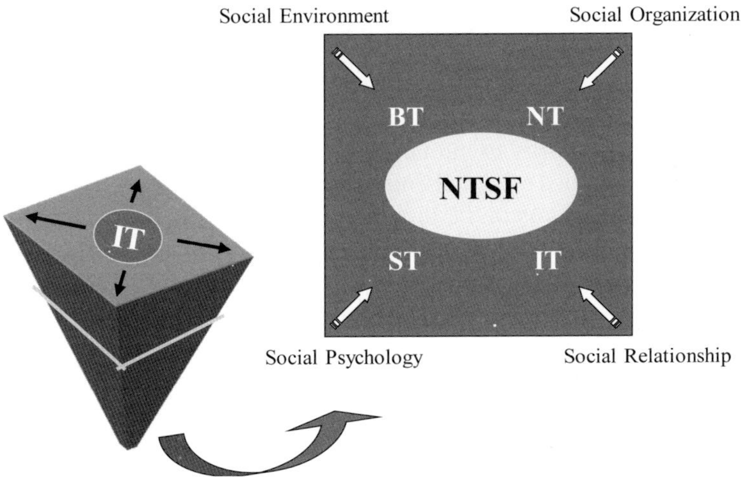

2. Prospect of Subsequent Transformations

This neo-technosocial formation, the extension of its primitive form of heterotopic society, has a series of following characteristics. First, it is marked by disequilibrium which could be analogized from the dictums “selection and concentration” or “tendency of 20:80 society.” Second, it has dynamism that is detectable from such words as “restructuring or structural innovation,” Third, it holds non-linearity that could be figured out from exponential growth model like “Moore's principles.” Fourth, the neo-technosocial formation contains self-organization which is found in new organizational principles such as “learning organization.” Finally, it has autopoiesis that is decipherable from the emphases on “originality” or “creativity.”

The neo-technosocial formation is a typical dissipative system that uses self-organizing power to promote creative development in a meta-stable state far different from an equilibrium one. It has the structure of a grid society with a complicatedly intertwined warp and woof, or the shape of a “rhizome society” which expands in more random, not predetermined way. Also, it is a “fluid society” where information circulates freely. Equipped with all these properties, the neo-technosocial formation can be defined as a “supra-open system of great complexity.”

V. Coda

As the new technologies of BT, IT, NT and ST add complexity and dynamism to the existing information society, the technosocial formation will encounter two serious problems in its development process. The first is that the society mat fall into a complexity trap. Order does not automatically come out of chaos. Instead, chaos can be aggravated, possibly leading to an irrecoverable catastrophe. The second is that a substantive trap may come out as a new social problem. Vulnerability to humanistic, ethical and aesthetic issues, quite different from the issues of social engineering, could get worse. To actively respond to these problems in the high-tech society of the future, it is necessary to replace “modern knowledge paradigm” based on a mechanical world view with “late modern wisdom paradigm,” which is more suitable for an increasingly complicated new social environment.

Section I

Structural Problematics

Chapter 2

From Hierarchy to Boundary

IT-based Social Inequality

Despite a persistent aspiration for egalitarian society, social inequality has long been a hot issue throughout human history. There has been a myriad of studies regarding causes, processes and effects of social inequality, while intense disputes and contentions among countless academic approaches have constantly existed. Regardless of different perspectives and methodologies, there remains one general primary proposition that "social inequality is a consequence of the unique characteristics or constitution of a given society." Just as inequalities of a traditional society are different from those of an industrial civilization, social disparities of the information age fundamentally differ from those of an era before Information Revolution.

In The Coming of Post-Industrial Society, Daniel Bell(1973) put forward "knowledge theory of value," a counter-argument against Karl Marx's "labor theory of value." In information society, it is highly likely that a system of social inequality will largely depend on the distribution of knowledge and information, which have risen to prominence as one of the most important socioeconomic resources. This is because the theory of digital divide based on accessibility of knowledge and information has become a dominant argument regarding social inequality in the information age. Yet, the conventional theory of digital divide has failed to capture a proper authority equal to the class theory of industrial society, because it only rested on the theory of information society, an optimistic view led by technological determinism, and placed too much emphasis on accessibility to informational media or facilities.

Today's society is deemed on a grand transition following Agricultural Revolution and Industrial Revolution, in that advanced information technology are not only establishing a new social order in diverse fields of social activities including economy, politics, education and culture, but they also create different social consciousness and personalities. In search of a theoretical framework to better understand social inequalities of the information civilization, this chapter attempts to focus on the following issues.

(1) Examining the validity of class theory derived from modern industrial society within a contemporary context, where societalization of advanced ICTs is widely facilitated.
(2) Expanding the idea of the existing theory of digital divide now mostly confined to the accessibility of information, to reconstruct a general theory that can explain diverse aspects of current phenomena of social inequality.
(3) Discussing the nature of social inequality unique to the 21st century contest and proposing an alternative paradigm to better explain it.

I. Problems of Social Inequality

By now, the problems of social inequality exhibit a disparity between theory and reality because class inequality is getting more consolidated and institutionalized while discourses regarding the issue are on the decline.

Despite the enhanced levels of living and increasing social mobility, a structural and perceptional gap concerning social inequality is not showing any sign of improvement. Since a system of inequality in modern society conventionally based on "the happiness of the few at the cost of the sacrifice of the many" is exhibited either by pyramid or diamond-shaped class structure, the size of middle class has been considered a crucial factor in apprehending the state of social inequality.

As rapid economic growth has increased employment opportunities and mass consumption has enhanced the condition of living both in advanced and developing countries, the middle class has long prospered even to the extent that Marxist class theory with a focus on polarization logic can be completely denied. Amid recent economic recessions coupled with deepening global competition, the decline of middle-class prosperity characterized by the 20:80 rule is coming to the fore.

Take the United States where the economy is thought to have taken an upturn after a series of oil crises and ensuing economic stagnations. Since the late 1980s, significant changes in both market environment and institutional systems have occurred to broaden the gap between rich and poor, including labor displacement resulting from deindustrialization, fierce global competition, industrial restructuring and massive unemployment. Such transformations have inspired the issue of "the decline of the middle class" or "the decomposition of the middle class" (Stier and Grusky, 1990; Weeden,

1999). As similar socioeconomic trajectory has been observed in many European countries, Marx's predictive insight into "the fall of the middle class" is currently drawing fresh attention worldwide. Even in Japan once proclaiming itself "the nation closest to Heaven" due to a drastic economic restoration after WWII and the Korean War, class disparity is now increasing, rather than diminishing, in terms of income, educational or occupational status, and inter-generational mobility, despite dramatic improvements in overall quality of life (Hara and Seiyama, 1999).

Korea is no exception. During the rapid economic growth period spanning from early 1960s to 1997, an ambitious neo-middle class mainly consisting of professionals, managers and technicians, rose to such a point that more than a half of national population contain a middle class consciousness. Therefore, it was generally accepted that the Korean society is heading toward a diamond-shaped class structure (Shin, Cho and Cho, 2003). After the foreign exchange crisis in 1997, however, followed a rise in unemployment rate owing to massive corporate bankruptcy and layoff, expansion of part-time and contract workers to promote a more flexible labor market and spread of neo-liberal ideologies emphasizing individual accomplishment. These adverse circumstances have inevitably led to a dramatic erosion in the middle-class population as well as middle class consciousness (Hong and Min, 2001).

Although the decline of the middle-class population can be regarded as a necessary condition for the collapse of the middle class, it cannot be positively affirmed that the former is always a sufficient condition for the latter. In this information age when workers armed with advanced knowledge and information are highly appreciated, unemployment anxiety coupled with economic stagnation tends to motivate professional knowledge workers into upper class while forcing the remaining ordinary workforce to fall to lower class. This middle-class decomposition appears to be a universal phenomenon witnessed across the globe. It was the middle class that suffered most from the employment fluctuation following the 1997 economic crisis and experienced harsh status downgrade after reemployment in Korea (Shin and Lee, 2000).

These developments suggest two implications: an increasing polarization of class structure and a deepening inter-class disparity. While the emergence of well-educated and upscale workforce epitomizing the rapid growth period of the past decades remains, the decline of middle class values with changes in employment status and breakdown of personal asset values has recently surfaced as a dominant trend. In short, through an ascendancy of top knowledge professionals labeled as a neo-embourgeoisment thesis and a massive degradation of middle class defined by neo-proletarianization thesis, current society is heading toward a 20:80 type characterized by two polarized sites:

the upper layer consisting of capitalists and knowledge professionals and the lower layer including a majority of ordinary, non-professional workers and the unemployed.

II. Theoretical Discussion

Class has been one of the most central issues in modern capitalist society. By emphasizing open economic opportunities, the Western bourgeois society attempts to regard individual achievement as a main driving force for the overall social development. In reality, however, individual resources, the ultimate means of social advancement, tend to be unequally distributed, and this is where such concept as 'class' needs to be adopted to explain the disparity in quality of life and lifestyle resulting from a serious discrepancy between personal input and output.

Observing the transformation of modern Western society triggered by the rise of industrial capitalism, Karl Marx, the founder of class theory, proposed macroscopic stages of historical development of human society based on a materialist framework. In the class theory, an integral part of historical materialism, he proclaimed the polarization thesis that described an inevitable conflict in a capitalist society between two antagonistic camps: the bourgeois and the proletariat (Marx and Engels, 1954). On the other hand, Max Weber, who put social inequalities in a much broader perspective to include social prestige, power relations as well as economic dimension, defined class as "a category of people sharing similar economic conditions in market situation". He also stressed that the identification of class structure or an understanding of class behavior was not that simple as Marx originally suggested (Weber, 1968).

The consecutive development of class theory originating from Marx and Weber has been dominated by both Neo-Marxian and Neo-Weberian traditions (Edgell, 1993). They are different in that the former is more focused on the relational property like relations of production based on exploitation thesis, while the latter is more concerned with the gradational property like life chances oriented toward exclusion thesis. Still, both schools share the same possessive viewpoint that a class system is largely derived from the appropriation of such economic resources as capital, living labor, assets, knowledge and skills. Those perspectives emphasizing the possessive logic and the primacy of economy do not seem to fully demonstrate their analytical potential in today's complex society, where internal differentiation and dynamic interactions within the class structure are greatly expanding.

Although diverse forms of social inequalities persistently remain, analytical power of class theory is ever degrading. There may be two hypotheses to explain this contradiction: one is 'no-class' hypothesis arguing that social class order tends to dissipate to the extent that a class question does not pose a serious issue any more; the other is 'theoretical lag' hypothesis claiming that a series of intellectual responses to the existing class reality have not been appropriately prepared.

The no-class hypothesis characterized by the declaration "There is no class whatsoever" finds its prototype in Paul Kingston's 'classless society thesis'. Maintaining a realistic view that class has its raison d'être as long as it can exercise a significant influence upon the social structure, Kingston diagnoses the current class system in American society in terms of a selection of criteria (inter- or intra-generational mobility, interaction patterns, cultural orientation, class attitudes, political behavior, etc.) proposed by Anthony Giddens' class structuration theory. Reflecting upon the numeric ratio of people who have inherited their parents' socioeconomic status, peer relations, neighborhood relationships, marriage pattern, lifestyle, in-group consciousness, and political commitment and behavior, Kingston draws a conclusion that "Class is dead." In a chapter titled "American Non-Exceptionalism," he also emphasizes a universal validity of theory of classless society by demonstrating peaceful class mobility and willful political association are commonplace in many other Western countries as well (Kingston, 2000).

Such ideas of no-class hypothesis have long been championed by some inequality researchers, who argue for class dissipation theory resulting from material affluence. It is beyond dispute that the expansion of wealth and the ensuing equalization of living conditions are likely to depreciate the salience of class differences. It appears unquestionable that hostile class awareness and class confrontations are less likely to occur as a majority of people enjoy a stable income and comfortable life patterns due to rising employment opportunities, diminishing individual or household income inequality, popular diffusion of home appliances such as TV sets and refrigerators, narrowing gaps in standard of living between urban and rural areas, decreasing class or regional differences in higher education, and weakening influence of family background.

Yet, there remains an inequality in high-end items even when the distribution of basic assets is leveled out to a large extent. Normally, we can buy a regular motor vehicle with ten thousand dollars or so, but when it comes to choosing types of car, the decision may involve much greater monetary expense (Hara and Seiyama, 1999). Therefore, the no-class hypothesis that claims the class order or the meaning of class will disappear in an affluent society which has achieved an equal distribution of basic commodities does not seem to do a good job in analyzing current class reality.

On the other hand, the theoretical lag hypothesis reflects the poverty of theory, claiming that the conventional class theory has become inappropriate to fully examine the constantly changing nature of the social inequality. This may lead us to an attainment view of class, which regards modern industrial society as a vehicle of opportunity for status attainment or social mobility, rather than an arena of fierce class confrontations (Sorokin, 1959). Even when discussions are confined to a rather orthodox class theory, there have been several opinions ascribable to the theoretical lag hypothesis.

First, from a perspective of affluence thesis mentioned before in relation to criticism over the no-class hypothesis, a clear evidence of theoretical lag phenomena is detected. Many dominant theories of the past, regardless of Marxian or Weberian traditions, championed a realist view of class based on the possession of tangible or non-tangible assets, recognizing the class consciousness and class behavior as its derivatives. Looking back upon human history since the modern era, however, the concept of class has often been used as an abstract notion to verbalize a diversity of social conflicts and disputes. In this regard, class is transformed into a nominal concept that indicates a specific position on the systematic continuum of social inequality; thus, class cannot disappear so long as whatever forms of social ladder persist. Yet, when it comes to non-material resources including knowledge, skills and symbolic assets, social measurements tend to be highly arbitrary, which may consequently obscure class difference or disparity.

Secondly, the current lag of theory phenomenon can also be explained by complexity thesis. To analyze today's complex class reality, Reinhard Kreckel has proposed a new conceptual framework of 'center and periphery', criticizing that class theory of the past is merely a partial paradigm that has only been applied to a limited population of workers and thus has failed to integrate workers and non-workers, men and women, and an unequal international division of labor. According to Stefan Hradil, social welfare policy designed to address inequality issues creates a new set of societal needs, including communication, social integration and self-fulfillment, which have a great affinity with such attributes as ethnicity, gender and age. Subsequently, Hradil predicts, a form of ascribed inequality, not achievement inequality, will exacerbate, and to scrutinize this new type of social woe, multi-dimensionality associated with inequality needs to be fully recognized (Yoon, 2000).

Due to continuous improvement of levels of living, expanding educational opportunity and enhanced social welfare policies, Ulrich Beck argues a new form of individualization, significantly different from that of during the rise of modern bourgeois, is underway and tends to undermine the collective basis of social inequality shifting the matter of class inequality from collective phenomenon to individual failure or personal crisis, which ultimately obscures traces of social inequalities (Beck, 2002). This systematic obscuring of inequality translates into a fragmentation, not dissipation, of social inequality, which in turn transforms social confrontations occurring during the individualization process into various forms of social discrimination, and brings the performance principle to the fore as a primary tenet of 'risk society.' That is because the performance principle attributes unjust class discrepancies to an outcome of personal fault or irresponsibility (Herman, 2002).

In contemporary society where class disparity does still exist along with increasingly elaborated and consolidated class order amid global expansion of the capitalist system, the decline of analytic approaches to class seems to be a stark contradiction. Rainer Lepsius and Peter Berger maintain that the root cause of such a phenomenon can be found in the indeterminacy of class structure. Orthodox class theorists keep raising a counterargument to the new perspective that emphasizes a qualitative shift in the mode of social stratification. Current criticism is largely focused on centrality of labor, validity of production paradigm, or politico-economic nature of welfare society (Youn, 2000). Yet, it is likely that such refutation takes an issue with fundamentally untestable propositions and thus instigates many counter arguments. In consequence, this paper attempts to design a broader perspective on the ever-changing status of social inequality, to examine the nature of contemporary class order, and finally to seek an alternative approach that can provide a better understanding of diverse social developments regarding class.

III. Contemporary Megatrends

Sociologists of the 1960s generally agreed that the process of industrialization in Western civilization could be characterized by three major driving forces: industrialization, urbanization and bureaucratization. More recently, many scholars who have been exploring macro-social trends in a contemporary context demonstrate a fact that the social adjustments over the past three decades are epitomized by informatization, globalization and decentralization.

Informatization is defined as a process through which the production, transformation, management and application of information have become a significant part of society. Combined with a dramatic advance in computer science and communication technology, this new social trend not only affects overall social activities including politics, economy, education and entertainment, it also acts on an individual's mode of behavior or mentality.

Globalization refers to a state of international interdependency intensified through ever-increasing cross-boundary exchanges of capital, technology, information, culture and human resources. Decentralization represents a condition where social resources, both tangible and non-tangible, diffuse into varied sectors of an organization or a spatial structure. Given that both trends accelerate amid recent information revolution, they are considered as epiphenomena accompanying the socio-technological process of informatization. However, these three contemporary megatrends promote societal transformation by enhancing structural flexibility and pluralism, and then it ultimately creates a supra-open system of pluralist flexible society, where boundaries between diverse institutional spheres diminish and dominance of any specific value declines. Such an open system is so complex and sophisticated that it defies a stereotypical analytic framework based on simple lines of logic. Contemporary society that places much value on individual needs and preferences takes on distinctive characteristics of a complicated system, which in turn builds up great social entropy and ultimately makes it difficult to apply a theory of social development according to a unitary criterion. Thus, it is assumed that the quantitative logic of growth will be gradually substituted by the qualitative logic of maturation.

Such observations have constantly been supported by several socio-philosophic visions: Yoneji Masuda (1980) claims GNS (Gross National Satisfaction), instead of GNP, should be a standard of national development; Ronald Inglehart (1990) puts a greater emphasis on non-material values than material interests; and Erich Fromm (1976) argues that central life interests of modern society are shifting from 'having' to 'being'. More recently, in his writing titled "From Possession to Access," Jeremy Rifkin (2000) logically accounts for a series of modern transformations.

In the age of access coming with a rapid advancement of information and communication media, Jeremy Rifkin suggests, markets are making way for networks, and a sweeping re-structuring of economic relationships is going to force a transition from industrial to cultural production. When combined with the logic of capital embodied by commodification, cultural capitalism is steadily replacing the current market system mainly based on property relations, market exchanges and material accumulation. In this new era of cultural capitalism, access to cultural resources, not possession and distribution of material property, is expected to create an unprecedentedly wide gap between the connected and the disconnected (Rifkin, 2000).

IV. Current State of Social Inequality

1. General Overview

Constant rearrangements in socioeconomic environment have led to an inevitable transformation in patterns of social inequality, which was once expounded by such a single parameter as distribution of material and symbolic resources, but now it requires an advanced level of analysis. Patterns of social conflict have turned out to be so pluralized, sophisticated and multiplied as indicated by those according to class, regional, generational and gender boundaries.

- Class Conflict: As income disparity has been gradually subsiding, class relations previously centered around the gap between rich and poor are expected to wane. Class differentiation primarily involving patterns of consumption, apart from the "money-making" issue, is emerging as a new source of class conflict.
- Regional Conflict: Due to extensive regional development and cross-national installation of public facilities, inter-regional conflicts tend to arbitrarily occur and an explicit social comparison between in-group and out-group is becoming obscure.
- Generational Conflict: Generational conflict, so far interpreted by the dual paradigm of conservatism and liberalism, has entered a more complicated phase with the emergence of a post-modern generation, who defies such a simple dichotomy. Today, intra-generational issues, not just inter-generational conflicts, are on the rise as well.
- Gender Conflict: Up to date, gender conflicts have been mostly concerned about gender roles or status, such as the division of household duties and equal opportunities for career activities, and now they have evolved into diverse human rights issues including sexual harassment and domestic violence.

The aforementioned changes in social inequality are considered inevitable consequences of ever-increasing complexity of recent social order. At the root of such transformations lie not only socioeconomic factors like power and wealth, but the desire for recognition directly associated with symbolic struggles for social prestige or social identity. In today's complicated conflict situation riddled with diverse principles and doctrines, including consumerism, regionalism, postmodernism and feminism, the issue of enhancing life chance is bound to be accompanied by a cultural issue epitomized by a fulfillment of proper lifestyle.

The struggle for recognition oriented toward symbolic values is in sharply contrast with the possessive desire for material resources in many respects. First, while material properties are within the boundaries of quantitative measurement, symbolic resources are not, which makes it fundamentally impossible to agree on a set of normative standards of expectation. Secondly, since recognition is mostly attained through interactive circumstances, each individual has his or her own idea of an optimum level of recognition, which can hardly reach a socially-conceded mediation or understanding. Finally, unlike material assets which are based on the distributive principle, symbolic resources manifest their values through the principle of distinction (Honneth, 2001).

2. Changing Nature of Social Inequality

With increasingly complex class order, the hierarchical structure of a society tends to build up invisibility and become elusive within the existing analytical framework. Main reasons for such a phenomenon are as follows:

(1) Factors of social inequality have been pluralized to include educational background, opportunity structure and social network, as well as wealth, power and prestige.
(2) Dimensions of social inequality have become multiplied as demonstrated in the collusion among politics, economy, media and cultural power.
(3) Social inequality has turned multidimensional, not only integrating class, but sex, age, region and ethnicity.
(4) An increase in intra/inter-generational social mobility adds greater dynamism to a social inequality system.
(5) The emergence of post-industrial values oriented toward non-materialism lays the confusion within existing hierarchical standards.
(6) A subjective evaluation that puts greater emphasis on self-actualization or self-esteem than on possession and distribution increases indeterminacy of hierarchical order.
(7) As individualization and self-determination intensify, collective solidarity, a referential basis of the traditional class system, has been diminishing.

These tendencies can be epitomized by a proposition of de-structuration. Table 2-1 compares characteristics before and after the transition.

Table 2-1 **Changing Nature of Social Inequality**

Structured Inequality	De-structured Inequality
Positional	Categorical
Upper-Lower	Highbrow-Lowbrow
Control	Exclusion
Static Structure	Dynamic Process
Objective, Tangible	Subjective, Intangible

Within a de-structured system of social inequality, quality of life will rise to prominence as a central value. An expectation for the qualitative improvement of life generally translates into a combination of life chances and lifestyle. The former refers to objective living conditions directly linked to material resources or power, while the latter involves a subjective aspiration for a desired life.

A determination function for quality of life can be categorized into the three following arguments. First is the primacy of life chance model, which contends appreciating a certain level of lifestyle largely depends on the advancement in objective standards of living. Next is the primacy of lifestyle model, which is based on a sort of counter-civilizational assumption that material affluence has created mental poverty. According to this model, existential value of life can be fully attained by pursuing self-actualization. Last is an integration model, which claims that theoretical discussions and implementation processes regarding quality of life should involve a comprehensive consideration of both life chances and lifestyle, under a proposition that life chances are not a sufficient condition for a better lifestyle, but they are a necessary condition to expand ranges of lifestyle options. This dual factor theory is thought to be most appropriate to capture diverse aspects of quality of life issues in modern times.

3. Toward a Sociocultural Class Analysis

In addition to a longing for an optimum lifestyle, class culture is taking on even greater salience as a means of grasping and properly responding to a changing class reality. As culture defined as entire ways of life is adding a new dimension to class order, what may be called as 'sociocultural class theory' needs to be presented as an alternative framework to traditional class theory that had been confined to the politico-economic or socioeconomic level.

A plausible solution to politico-economic inequality closely related to an unequal appropriation of power and wealth can be found in a reform of distribution structure. The current state of social inequality which is being extended to a problem of meaning beyond a matter of deficiency is however epitomized by an 'enculturation thesis.' Such forms of social inequality intertwined with symbolic elements tend to obscure patterns of vertical differentiation under the pretext of distinction and preference, not discrimination or coercion, but eventually they are highly likely to reproduce flexible forms of social inequality (Bourdieu, 1984).

Social inequality in future society is expected to go through a de-structualizing process of conventional hierarchical order based on the differential distribution of socioeconomic resources. To effectively observe and respond to such social transformations, it is urgent to develop an alternative conceptual paradigm considers the cultural embeddedness of social order.

Cultural differentiation differs from previous class models in that it stresses a symbolic boundary, which cannot be easily crossed just by mobilizing material resources. Accordingly, class inequality in the near future is expected to be represented by a phrase "from hierarchy to boundary."

V. Discussion

As knowledge and information has emerged as a significant part of social resources, a great transition in the social inequality system is on the move. The social transformative power of knowledge and information has long been acknowledged by information sociologists, who are focused on historical implications of the Information Revolution following Agricultural and Industrial Revolutions. More recently, such informal categories of knowledge as practical or tacit knowledge have also been emphatically asserted by advocates of knowledge revolution more than ever.

With the advent of qualitative transformation of an inequality system that extends beyond simple inter-class mobility and reversion, the purpose of this chapter is to shed light on the nature and dynamics of new vertical social order and to observe a future prospect of social inequality.

A developmental value of modern society is more focused on a qualitative advancement of life than material affluence. Quality of life is a concept that implies an enhancement of lifestyle involving self-actualization, not merely confined to objective living conditions such as wealth and power. As needs for autonomous life design, along with an inspiration for self-actualization, augment, the nature of class order has become multilayered, complicated and sophisticated, shifting from merely being linear or unidimensional.

With the decline of modern rationality, a previously dominant dichotomy demonstrated by logos vs. pathos, cognition vs. affection, sense vs. sensibility or head vs. heart is now going through an implosion. Likewise, as mutual penetration among politics, economy and culture is expected to become intensified, it is generally accepted that material wealth itself cannot automatically guarantee a social status, which now must be hard earned by living up to a proper lifestyle of the upper class. In other words, class order is diffusing throughout the realm of life-world going beyond politico-economic domains. Therefore, combined with the establishment of a new social inequality system fully integrating a range of symbolic factors, a matter of boundary that transcends a matter of hierarchy will emerge as a more crucial issue in future society.

As a cultural dimension of social inequality, which generates a formally open but closed boundary permitting no crossover, has come in sight through recent changes in class system, inequality studies in future society need to extend to integrate socio-cultural boundaries, exceeding a stage that only detects hierarchical rank order based on distribution of tangible resources.

Chapter 3

A Critical Reexamination of Digital Divide

Introduction

Some researchers who have tracked the trends of information-based society have argued that rapid progress in information technology will accelerate the monopoly or disproportionate distribution of information by a handful of privileged people and thus solidify the existing inequality (Compaine, 1985, 2001; Slevin, 2000). Given the notion, digital divide has emerged as one of the challenging problems not only in the U.S. and other developed countries equipped with solid information infrastructure but also in less wired countries which are trying to ride on the information bandwagon. Now, digital divide has become an important issue in the interest of individual countries and international relations as well, as it is being discussed at summit meetings and international conferences (OECD, 2000, 2001).

This chapter attempts to lay a logical foundation for coping with digital divide, which is about to challenge the rosy picture of the future society depicted by proponents of information-based society. First, it outlines the future of the information society, examining previous studies about digital divide and analyzing the present states of information gap. Then it attempts to reconstruct the notion of digital divide based on of empirical data and explores ways to solve the problem of widening digital gap. It is hoped that an extensive study on the issue of digital divide and the exploration of policy alternatives will contribute to bridging digital divide in the following ways: 1) Governments will be encouraged to offer a vision of a society where information equality is guaranteed, i.e., "information-based welfare society"; 2) organizations will be inspired to create information-oriented learning process that will narrow digital divide among different classes, generations, sexes, and regions; and 3) individuals will be motivated to enrich their information competence to accept the dynamic changes in their future lives.

I. Theoretical Background

Researches examining information inequality in connection with the media began with Phillip Tichenor and others who formulated the hypothesis of knowledge gap in 1970. Until the early 1980s, studies were widely conducted on the influence of the mass media on unequal distribution of information (Tichenor, 1970). But the notion of information gap attracted little attention as a social issue. That is because the notion of the mass media functioning as a cause of information gap became less persuasive by the rapid supply and wide use of radio and TV, although a social gap between the literate and the illiterate has been aggravated by the introduction of newspaper and other printed materials.

Researches in information gap faced a turning point in the late 1980s when the Internet began to be widely used because of the integration of computers and communication technologies. Compared with the previous mass media, the Internet was not only entertaining and informative but also expensive and complicated. For the latter reasons, class and regional differences clearly manifested in the use of the new medium, resulting in social and regional gaps in information distribution. In late 1980s, debates over the unequal distribution of the new media became prevalent. Since 1989, when the summer issue of the Journal of Communication ran a special article about the information gap created by new communications technology, digital divide came to attract attention as a subject of academic debates (Croteau and Hoynes, 2000).

In Korea, too, where the enthusiasm for information technology is second to none, digital divide has become an important academic and social issue. Despite a wealth of debates, the quality of research findings remains unsatisfactory. Academic circles and research institutions have conducted many studies, but they have focused on information accessibility, ignoring problems related to information inequality and largely indifferent to the need to work out practical strategies or policies for closing the gap. This is problematic because the information industry—a branch of industry that produces, manufactures, processes, distributes, and utilizes information—has become a driving force of economic development and is making inroads into traditional sectors like agriculture and the manufacturing industry. Academic circles and policymakers, therefore, will have to assess digital divide comprehensively and produce solutions for heightening people's awareness of the information society and for improving the user-friendliness of information media and information technology (Jordan, 1999; Yun, 2000).

II. Dimensions of Digital Divide

Scholars of the information society are divided over whether social inequality decreases or increase in information-based society. However, they generally agree with the idea that inequality in the information society is fundamentally different from that of industrial society. As informatization progresses in society, the cause and structural nature of social inequality changes as well.

It seems that the information society expands the quantity of information available to the members of a society by revolutionizing the ways of using and exchanging information. But such a view is a superficial analysis based on the quantity of information supplied by various forms of the mass media. A different interpretation is possible when the actual amount of information acquired by the user is considered. In fact, the more information flows throughout the entire society, the wider the gap becomes between "information haves" and "information have-nots," leading to digital divide that refers to differential aspects of information-based society (Webster and Robins, 1986; Knights and Wilmott, 1988; Schiller, 1996).

According to the previous studies, digital divide has been caused by four major elements: class, sex, generation, and region. In terms of class, digital divide exists among different types of workers — knowledge workers, conventional workers, and marginal laborers — and between the upper or middle classes and the lower class. Regarding sex, digital divide exists between men and women. There is also a huge class and generation gap among women themselves. The greatest disparity, however, is between the net-generation, conversant with personal computers and the Internet, and the older generation, accustomed to an industrial society (U.S. Department of Commerce, 1995, 1998, 1999, 2000; World Bank, 2001; Park, 2003).

The net-generation is comfortable with the Internet and other new media, regarding them as indispensable part of life as air. The older generation, on the other hand, finds the new information-related culture and the resulting changes repulsive and burdensome. Regional gap, in terms of information accessibility, occurs between cities and rural areas as well as between big and small cities. Information gap can also occur within a city itself. In addition, international digital divide exists between the developed and the underdeveloped, which is epitomized by the fact that more than 90 percent of internet servers in the world are in developed countries and that New York City has more Internet servers than all servers in Africa combined. (Figure 3-1)

Figure 3-1 **Dimensions of Digital Divide**

Dimension of Digital Divide	Points
Sex	Men and Women (especially within older Generation)
Generation	Net-generation vs. Non-net-generation
Class	Knowledge Workers vs. Conventional Workers vs. Marginal Laborers
Region	National: Cities vs. Rural Area, Big Cities vs. Small Cities International: Developed Countries vs. Underdeveloped Countries

III. Mechanism Producing Digital Divide

Digital divide is created, reproduced, and aggravated through a complex process. Initially, it can be said that economic inequality leads to digital divide, but that does not describe the whole picture. Financial ability does not guarantee the desire to access and use information. Then, what factors influence information access and usage? So far, such key factors as economic power, social status, educational level, and occupation have been mentioned.

Eonomic power is the most important factor. Because information services that the new media provide are marketed as commercial products, lack of money is the biggest hindrance to accessing information devices and software. That is why economic ability is directly linked to the gap in access to new technology and information. In fact, to return profit for huge investments in product development, businesses have devised strategies to shorten product life cycles and target rich people. It is noteworthy that economic disparity leads to a gap in access to information and information devices, the initial and most fundamental component of the information society.

Socio-demographic factors are also important. Attitude toward information and Information accessibility and use vary significantly according to social status, occupation, education, and age. These factors change the conditions under which people interact with others and have access to the media. They also change the content of and opportunity for education. And, all of this changes the level of information mindedness.

The "exponential property" of information is another significant element. Generally speaking, information tends to flow toward the information haves. That is because they are more eager than information have-nots to acquire information and more competent to understand information. It is true that people with a higher level of information competency can understand a given message more easily than those with a lower level of information competency. Although a clear explanation of the internal mechanism is not available, a significant correlation does exist between the level of accumulated information and the desire to access new information devices and information. The exponential property of information provides a clear explanation of the obvious advantage of both knowledge leaders and early participants in the information sector.

Another important aspect that has been overlooked in studying digital divide is the multidimensionality or the multiplicity of digital divide. So far, digital divide has been recognized as a comprehensive concept that converges into a single construct. As a result, the multidimensional/multiplex aspects of digital divide have been ignored in researches. However, it is possible to attempt multidimensional analyses for understanding the complexity of digital divide. Digital divide can be categorized into three levels and conditions: access to information devices and information (media accessibility); the ability to utilize information resources (information mobilization); and the will to use information devices and information resources properly (information consciousness).

Media accessibility: So far, digital divide has focused on the gap in access to information media, which are relatively more expensive and have a shorter lifecycle than ordinary products. Information media accessibility is influenced by economic power, which serves as a major element of digital divide.

Information mobilization: Information mobilization refers to all activities related to using information materials, including the operation of information devices, familiarity with software, and the ability to search information. Users who possess information media or have information accessibility but are not intelligent enough to use them will not be able to fully utilize information resources. On the other hand, if users who have access to information media and are intelligent enough to use them keep gathering useless information, they can be said to be bringing upon themselves information deprivation. In this context, the wide use of the Internet log-in hours as an indicator of informatization leaves much room for reconsideration. The time spent on games and on-line chatting does not constitute the application of useful information services for gaining valuable information resources.

Information consciousness: Information consciousness, often expressed as "information mindedness," refers to the user's ability to judge whether the information in question is good or bad. The mode of utilizing information, which is central to information mobilization, is a matter of the user's habit and practice, while information consciousness is directly linked to the user's subjective life-world, or his reflective power in accordance with the characteristics of the "subculture" to which the user belongs.

But most of studies on digital divide have focused on the gap in access to and ability to use the hardware and software of various media, disregarding information consciousness that can be considered a "humanware" as irrelevant. Information consciousness has been discussed only in respect to cultural or ethical aspects of information, out of the realm of digital divide.

This paper, however, views the information consciousness gap as a part of a complex phenomenon. In view of this, the paper will establish various phases or stages of digital divide, and then provide solutions for problems at each phase of digital divide. Recently, personal computers have found their way into many homes, regardless of education and class, increasing information media accessibility. Nevertheless, a gap in computer usage and information consciousness keeps widening among classes. So, it is important to apply multidimensional analyses to understand the full spectrum of digital divide as well as to provide appropriate solutions. (Figure 3-2)

Figure 3-2 **Complex Mechanism Producing Digital Divide**

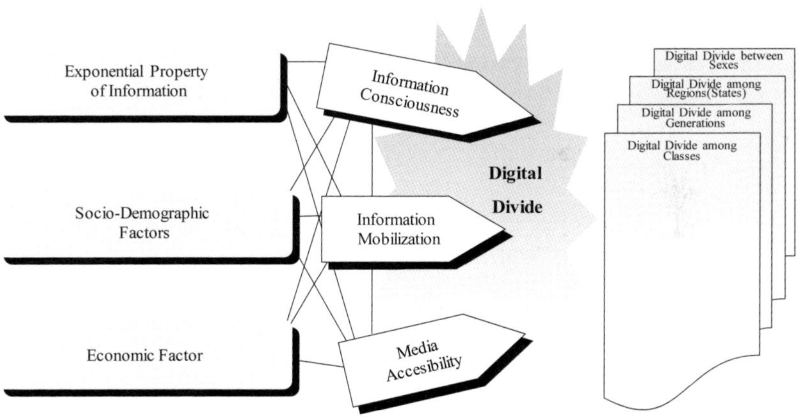

IV. Stages of Digital Divide

Basically, digital divide is created by socio-economic factors that have influence on access to information devices. Along with computerization process, the core issue of digital divide tends to shift from who has better access to information media or can acquire more information to who makes the right use of the acquired information or what stance a user has on information itself. In other words, the key issue of digital divide is switching from the issue of universal possession to the issue of autonomous reception.

Therefore, on the assumption that digital divide will widen further with the progress of informatization, this paper will examine the current state of digital divide and provide possible solutions by making a tripartite model that consists of the first, second, and third differentiation processes. In the first differentiation process, information accessibility will differentiate users, followed by information utilization in the second, and information receptiveness in the third.

Information accessibility is closely linked to the economic conditions under which users can access information technology. Information utilization is intimately linked to the social environment where users can obtain and process information as well as create added value using information technology. Information receptiveness is about whether users can use information to enrich their own lives intellectually and culturally. Information accessibility and information utilization, both of which are related to the expansion of life chances, and information receptiveness, which pertains to the enrichment of the quality of life, will serve as indicators of the level of individual, organizational, and societal informatization. (Figure 3-3)

Figure 3-3 **Stages of Digital Divide**

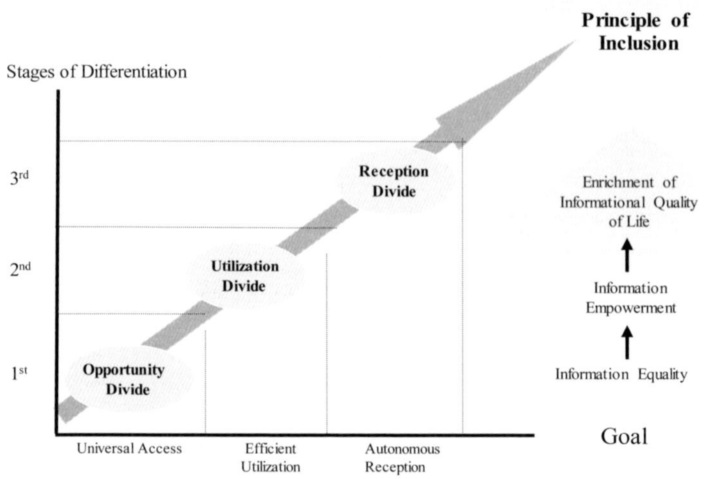

1. The First Differentiation: Information Access

Digital divide is first and foremost evident in the user's access or lack of access to PC, modem, phone lines, and another Internet equipment. Information in the information society is transformed into binary digits, saved as an electronic file, and circulated through information media, such as computers, cellular phones, and the Internet. Information providers gather, treat, and process information in the digital form, and charge fees for information they provide in to return profit for their investment. On the other hand, information users buy computers and modem, and pay fees for access to information. People who are not rich enough to pay fees are most likely to be excluded from the benefits of informatization. In the information society where information users have to pay for both hardware (information devices and machines) and software (data resources), poor people and underdeveloped countries will have a limited opportunity for access to information (Mosco and Wasco, 1995; Thomas, 1995; Norris, 2001; Compaine, 2001).

As explained above, digital divide at the first stage can be defined as a sort of "opportunity divide," given the fact that opportunities for access to a medium play an important role in dividing between "the upper and the low" echelons. Furthermore, the disadvantaged group is characterized as being "computer-illiterate". At this stage, whether users have opportunities for access to information depends mainly on their economic resources.

2. The Second Differentiation: Information Utilization

The primary benefits from the information society go first to people who are rich enough to pay fees for information and are intelligent enough to need and use information. As information technology develops further, people who are excluded from those benefits find it harder to catch up with the early information users. Early adopters of information, who were able to pay for information devices and information-based education, are now enabled to retain an advantage over others in using information. With an increase in the quantity of information, there emerges the demand for enhanced information utilization and for information equipment with a bigger capacity and better performance. The early adopters are rich enough to upgrade the capacity of not only their equipment but also their competence to obtain and understand information. In this process, initial digital divide between the early adopters and non-adopters is highly likely to widen further as information technology continues to make progress, as the quantity of information expands, and as the complexity of information utilization become greater (Salvaggio and Bryant, 1989).

Ironically, a gap in the level of information utilization itself is sometimes seen as being symptomatic of economic inequality in the real world. The current upward mobility of venture capitalists or professionals in the digital sector clearly shows that information utilization exerts an important influence on economic power. In the second differentiation process, therefore, a full utilization of information resources plays an important role in dividing between "the upper and the low echelons." In that sense, digital divide at this stage ought to be termed as a "utilization divide." Another required element is "network capital," comprising both personal and physical networks, which is as important as information accessibility for full information utilization (Kling, 2000; Kling and Lamb, 2000).

In this differentiation process, the possession or lack of such network capital divides white-collar workers into either gold-collar workers or routine knowledge workers. And as the framework of the capitalist market undergoes fundamental changes, large corporations will lose their monopoly while some IT businesses armed with the network capital will loom large.

3. The Third Differentiation: Information Receptiveness

Economic power is considered a prerequisite for accessing information devices and utilizing information, the two key components of digital divide. It is undeniable that economic power is the primary cause of digital divide, but it is inappropriate to say that economic power determines all dimensions and levels of digital divide. According to studies on technology diffusion theory, non-economic factors like social or cultural needs and information mindedness are as significant as economic factors in accessing information device and utilizing information. In other words, what emerges as a key to bridging digital divide is not access to or utilization of high-tech information devices or facilities but whether the user knows how to use them for the betterment of their quality of life. For example, the same information technology can become either "informative" or totally useless. The door to a mature information society opens only when quantitative increases in information utilization develop into qualitative increases in information content (Michael, 1972). In many respects, this is not happening in Korea. It is often said that non-economic factors like information consciousness will be converted into economic factor eventually. But when people deal with information, many of them tend to make decisions in favor of non-economic factors, indifferent to their economic interest.

When the information society advances further, the gap in access to the Internet will be narrowed considerably. Then, the focus of debates over digital divide will shift to the question of who will have dominant power under what conditions in the cyberspace. In other words, the focus of studies will move from the issue of unequal access to the cyberspace to the issue of digital divide among participants of the cyberspace (Rao, 2001). It is also possible that research interests will shift from economic power to social power and then to cultural power.

In this regard, it would be helpful to look at the interactive communications and behavior patterns of the members of the Usenet groups that are leading the pack of virtual communities. The members of the Usenet groups create and share unequivocal messages in written form to convey physical, emotional, and behavioral signs and meanings. As a form of society based on language, Usenet groups are dependent on symbols, analogies, and metaphors to reconstruct or represent events or behaviors that occur in the real world.

In a networked society like the Usenet groups where a written language plays a dominant role in conveying messages, "the knowledge of language and other cultural elements" is a key factor in discriminating the members. As a result, a good command of language is more valued than in the real world. Consequently, it serves as a new source of power that adds to the actual power that the Usenet group members enjoy in the real world. In other words, the verbal ability to offer a persuasive assertion or to bring up a counterargument will serve as a core source of cultural power (on the assumption that cultural power as such exists) for the members of the cyberspace. So, the members participate in a continuous cycle of statement and reaction to prevent their cultural power from dying out and ceasing to exist (Mackinnon, 1995).

As suggested by the case of the Usenet groups, the future generation that will spend more time in the cyberspace will see that the popularity of their messages, the number of "hits," persuasive power, quickness to response and reputation will serve as key components that determine their controlling power in the cyberspace. Those competencies, however, are not available to users who spend many hours on on-line games, chatting, on-line shopping, or cyber stock transactions.

To obtain those competencies, it is necessary to enhance cultural abilities by reading books, engaging in discourse, or experiencing meaningful personal relationships in the real world. In that sense, the elite status in the new cyber society will probably go to "Bobos" who set one foot in the bohemian world in pursuit of cultural creativeness and the other foot in the bourgeois territory filled with ambition and economic success (Brooks, 2001).

About the situation in Korea, surveys find that although the spread of information technology has reached the level of economically advanced countries, Koreans read far fewer books than the Japanese and the people of other developed countries. As exemplified by reports that the more hours young students spend on computers, the less hours they spend on books, Korean youths' explosive enthusiasm for the Internet makes it harder for them to find time for reading and contemplating. That seems to serve as a huge obstacle to narrowing digital divide, so we have no choice but to find solutions by offering extensive cultural experiences and expanding discourse opportunities so that young students can exchange their thoughts and feelings in the real world.

In the third differentiation process, what matters is not the universal possession or utilization but the autonomous reception of information. In addition, cultural capital has the dominant influence, since what is important is not the "degree" or the "width," but the "depth" of knowledge. People who find it difficult to access information can become not "computer illiterate" or "net illiterate" but "cultural illiterate." So, it is necessary to come up with solutions that encompass cognitive-emotional dimension beyond instrumental-dimension. (Figure 3-4) (Collins, 2000).

Figure 3-4 **Levels and Characteristics of Digital Divide**

	First Differentiation		Second Differentiation		Third Differentiation
Type of Incompetence	Computer Illiteracy	→	Net Illiteracy	→	Culture Illiteracy
Dominant User Type	Skillful Operator	→	Versatile Data Miner	→	Mature Netizen
Learning Process	Training	→	Experience	→	Reflection
Body Image	Hand	→	Hand/Head	→	Hand/Head/Heart
Site of Solution	Hardware	→	Software	→	Humanware
Type of Digital Divide	Opportunity Divide	→	Utilization Divide	→	Reception Divide
Nature of Digital Divide	Information Access	→	Information Utilization	→	Information Reception
Source of Digital Divide	Economic Capital	→	Network Capital	→	Cultural Capital
Type of Knowledge Base	Degree of Knowledge	→	Width of Knowledge	→	Depth of Knowledge
Nature of Knowledge	Simple Knowledge/ Formal Knowledge	→	Formal Knowledge/ Practical Knowledge	→	Practical Knowledge/ Cultural Knowledge

V. Density and Volume of Digital Divide

In the first differentiation process, short-term investments can help bridge digital divide to some extent. In that sense, digital divide at that stage is characterized by relatively low "gap density." But as digital divide evolves from the second stage to the third, gap density will increase gradually, making it harder to narrow digital divide at later stages. That is because the narrowing of digital divide can be achieved not through simple increase in investment but through long-term efforts like general, social and cultural learning. In short, with the development of information technology, quantitative digital divide will decline while qualitative divide will emerge as a new problematic. Therefore, the more stages the divide goes through, the bigger efforts are necessary to close the gap. (Figure 3-5)

Figure 3-5 **Density of Digital Divide**

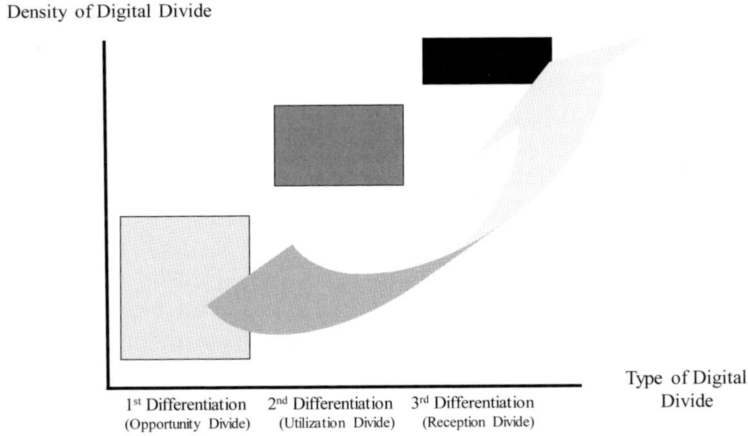

At the same time, due to exponential property of information, digital gap tends to increase in a cubical fashion where three types of knowledge base – degree of knowledge, width of knowledge and depth of knowledge – are intermingled with each other. Accordingly, discussion on digital divide is not likely to decrease but rather intensify. (Figure 3-6)

Figure 3-6 **Volume of Digital Divide**

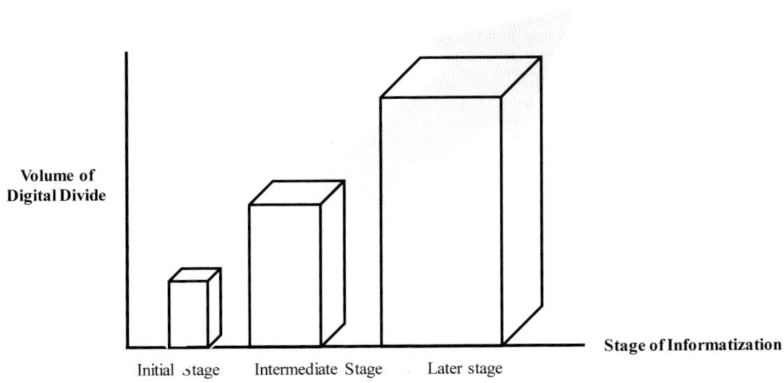

VI. Measures for Narrowing the Digital Gap

Digital divide in the information society develops differently according to each stage. So, it is necessary to devise countermeasures for each stage. At the first phase of digital divide, it is of vital importance to enhance the availability of information media. For this, various policies can be applied, like lowering the price of PC and modem, developing cost-effective Internet equipment, and lowering the service fees to a reasonable level through heightened competition among Internet service providers. In the process the public sector, including the related government agencies, can take the initiative in enhancing the availability of information media by assuming the role of a supporter or coordinator. Another important measure is to make it easier to access the Internet by lowering the service fee of high-speed communications networks that are in wide use across the country.

But the availability of information is not a complete cure for bridging digital divide, since digital divide is a complex issue that goes beyond the media availability. Another critical factor that corresponds to the next stage of digital divide is the user's information mobilization power that refers to his or her ability to accommodate information resources.

According to research findings so far, young people in their teens and twenties make the best use of the information media, while older people are less inclined to do so. A chief reason for this seems to be that the formal education of young people included instruction on the use of information media. In terms of competence for information usage, people in their thirties seem to be least apt. However, education programs for enhancing computer and Internet competencies have consistently targeted housewives and elderly citizens, exposing their limitation as a temporary measure. So, it is necessary to set up extensive plans to educate more people on a regular basis.

One of the practical options is to fully utilize the existing continuing education infrastructure. It is widely known that the existing social education programs, built under the banner of lifelong education, have fulfilled the learning aspiration of the underprivileged by offering various courses for free or at a low price. So, it will be a cost-effective option to narrow digital divides among different age groups by providing information education using the existing continuing education system.

However, reinforcing information education with the existing social education infrastructure does not guarantee an improved information competence of the underprivileged. As digital divide goes through the second and the third stage, additional efforts are required, for there emerges the need to enhance not only information accessibility but also the ability to utilize comprehensive information resources. The prior conditions for the solution mentioned above are to form a social consensus on the necessity of providing more people with opportunities to access information resources and to create an environment where creativeness and imaginativeness are valued as precious social assets. In short, it is necessary to transform the entire society into "a learning society at large." At the same time, self-controlling measures should be devised to prevent the cyberspace from serving a channel for addictive or hedonistic behaviors. What this means is that efforts to bridge digital divide should be expanded from enhancing merely information media skills to improving the overall ability to mobilize information resources and eventually raising the information consciousness, thereby stimulate social communication.

Human communication has been an integral part of society in any period and place. As informatization progresses even further, communication itself will define and confer meaning to human life. Then, it is impossible to lead a daily life without efficient communication, as information exchanges will shape most of human activities. Communication will become not so much an instrument for conveying messages but a critical factor in enhancing the quality of life. So, it is necessary to implement measures to not only increase the media availability but also improve communicative competencies at home and work (Kling, 2000; Blendon, et. al., 2001).

Meanwhile, indicators that are used to determine international digital divide are the number and density of information service providers, number of hosting servers and Internet users, the number of organizations equipped with the networks, the Internet permeation rate, the volume of the Internet content in their own languages, and the usage rate of Internet contents by the major sectors. As of 1999, Finland had more Internet hosting servers than all servers in Latin countries combined, while New York City had more servers than all servers in African countries combined. But now, as informatization has progressed even further, the most critical factor in widening digital divide among countries is language, for English is used in 80 percent of the world's Internet contents. Language is increasingly becoming a determining factor in the widening information media accessibility gap among non-English speaking countries as well as between information-rich countries and information-poor countries. In the English-dominant Internet, non-English speakers find it hard to use the Internet, however advanced their computer skills may be. Though graphic icons were created to solve that problem, the icons still reflect the English-speaking culture and icon usage is explained in English, making it hard for non-English speaking users to understand. The language used in chatting and message boards in the Internet is resonant with expressions popularized by the young generation, so the older generation has difficulties understanding. It is natural then that the older generation regards the cyberspace as an inaccessible, unknown world, because the language in currency is very much youth-oriented and is strange to the older generation

(Auh, 2000).

To solve this, it is necessary to develop computer terms or online languages that are in accordance with the everyday language. Though languages used in the cyberspace are not always wrong, the current language usage needs to be changed so that everybody feels free to express his or her opinion and communicate with other people in the cyberspace. If the language barrier in the cyberspace estranges users from each other and divides them into groups by age, generation and class, it runs counter to discursive democracy that is the goal of the information-based welfare society. But lowering the language barrier in the cyberspace is achievable only when users can understand their own linguistic culture and socio-cultural implications.

At the second or third stage of digital divide, where multidimensional information utilization and autonomous information reception becomes the matter of concern, major factors in digital divide reflect on the user's life-style. So, information providers should make efforts to provide information that is useful to daily life of ordinary people. Specifically speaking, computers and the Internet are in wider use among men than women, which seems to result from the fact that information service providers target male users as main customers. The main functions of the computer — a word processor, a database, and a presentation tool — are useful to male workers but not to housewives. The user's occupation is another factor in deciding Internet access. Knowledge workers and students access the Internet and search information more frequently than factory workers and administrative workers. The difference also reflects the importance of the relationship between the Internet content and the user's life-style. Therefore, it is necessary to not only identify what information have-nots need and demand but also to provide them with user-friendly information services (Stephenson, 1991).

The essential factor in information receptiveness is information-mindedness. That is because one's receptivity of or apathy to informatization itself can lead to digital divide. Apart from their socio-economic status or other institutional considerations, whether users are information minded or not will affect their ability to utilize information media.

Various approaches are possible to boost information-mindedness. Among others, it is preferable to hold informatization events that target diverse groups in terms of class, sex, generation, and region. So far, "Information Hunting Contests" have been held for the Internet users to boost interest in information-based society. But they were just shows, targeting information haves who are already armed with the information-mindedness. Those information haves need not be targeted for promotion campaigns, for they have no difficulty in participating in the march to the information society. And yet, the events sponsored by internet communities and Internet service providers often target information haves and they are the ones who stand out. Even government-sponsored contests tend to target well-educated people who are good at using information media. Those contests may be effective in intensifying the information haves' participation in the informatization process but are likely to widen the divide between information haves and have-nots, alienating the latter from the information-enhancing process. To overcome that situation, it is necessary to draw up policies and offer occasions to help the information have-nots. With those policies and occasions, it is possible to cultivate information mindedness as many people as possible and obtain the desired outcomes of narrowing digital divide. Communication is impossible when there is only one party. In that sense, we will say that inviting information have-nots, as the other party, into communication is a way to fulfill Habermasian idea of promoting social rationality in pursuit of ideal speech condition by overcoming oppressive and distorted communication.

VII. Discussion

The goal behind efforts to dismantle the new unequal system created by digital divide is to realize an information-based welfare society. The welfare society refers to a society where people can fully exhibit their potential and creativeness and where they are evaluated according to their contributions to the collective good. In the information era, all members of society should be guaranteed equal rights to have access to information, obtain useful information, and enjoy information autonomously. In other words, with the progress of the information society, the citizens need to be guaranteed, as civil rights, the rights to information media access, basic information services, better information utilization, and information welfare.

With the rise of civil society, the notion of civil rights has surfaced to protect basic human rights, such as personal liberty and freedom of thought, political rights, such as the right to vote, and social rights, such as the right to social participation and the right to welfare. In the information society, on the other hand, the new version of civil rights—the right to information welfare—will have to be guaranteed to protect the rights to information access, information utilization, and information receptiveness. Only when information welfare rights are protected along with civil rights, can we find a fundamental solution for the widening digital divide and leap toward a mature information-based welfare state. (Figure 3-7)

Figure 3-7 **Output Image of Information-based Welfare Society**

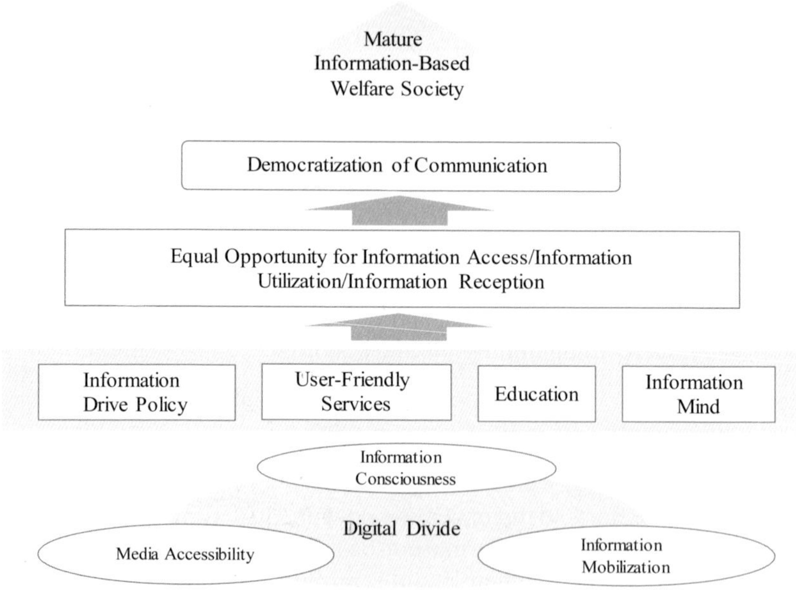

Section II

Life-world Transformation

Chapter 4

Cyberculture

Emergence of New Cultural Consciousness

I. The Advent of Cyberculture

The term 'cyber' comes from the Greek terminology, "κυβερ," which meant coordination, control, or guidance. Since Winer denominated the system of information processing with some feedbacks as cybernetics, the term came into wide use. With the rapid progress of computer technology, the prefix, 'cyber,' gained currency as a term indicating control systems utilizing computers in general. Cyberculture denotes the newly emerging cultural system brought forth by the progress of cutting-edge technology for information and communication as represented by the internet.

As can be inferred from the concept of 'cultural lag,' which means the gap or the time distance between external and internal changes, it might have been that the existence of cyberculture was not felt quite clearly at the early stage of the progress of information technology, because the change in the system of consciousness, including the notion and mind, lagged the reality. However, with the progress of 'informatization', brought forth by social diffusion of the technology for information and communication, infusion of technology and culture is more facilitated and the cyberculture, as a ramification of the techno-culture, is getting more and more influential in human society.

The genesis of cyberculture can be traced back to the flexibility stage when significant changes arise in modes of thinking and patterns of behavior in our daily life, especially with reference to customs, norms, ethics, rituals and other institutional arrangements. However, cyberculture as a new cultural pattern seems to proliferate from the outset of cyber-stage when the effect of information technology permeates deep into the inner world of our consciousness. The developmental process during the first three stages from automation to flexibility stage is likely to be related with changes in our external objective conditions of life. However, as the production activity, the social relationship and the societal networking expand and increase, the societal degree of freedom tends to expand accordingly to the point that "In what way shall we live?" seems to be the question more significant than "how well do we live?" People tend to be more concerned with lifestyle than with life chance. Accordingly, culture, which is defined as the entire ways of life, gains salience as the main component of our quality of life.

This new cultural consciousness is facilitated by such tendencies as (1) the increase of free time and dispensable income, (2) the diffusion of postmaterialist values along with the continual growth of material levels of living, (3) the growing concern for self-actualization due to the upgraded need level, (4) the expansion of cultural opportunities via new media, (5) the surge of culture industry which aims to realize the surplus value.

As such, changes in the opportunity structure, value system, need disposition, media environment, and mode of capital accumulation are leading to the state described by a series of 'post-' themes like post-industrialism, post-materialism, post-modernity or post-Fordism. Also, it turns out to be the result of the reciprocal interaction between advanced IT and concomitant social transformation.

II. Mapping the New Behavioral Patterns

Members of the advanced information society are likely to adapt themselves to changing environment by appropriately adjusting their behavioral motive or strategy to the new circumstances where societal degree of freedom is being continually increasing. Their responses can be examined in terms of dual aspects: internal mode of thinking and external mode of action.

1. Mode of Thinking

People living in the open society opt for pluralism as a response to the changing environment. Under the circumstance of pluralist values, any idea or attitude may not be denounced or rejected; rather, each finds its own raison d'être. Given the state where dissensus is not seen as conspicuous as consensus, free associations of oppositional components are widely accepted, and associative thinking becomes prevalent. This holds true in the objective aspect like time or space as well as in the subjective dimension of values or preferences.

In the constitutional time-perspective where the natural time order is transcended, past events or behaviors are a part of representational portfolio which can be freely rearranged at will. In parallel with the progress of informatization, the time-constitutional mode of thinking tends to diffuse into every corner of the society. "Synchronic coexistence or simultaneous occurrence of diachronic beings or affairs" is no longer thought to be pathological. It tends to be accepted and even hailed as part of normality.

As an evidence of constitutional spatial perspective, we can point out the blooming image of 'global village' where news from opposite side of the globe is instantly known to people on this side and the world keeps on shrinking to become a single unit (McLuhan, 1994). The perceptional space compression is accelerated by the popularization of online activities on the cyberspace such as e-commerce, tele-work, tele-conference, electronic voting and one can even envisage a possibility of anti-spatial thinking which totally denies spatial distance or distinction.

In the conventional conceptual framework, "the order of things" is quite apparent between true and false, good and evil, beautiful and ugly, superior and inferior, and the like. In the constitutional perspective where the value of every existing thing is acknowledged, emphasis is given to the logic of différance, by which the observable difference is seen as not substantial but rather coming from the manifestation or reservation of specific elements. At the root of the différance logic, there lies a belief in mutual homogeneity (Derrida, 1978). For instance, in the conventional empirical perspective where the ostensible difference is stressed, the male-female distinction is taken to be an irrefutable truth. However, in androgynous perspective where both the male and the female are sharing the maleness and femaleness at the same time, both sexes are not regarded seen as discrete categories and homosexuality is recognized as being permissible as heterosexuality. Such ambivalent conceptual scheme helps overcome the dichotomous thinking represented by 'the sacred' versus 'the secular,' and thus enhance the realization of hybridism which embraces conflicting elements. Modern classic, crossover music and fusion food seem to be the most typical cases. So is the animated film, "Beauty and the Beast," which deals with the romantic love between a human and a non-human. It illustrates that the associative thinking, which advocates the fusion of traditionally incompatible elements, becomes the 'Zeitgeist' of the current era.

2. Mode of Action

One of the characteristic traits of overt behavioral pattern of the present sharply contrasted to that of the passing period is the arbitrariness. The postmodernist slogan of "Anything goes" may be the direct expression of the current scene best represented by a series of volitional actions.

At present, many people can play actions according to their will by the power of constitutional thinking. Unlike those of the pre-modern community who blindly followed the traditions rules or conventions and those of the modern society who stick to utilitarian interest or legal responsibility, people of the present possess a wide spectrum of behavioral assets which enable them to select, practice and experiment patterns of behavior in terms of their subjective criteria. Moreover, increasing flexibility in thought style may well foster many transgressional actions which are not easily explicable by the conventional logic. Thus far, most transgressional actions have been abhorred and suppressed. However, in the near future when diversity is accepted and even encouraged, many transgressional behaviors, excluding the criminal behaviors having apparent victims or damages, will be generously accepted in the name of human rights or individuality.

This volitional behavioral pattern tends to be consolidated with the growing concern of semantic value given to a certain object or phenomenon. According to the semiotics of post-structuralists, things or phenomena convey meaning through the process of signification which connects the signifier and the signified. Thus, meaning can be conveyed not only by its property which can be empirically perceived and experienced but also by some association which may occur even without any real experience (Barthes, 1973). The more the content of association deviates from the empirical world, the higher the symbolism of the things and phenomena would be. At the extreme, we may envisage the circumstances under which the signifier gains the absolute control of meaning over its signifier (Baudrillard, 1983). As information technology reaches a certain point of maturity and the expression of the meaning of all things or phenomena is utterly digitalized, it would be quite probable that the relationship between the signifier and the signified will be decontextualized, and thus volitional behavioral patterns are highly commonplace.

III. Supporting Evidence

To confirm the making of new behavioral traits, a survey was conducted for 450 teenager sample in South Korea and their behavioral tendencies were compared with those of different age groups reported from other survey research. The distinctive behavioral characteristics Korean teenagers are summarized in Table 4-1.

Table 4-1 **Behavioral Characteristics of Korean Teenagers**

Behavioral Characteristics	Supporting Evidence
Estheticism	fancy goods / plastic surgery
Idiosyncrasy	hip hop fashion / colored hair

Event-Orientation	commencement extravaganza / pre-SAT party
Pursuit for Spectacles	mammoth concert / multi-vision wide screen
Multiculturalism	fusion food / jazz dance
Adventurism	extreme sports / venture business
Nomadism	convenience store / mobile phone
Velocity	abrupt meeting / fast food
Casualism	sitcom / internet café
Frivolity	mini-component / light beer
Participation	Karaoke & DIY (Do-It-Yourself)

If we collapse these behavioral tendencies into broader categories, expressiveness and voluntarism can be articulated as the dominant behavioral trends. If we further explore, "identity claim," represented by the attempts to realize one's own identity, turns out to be the most comprehensive behavioral attribute of current Korean youngsters.

IV. Nature of Cyberculture

Cyberculture is the cultural content that resides in its vehicle, cyberspace. Along with the extensive use of cyberspace, the effect of cyberculture can reach our intrapersonal mentality and new behavioral patterns corresponding to the changing environment tend to arise.

Cyberculture is the new ways of life of identity-searching individuals who have been socialized under the context of cyberspace of high degree of freedom. Since the objective environment works as the frame of reference, one may predict that the new cultural consciousness of cyberculture is the result of the interaction between the objective world of cyberspace described by those characteristics such as connectivity, anonymity, manipulability, temporal-spatial variability, virtuality, multiplicity, complexity and self-constructiveness and the subjective world of actor's behavioral orientations eventually attributable to "identity claim." Then, basic principle of cyberculture can be identified as neither pleasure nor reality, but transcendental one (Figure 4-1).

Figure 4-1 **The Formation of Cyberculture**

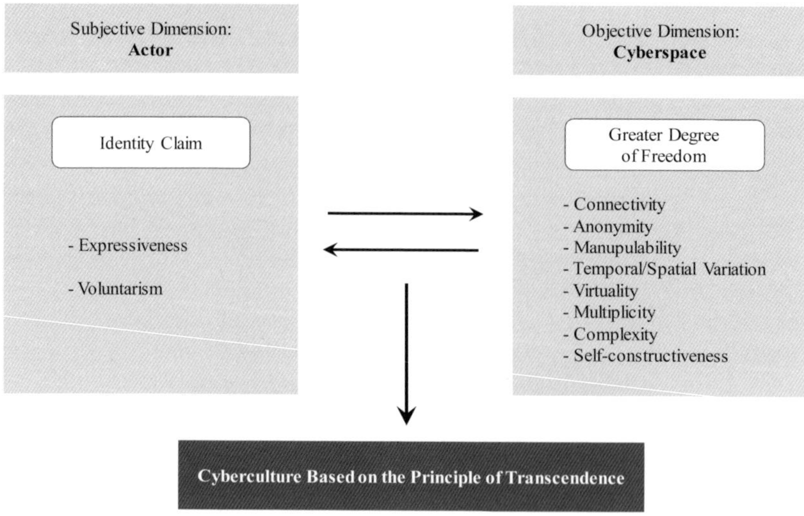

V. The Dynamics of Cyberculture

The rudimental dynamics of the cyberculture comes from the interplay between actor, the subject of a cultural activity, and the new cultural environment engaged with cyberspace. But, the underlying dynamism can be further explored from the discussions of the interface between (1) technology and culture, (2) center and periphery and (3) cultural system and its environment.

1. Technological Logic and Cultural Logic

As far as cyberculture is seen as a compound of culture and advanced ICTs, the association of technological logic and the cultural logic is of crucial importance for understanding the underlying dynamism of cyberculture.

Throughout human history, technology has remained as a part of culture system that comprises all the know-hows of any sort. Since early 17th to early 20th centuries, however, traditional congruence between science and technology were dissolved and the conflict between the two grew idle (Snow, 2012[1959]). Currently, technology and culture seem to enter another new age of accord and the barrier between technology and culture has been gradually alleviated. Cyberculture is a new phenomenon that implies the reunion of technology and culture.

2. Center and Periphery

Owning to its mixed property, cyberculture can contribute a lot for dissipating lateral or vertical boundaries. Even the case, the dynamism of cyberculture may aggravate certain conflicts and bring about radical social change through cross-valorization.

Past discussions on the relationships between center and periphery have been centered on the conflicts between the advantaged and the disadvantaged in terms of resources or opportunities available to them. However, under the current social condition where such dictum as "from quantity to quality," "from having to being" or "from life chance to lifestyle" prevails, cultural conflict may not be fully explained in terms of political economy regarding the issue of distribution since central life concern is now shifting from interest to identity (Taylor, 1992).

In the case of interest conflict, distribution of resources or opportunities is visible enough to make consensus or compromise. In contrast, in the case of identity conflict, the evaluation criteria are so vague that even those who are directly involving in the conflict process can hardly figure out its satisfactory level. Moreover, since identity conflict usually accompanies by serious emotional antagonism, its damage may be more serious than that of fierce interest conflict.

3. Cultural System and Its Environment

The advanced information society is prone to lead its cultural system to the chaotic state of greater complexity. In addition, the transcendental principle of actors and their action field of cyberspace allow greater variability in constructing ways of life. Off and on, this variability gives rise to a gloomy prospect that cultural life in the future may reduce to an irreversible state of anarchy. However, this line of prediction should be regarded as a one-sided view which overlooks the autopoietic potential of the cultural system. Autopoietic system, by its emergent properties, seeks to attain to the higher level of order.

ICTs have provided us with new challenges and opportunities. Moreover, virtual experience in the cyberspace enables people to reflect, reformulate and reorganize the goals they are searching for. People tend to cope with the complexity of the real world through the flexible action frame. So, the cyberculture itself should be taken as an outcome of autopoietic system that reflects the system's desire seeking an order from chaos.

This interpretation seems to be quite compatible with Stephen Crook's perspective (Crook, et al., 1992), which tried to understand modern society as post-modernity in terms of the concepts like hyper-differentiation, hyper-rationalization and hyper-commercialization.

It is Niklas Luhmann who spells out the principle of autopoietic growth and evolution. He argues that faced with the chaotic external environment referred as 'super complex circumstances,' system tries to diminish complexity by way of the response of selection, maintain the differentiation between itself and its environment, and elaborate its own internal structure (Luhmann, 1995). If we admit such autopoietic potential of cultural system, cyberculture is expected to undertake the positive function continuously creating new cultural values.

VI. Discussion

Peter Berger once saying that "the ultimate human terror is not evil but chaos," stresses that the basic function of culture is to enhance the sense of order out of the seemingly chaotic state (Berger, 1967). Originated by the rapid progress and diffusion of ICTs that has evoked additional source of confusion or complexity, cyberculture is thought to be the reflection of new cultural aspiration to "make sense of the world" in the chaotic digital world.

Then, what will the future of the cyberculture where mutually contending, multiple small narratives in lieu of great ones are prone to dominate current field of discourse? Some futurologists predict that information society led by the technological progress will be eventually replaced by sensational or emotional state filled with mythical fantasy that in the future we will find ourselves in a 'dream society' where stories are collected, created traded and consumed, thus implicitly suggesting the possibility of continuous increase of cultural entropy (Jensen, 1999).

With the demise of modern rationalism, we will not be able to refute the assertion that the dualism, often represented by the dichotomies like logos vs. pathos, cognition vs. affection, sense vs. sensibility, head vs. heart will continue to implode. Accordingly, the influence of cultural life-world vis-a-vis the politico-economic sphere is expected to flourish. Such a prediction can be supported by the fact that, recently, topics like life politics, cultural economy or managed heart are appealing more than ever before.

Although many people throw a doubt on the cultural life of the future, I do believe that cyberculture is a product of dynamic process searching for higher order on the 'edge of chaos' and it will fulfill the function of 'meaning giving', the unique function of culture, and thus help to overcome cultural anarchy.

Chapter 5

Online Buddhist Community

An Alternative Religious Organization

I. The Coming of Information Society

Passing the turn of the millennium, human society is undergoing a very dynamic process induced by an array of historical events such as technological revolution, globalizing economy, the decline of Marxism-Leninism, diffusion of postmodern lifestyle, and new forms of relationship between state-economy-civil society. Unlike the previous transition of industrialization driven by labor-saving mechanical technology, information technology is playing such a significant role in the current social transformation that 'information society' has become a catchword of our time.

There is not one but are many different perspectives on the information society (Lyon, 1988; Webster, 1995; Castells, 1996). Despite some clear differences, however, there exists consensus on characterizing the information society. As indicated by the massive mergers of major information and entertainment conglomerates during the past several years, new technology tends to be not just an informing tool but means of production, communication and leisure activities restructuring our working and non-working lives. Therefore, it becomes harder and harder to discuss contemporary society without referring to the magnificent effect of the new information technology (Kling, 1996).

II. Dynamics of Information Society

Informatization process does not portray a smooth and continuous path. Rather, it can be stated by a series of distinct steps having unique features and arrangements. There are many social scientific studies dealing with the societal transformation attributable to new information technology. Among a large body of specialized research studies, only a few authors have attempted a broad historical sweep and bold theorizing. To my knowledge, Manuel Castells seems to be the most remarkable.

In the trilogy, The Information Age: Economy, Society and Culture, Castells concludes decades of research by presenting an empirically grounded, cross-cultural account of major social, economic and political transformations which have reformulated the landscapes of human knowledge and experience across the globe. The basic model underlying his trilogy is a dialectical interaction of social relations and technology, or, in Castells' terminology, 'modes of production' and 'modes of development.'

Admitting that the evolution of the capitalist modes of production is driven by private capital's competitive pressure to maximize profits, Castells makes it clear that modes of development evolve according to their own logic. He defines the evolutionary logic of the current 'informational modes of development' according to 'Information Technology Paradigm.'[1] But he has not portrayed a comprehensive outlook of informatization process yet.

III. Stages of Informatization

Social transformation driven by advanced information technologies never occurs in a gradual and continuous fashion. It is widely open to sectional, functional, temporal variations. Taking all those variations into account, I construct a progressive model of social informatization presented in Figure 5-1.

The initial phase called 'computerization stage' is a state characterized by the construction of technological infrastructure including the installation of computer hardware. The effect of computerization lies in automating repetitive tasks and reducing working time and energy. The information technology at this stage remains instrumental in so far as it involves the enhancement of job efficiency without influencing other aspects of human activities.

1) Characteristics of "Information Technology Paradigm" described by Castells are; (1) Information is the raw material as well as the outcome. The new technologies act on information rather than on matter. (2) Because information is an integral part of all human activity, these technologies are pervasive. (3) Information technologies foster a networking logic, because it allows one to deal with complexity and unpredictability, which in itself is increased by these technologies. (4) The networking logic is based on flexibility. (5) Specific technologies converge into highly integrated systems (1996: 60-65).

Figure 5-1 **Developmental Model of Information Society**

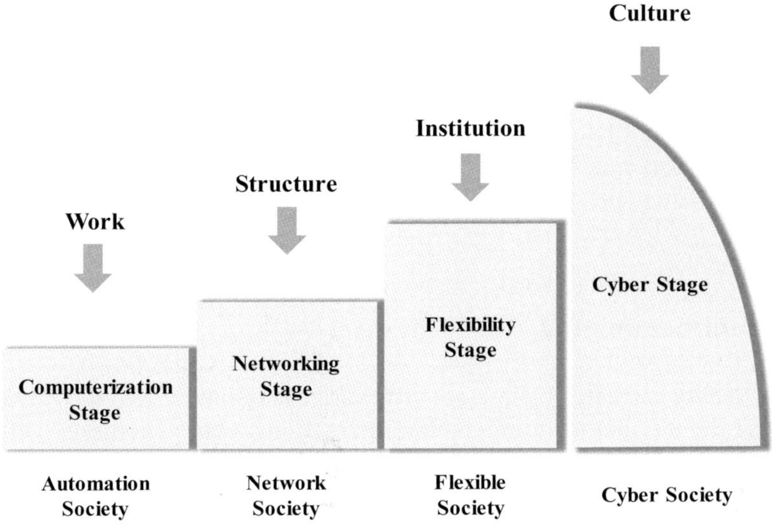

Next, follows the 'networking stage' where computing and telecommunication functions are incorporated. At this stage, the fusion of computing and telecommunication(C&C) technologies constitutes an extensive 'informational grid' linking people, homes, schools, factories, offices, shops, banks, hospitals, etc.

In the third 'flexibility stage,' 'borderlessness' emerges as the most prevalent phenomena. Until the modern industrial era, divisions between groups, organizations, sectors, regions, nations were rather clear-cut and often legally protected. But an extraordinary increase in the social networking tends to dissolve those divisions. Massive exchange of information beyond the time-space limitation dissociates all the boundaries.

The pinnacle of the informatization process is cyber-stage, an outcome of the fusion of advanced information technology and (multi-) media technology. Compared to the previous three stages - computerization, networking and flexibility, the last cyber-stage looks far more epochal, since cyberspace is a timeless-boundless space of infinite freedom.

IV. Cyberspace

Cyberspace, the constitutive element of the cybersociety, is defined as 'a conceptual space of interaction where words, data, wealth, power and affection are exchanged by people using CMC (Computer-Mediated Communication) technology (Rheingold, 1993b).

Cyberspace is an unbounded space within which anyone can contact anyone else exchanging whatever he or she wishes to trade. It is the place of anonymous encounter. It is characterized by a multilateral-multiplicative structure of 'hyperlink'. Further, cyberspace is atemporal and aspacial in the sense that it is not bound up with time or space at all. But, the most distinguishable trait of cyberspace may be its virtual property (Loader, 1997). That is why the term cyberspace is often used interchangeably with that of virtual reality.

V. Virtual Community

Virtual reality is created by interactivity. Varieties of online activities greatly increase the number of interpersonal interactions. Online communication is marked by its high frequency of exchange. Yet, a more significant aspect of cyberspace is the depth of exchange. With offline print medium and snail mail, it is difficult to have several rounds of conversation or discussion on the same subject. But online it is easy. One topic discussed for several days may generate hundreds of messages, so that there is an ample opportunity for in-depth discussions. As a result, it can foster a sense of community and create what Howard Rheingold calls virtual community (Rheingold, 1993a).

Is virtual community-building able to stop the fragmentation of social human relations? Thus far, many people suspect it and tend to regard virtual community as a pseudo-community. But, it may not the direct physical presence but social presence that gives rise to social integration. For some people, it turns out that virtual community has a great influence upon their daily lives not less than traditional local community (Jones, 1995). Indeed, such a prediction might be true in the case of virtual religious community in cyberspace.

VI. Social Functions of Religion

Religion is generally defined as a system of commonly held beliefs and practices that are oriented toward some sacred, supernatural realm. Modern sociologists who have studied the relationship between religion and society articulated social functions of religion as follows.

(1) Provision of meaning: Religion provides theodicy that gives meaningful answers to ultimate and eternal questions about human existence. Basically, we are living under conditions of uncertainty and insecurity.

But our capacity to control the conditions of our lives is very limited. Being perplexed and helpless in such an insurmountable, frustrating world, we feel the necessity of some sort of explanation. At these 'breaking points', religion provides meaningful answer that offers the prospect of hope of spiritual intercession (O'Dea, 1966).

(2) Legitimating social arrangement: Religion can function to legitimate, that is to provide justification for an existing social order (Berger, 1967). Religion does this by reinterpreting the realities of everyday life as part of a greater cosmic scheme. By placing everyone's daily existence in the context of a broader system of order, religion makes the status quo seem difficult or impossible to change.

(3) Promoting a sense of belonging: Religious organizations provide opportunities for people to associate with others who can exchange ideas, benefits, lifestyles, tastes, and so forth. Based upon the study of Western converts to Eastern religions, Harvey Cox (1977) argues that what they are looking for is friendship, companionship, acceptance, warmth and recognition. For many people in modern society, membership in a religious organization provides a sense of community to cope with their loneliness and isolation.

(4) Promoting social solidarity: Religion functions as a form of social 'cement.' It unites the believers by regularly bringing them together to enact various rituals and by providing them with the shared values and beliefs that bind them together into a unified moral community (Durkheim, 1947).

If we combine the first two functions into 'interpretive one', social functions of religion mentioned above may be subsumed under the notion of 3 'I's, i.e., 'Interpretive', 'Interactive' and 'Integrative'. Based on this tripartite classification scheme, it may be possible to differentiate types of religious community into 'Belief Community (BC)', 'Relational Community (RC)' and 'Affective Community (AC)' where 'need for otherness', 'need for affiliation' and 'need for collective identity' prevails.

VII. Religion in the Information Age

1. Religion and Technology

Religion and technology seem totally unrelated. They look quite incompatible since each deal with very different aspect of reality. Religion speaks to humanity most powerfully and authoritatively at the limit of human control over daily life. On the other hand, technology aims to extend the boundaries of human control, and consequently tends to diminish the operating arena of religion (Brasher, 2001).

Such a contrasting view was most conspicuous during the transitional period from medieval to modern ages. In Western history, the former dominated every aspect of human life throughout medieval period, while the latter gained salience from the outset of modern period. Thus, the oppositional relation of the two is, by and large, the result of the conflict between the medieval religious creed and modern technological civilization initiated by Victorian idea of science. Since then, debate over religion and technology has comprised the issue of religion versus science.

It is often said that the 'God of the physicists is cosmic order' (Pagels, 1984). At the very bottom level, religion and science may share the same purpose, i.e., searching for the fundamental order of the universe. Among those who support the non-confrontational view of science and religion, some maintain convergence model by saying 'All truth is God's truth.' A Liberal Protestantist theologian Friedrich Schleiermacher, who reinterpreted Christian faith in accordance with the accepted wisdom of the age is a good example. Another example is the process theology which has actively sought to adapt the Christian tradition to the insights of the natural science (McGrath, 1999).

But, more persuasive than such overarching conceptualization is the complementary view that stresses the distinctive nature of religion and science. The emphasis on the distinctiveness of the two has been obvious in the writings of Neo-Orthodoxy theologians. Langdon Gilkey (1959) argues that theology (religion) and the science (natural science) represent independent and different ways of approaching reality. The natural sciences are concerned with asking 'how' questions, where theology asks 'why' questions. The former deals with secondary causes (that is, within the sphere of nature), while the latter deals with primary causes (that is, the ultimate origin and purpose of nature). Yet, based on the complementarity logic, they yield answers which are harmonious and mutually enriching, rather than conflicting and divergent (McGrath 1998)[2]

2) The idea of complementality is derived from Danish physicist and philosopher Niels Bohr and the Copenhagen School of quantum mechanics. Bohr's principle of complementarity is originally concern with the wave and particle models of light and matter. For Bohr, the two models were both required to explain the behavior of light and matter. So, whatever the nature of light may be, its behavior can be explained in the basis of wave and particle models, and the complete description of the behavior rests upon the bringing together of what are, in effect, mutually exclusively ways of representing it. This principle of holding together two apparently irreconcilable models of a complex phenomenon in order to account for the behavior of the phenomenon is known as the principle of complementarity (McGroth 1998: 187-195).

2. Religion in Cyberspace

Recent development of information and communication technologies provides another opportunity for us to reflect upon the relationship between religion and science in terms of 'new principle of complementarity.'

According to British philosopher Alfred Whitehead, religion is defined by what people do with their solitude. To the deeply pious members, religion is the main activity through which one's deepest, ultimate concerns are expressed (Brasher, 2001). But to the lay people, religion is a source of social interaction while something sacred is still the matter of interest. Thus, religion is a way of making communion. To the extent that most religious expressions take the form of communication, they should be accompanied by relevant means of communication.

Throughout history, religion has quickly adapted to almost every new communication technology. Bible may be its first noticeable product. Thanks to Johannes Gutenberg's printing press, the fifteenth-century Europeans were able to get an access to the religious documents that were formally limited only to an affordable few. Radio and television had the similar impact upon religion. With the advent of those mass broadcasting technologies, people started to think of themselves as audience and demanded the quality of the worship event. The popularity of mega-churches soared; religious radio survived in almost every city; televised worship drew huge local and national television audiences; cable television and its satellite distribution proved an even more ground for their evangelical use. Internet is playing a powerful role in religious communications (Soukup, 1999).

Religious organization is formed, maintained and reformed by the group of people called communion. Recently, more and more online religious organizations flourish and diversify. Then, what makes them so proliferate? Online religion provides immediate access to a wide range of religious information, usually more quickly than do the traditional channels of distribution. Online religion is the media that provide us the experience of co-presence without having any temporal-spatial constraints. Online religion also provides means of candid discussions that are relatively free from the influence of pre-existing religious authorities. In addition, owing to its virtual character, online religion can create the spectacles that help to provoke enormous religious experience. But more than anything else indicated in Table 5-1, only within cyberspace we are getting to enjoy a highly privatized, focused and multi-way communications. Accordingly, the online religious communities are thought to be the locale where people can directly find a spiritual sanctuary under a very unrestricted speech condition.

Table 5-1 **Media Characteristics regarding to the Attributes of Communication**

Medium	Attribute			
	Privacy	Audience	Direction	Temporality
CMC	High	Focused	Multi-way	Variable
Phone	High	Focused	2-way	Immediate
Mail	High	Focused	2-way	Delayed
Radio	Low	Broad	1-way	Immediate
TV	Low	Broad	1-way	Immediate
Print		Broad	1-way	Delayed

(Boehlefeld, 1996: 147, Revised)

VIII. Online Buddhist Community in Korea

With the rapid expansion of information highway driven by ambitious National Information Infrastructure policy, the commercial telecommunication network began to flourish since early 1990s and four major information service providers – Chollian, Hitel, Nownuri and Unitel – appeared thereafter.

1. Buddhist Communication on the Internet

Overall, 24 religious communities were found in aforementioned major information service providers. Their distribution with respect to religious denomination is summarized in Table 5-2. Buddhist online communities include BUD and BOSAL in Chollian, BUD in Hitel, BUD in Nownuri, BUD in Unitel.

Table 5-2 **Religious Communities within Major Information Service Providers in 1997**

Religion	Chollian	Hitel	Nownuri	Unitel
Protestant	3	1	3	2
Catholic	1	1	1	1
Buddhism	2	1	1	1
Won Buddhism	1	0	0	0
Unification Church	0	1	0	0
Other	1	1	1	1

(Park, 1997: 4-5, Summarized)

Unlike most online religious communities initiated or supported by established religious institutions, most online Buddhist communities were developed spontaneously because Buddhism traditionally emphasizing 'Anitya' (impermanence of existence) would not pay much attention to the dynamics of external world. Thus, Buddhist communication on the internet has been characterized as being more autonomous, private, informal and unbounded compared to that of other religious denominations.

2. Chollian Buddhist Club

Chollian Buddhist club (C-BUD) formed on September 6, 1991. Due to its history, scale and activities, C-BUD composed of more than 300 communities was regarded as one of the most successful online religious communities until the late 1990s when web-based online communities began to upsurge. Three main menus, a supporting menu and submenus belonging to them are listed in Table 5-3.

Table 5-3 **Menus and Sub-menus in C-BUD**

Main Menu			Supporting Menu
Learning Sector (LS)	Relieving Sector (RS)	Sharing Sector (SS)	Office Sector (OS)
LS1: Beginner LS2: Counseling LS3: Bible Study LS4: Debate	RS1: Café RS2: Inner Circle RS3: Personal Affairs RS4: Guesthouse RS5: Open Letter RS6: Chatting Room	SS1: Sermon SS2: Meditation SS3: Buddhist Culture SS4: Event SS5: Library	OS1: Newsletter OS2: Newcomer OS3: Membership OS4: Management OS5: Voting

(Park, 1997: 46, Rearranged)

Nowadays most online communities are located in search engines or portal sites. Complying with such a new trend, C-BUD members decided to transform their online community into web based one and launched their own website on the internet in August 30, 2001. Unlike most religious communities registered in a specific search engine or portal site, C-BUD is having its own service solution with independent domain (http://www.buddhasite.net). That is why C-BUD has been most successful in soliciting loyalty from its members and maintaining a solid group identity. Furthermore, contrary to café-type religious communities simply providing scriptures, liturgies, events, news, chat room services, etc., C-BUD has been gaining qualifications that make it possible to evolve into an alternative religious organization.

IX. Analysis

Despite a growing concern for information society and persistent research interest in religious community, a scant attention has been paid to the complex phenomena of online religious community. Thus far, only a countable number of studies have been reported concerning the issue of online religious communication in Korea (Park 2000; Kim 2000). What made things worse is that they were polarized into either very preliminary case description or illusive conceptual discussion. This study may be the first and only empirico-theoretical approach to online Buddhist communication in Korea.

Triangulation strategy, combined methods of content analysis, participatory observation and interview were adopted. To figure out basic communication patterns, content analysis was conducted. Participatory observations were carried out to ensue what was going on in chatting room and various offline meetings. Interviews with past and current executive members were also included for more valid interpretations.

The data were collected between September 1996 – August 1997. It was the time when most independent ISP-based online communities were incorporated into huge search engines or portal sites. However, since ISP-based religious communications were usually composed of the participants who are willing to pay for their membership fee, it was able to maintain a strong group solidarity and identity. Thus, more recent web-based online communications are not included in this study.

1. Findings

1) Users' Profile

Not far from the general patterns of internet users, male users of twentieths and thirties comprise most of C-BUD members. Sex and age distributions of 1,146 members who registered between April - October 1977 are summarized in Table IV.

The results are quite opposite to the distributions of the people who declared themselves as Buddhist listed in the third column of Table 5-4.

Table 5-4 **C-BUD Membership Composition by Sex and Age (%)**

(N=1146)

Sex		Age				
Male	Female	-19	20-29	30-39	40-49	50+
71.8	28.2	8.0	56.7	26.7	7.5	1.1

(Lim, 1996: 24)

Among 530 members whose occupations were identifiable, college students occupied the highest proportionv (32.1%) and next followed white collar workersv (23.2%), professionalv (8.7%) and middle/high school studentsv (7.7%) in sequence. The monthly connection time amounted to 903:33 1819:37 hours in March 1996 and September 1997 and average connection time were 51:46 and 58:32 respectively. The fact that busy daily workers are actively committed to online religious communications may be an additional evidence that can predict the emergence of alternative religious organizations in cyberspace.

2) Purpose of Communications and Activities

If we review major online menus of C-BUD, their explicit purpose tends to bifurcate into "Intimacy" vs. "Information." For instance, those menus such as "Café", "Open Letter" and "Personal Affairs" are designed to consolidate the intimacy, while "Sermon," "Mediation," "Beginner" and "Bible Study" are intended to increase religious information. On the other hand, "Chatting Room" aims to do dual function of intimacy and information, while "Debate" is deemed to perform another dual functions of information exchange and religious practice.

Besides those verbal activities, there are several offline activities in C-BUD, such as "Cohort Meeting," "Abrupt Meeting," "Regional Meeting," "Community Service" and "Regular Communion". Apparently, "Cohort Meeting" and "Abrupt Meeting" aim to increase intimacy, while "Community Service" is for better religious practice. Two other offline activities, "Regional Meeting" and "Regular Communion," are supposed to meet a triple purpose - intimacy, information and religious practice – which seem to quite comparable to the three different orientations of religion – people-orientation, knowledge-orientation and action-orientation. The major online communications and offline activities with respect to their expected purpose are illustrated in Figure 5-2.

Figure 5-2 **Intended Purpose of Major Online/Offline Activities in C-BUD**

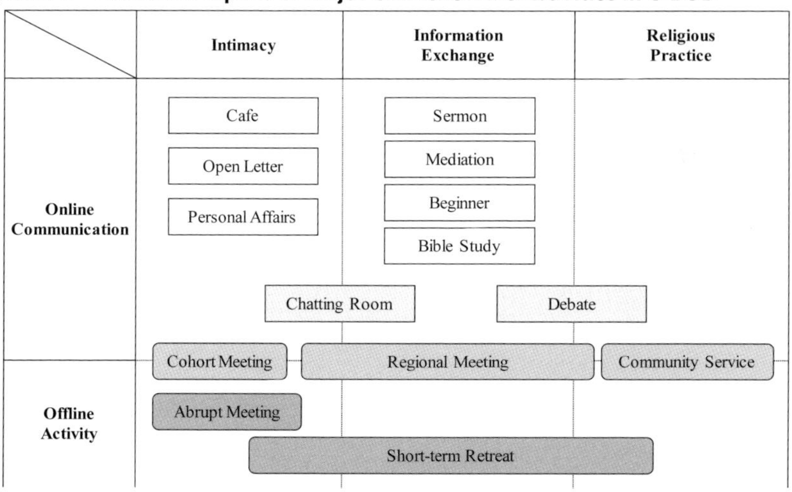

2. Summary and Discussions

Past studies of virtual community propose that (1) The development of virtual community can be explained as a reaction to the decline of traditional community. (2) Community ties are to be consolidated when people meet on a regular basis in cyberspace. (3) The members of virtual community meet online to do just about everything that other people do in face-to-face interactions. A case study of an online Buddhist club is carried out to test those propositions. Users' characteristics, formal structure, and verbal/behavioral activities are examined. In general, strong empirical evidence supporting the propositions is obtained.

Then, online communications and activities of Chollian Buddhist Club were analyzed in terms of three basic functions of religious discussed in Section 6. By and large, three main menus that comprise the substantive part of the Chollian Buddhist Club, Learning Sector (LS), Relieving Sector (RS) and Sharing Sector (SS) seemed to exactly match three basic functions of religion - interpretive, interactive and integrative function respectively. Simultaneously, five submenus of the supporting menu - from OS1 to OS5 - could be deployed into the three basic functions of religion mentioned above.

However, when we further investigate the contents of actual online communications performed within each submenu, we can draw a conclusion that not all the submenu activities are performing what was originally designated by their top menus. What is going on in RS2 and RS3 are closer to integrative function, and so are the activities of SS1 and SS2 to interpretive function. And, a part of activities of SS3-SS4 and OS1/OS2/OS3 seems to have something to do with totally different function that may be labeled as 'instrumental function' for profit seeking through online interaction constituting utilitarian community (UC) (Figure 5-3).

In addition, if we compare the number of connections across the types of community, the highest is the RC and next are BC, AC and UC in sequence. Overall, functional composition of the interactions occurring in C-BUD turns out to be quite like that of established Buddhist Church where BC is playing a dominant role over AC or BC. Anyhow, the most conspicuous aspect in C-BUD is the manifestation of utilitarian community that used to be obscured by sacred religious creed in existing religious institutions.

Figure 5-3 **Functions and Functional Relocation of C-BUD**

Function & Community Type	Formal Menu	Activity
Interpretive Function - Belief Community (BC)	Learning Sector (LS)	LS1: Beginner LS2: Counseling LS3: Bible Study LS4: Debate
Interactive Function - Relational Community (RC)	Relieving Sector (RS)	RS1: Cafe RS2: Inner Circle RS3: Personal Affairs RS4: Guest House RS5: Open Letter RS6: Chatting Room
Integrative Function - Affective Community (AC)	Sharing Sector (SS)	SS1: Sermon SS2: Meditation SS3: Buddhist Culture SS4: Event SS5: Library
Instrumental Function - Utilitarian Community (UC)		
System Operation	Office Sector (OS)	OS1: Newsletter OS2: Newcomer OS3: Membership OS4: Management OS5: Voting

Figure 5-4 **Comparing Composition and Hierarchy of Community Types in C-BUD**

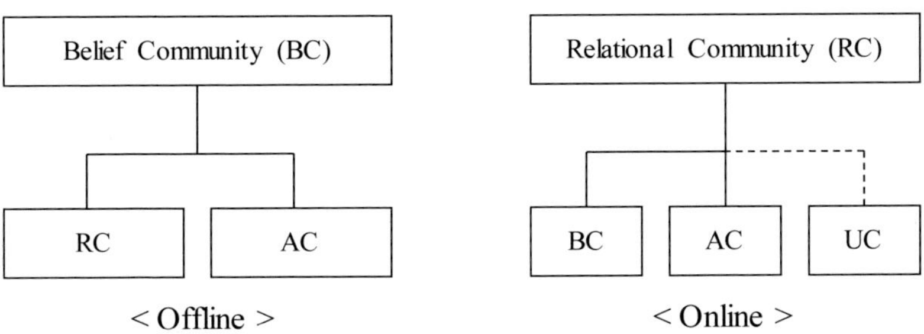

X. Discussion

While more than 80% of the whole population are concentrated in cities, most Buddhist churches (temples) are still scattered in rural mountainous area. Therefore, to busy full-time workers, it is hard going to temple on a regular basis. That is why Korean Buddhism is now said to suffer from "elder/female excess phenomenon." In this sense, Chollian Buddhist Club (C-BUD) that is now drawing many people who regard offline meeting too demanding appears to be a possible alternative to the pre-existing religious organizations. Such a prediction sounds quite valid when we examine age and sex distributions of the Chollian Buddhist Club users that are sharply contrasted to that of offline congregational members (Table 5-5). Particularly, the openness and anonymity of most online communications promote active participation of the members who might feel reluctant to participate in formalized offline patterns of worship.

Another remarkable difference between online and offline religious communications can be found in the manifestation of utilitarian community by the process of 'functional dislocation.' Accordingly, it can be argued that online religious communication is more inclusive than offline religious affiliation since that the former contains the utilitarian community that is not so explicit in the case of the latter.

Perhaps, the most important finding may be the emergence of spiritual community through functional dislocation. To its members, online religious co-experience with like-minded individuals seems to have a great influence on their everyday lives, not much less than that in traditional offline religious organization at all. It must be a strong counter-evidence to those who suspect the virtual community-building or regard virtual community as a pseudo-community.

The findings also suggest that the online Buddhist Club is performing multiple functions (1) as a belief community providing a system of beliefs and practices relative to Buddhism, (2) as a relational community that helps satisfy the need for affiliation in a heartless world, (3) as an affective community to provide a kind of group identity for those who seek it, plus (4) as a utilitarian community providing an effective means of resource mobilization for the pursuit of individual interest as well.

It challenges the conventional idea on modern societal transformation, generally described as 'form primary group to secondary group, or from Gemeinschaft to Gesellschaft (Cooley 1992; Tönnis 1988). Thus, a new ideal-typical construct that considers the multi-functions of contemporary religious organizations, - interpretive, interactive, integrative and instrumental - needs to be further explored.

We can also witness the changing role of online religion, 'the shift from media to life-world.' which is quite analogous to Marshall McLuhan's dictum, 'Medium is Message.' Nowadays Online religious organization is shifting toward a locale of spiritual community of like-minded individuals. Accordingly, 'sanctuary model' instead of 'tool model' seems to be more appropriate in understanding the current development of religious organization. More than an additional locale for religious practice, online religious community is moving toward an alternative religious organization that satisfies the needs of contemporary individuals who are trying to pursue a 'biographical solution to systemic contradictions in the individualized world.'(Beck and Beck: 2002: XVI)

Section III

Changing Self and Identity

Chapter 6

Lifelogging and Changing Nature of Self

"I write, therefore I am." As this famous statement asserts, human beings are distinguished from other creatures as Homo Scriptus, who keeps track of their experiences. To fulfill such desire, 'lifelogging' is largely classified into manual and automatic documentation. Manual lifelogging represented by journal writing traces back to the era of script. Meanwhile, lifelogging using diverse devices has moved into high gear along with the expansion of advanced information technology: in this study, the latter will be the focus of discussion.

Lifelogging has come into our daily lives with the appearance of mobile devices and sensors. As the Internet of Things helps to expand the networked connection of 'people to people,' 'people to things,' 'things to things,' 'everything to everything' and the intelligent 'Ambient Internet of Everything' integrating virtual reality, lifelogging has become an unusual phenomenon of modern society (Gurrin, Smeaton and Doherty, 2014). There lies a reason for a thorough examination regarding its effects on both an individual and society as a whole.

Extra attention needs to be paid to the influence of lifelogging on self, an interface between an individual and society, as the accumulation of personal information caused by lifelogging brings about sweeping changes in the concept of self. Regarding self in an era of lifelogging, some fundamental questions can be posed: is it losing its autonomy as it gradually separates from a subject? or is it reinforcing its autonomous capability as advanced digital devices, which are getting lighter, slimmer, shorter and smaller, help it have the world in the palm of hand.

Accordingly, this chapter intends to (1) review the development and social effects of lifelogging technology with a focus on wearable technology and the IoT, (2) examine changing perceptions of self-caused by lifelogging from different perspectives, (3) propose theses on self in an era of lifelogging, and (4) suggest imminent issues and countermeasures with regard to self-changing with the expansion of lifelogging.

I. Lifelogging Technology: Development and Social Effects

1. Development of Lifelogging Technology

Lifelogging is defined as a practice of digitally collecting, processing and reenacting life experience data gathered by diverse sensors. Fundamental technologies behind lifelogging include microelectronics technology, IT technology leading the development of computers and the Internet, advanced biotechnology, and nano-technology which controls the bulk technology at a molecular level. Data of life experiences, which consist of the main body of lifelogging, are partly broadcast via such IT devices as personal computers and mobile phones, but basically, they are established through wearable sensors and, regardless of lifeloggers' intention, automatically accumulated in daily environment: hence, wearable technology and IoT are core technologies of lifelogging.

Wearable technology has been enhanced to develop light-weight devices suitable to be worn, reinforcing physical and sensory activities. Early-stage wearable technologies initiated for military purposes once had weight and shape issues and functional confinements. Yet, with weight reduction based on nano-technology, functional diversification using biotechnology, and the IoT service introduced in the 2010s, a wide use of wearable technology has been rapidly facilitated.

Starting 1994, Steve Mann, a mechanical engineer and performance artist, transmitted his everyday life over the Web using a wearable camera and display, and exchanged live feeds and messages with other people in real time. During this project, he devised a way to attach computers, keyboards, screens and wireless transmitters to human body (Mann, Nolan and Wellman, 2011). In the beginning, their practical values failed due to heavy-weight computer devices, but later, as web cams emerged followed by Google Glass, Apple iWatch, and Nike+ with the development of nano-technology, life capturing has become much easier.

Designed to intelligently connect everything using information technology, the Internet of Things generally refers to the technology and services, which sense and communicate with surroundings, and properly process and control data linking everything with the Internet anytime anywhere without direct human intervention. The Internet in the 1990s was interpersonal involving exchanges of necessary information between individuals, but in the future, where the IoT will be in wide use, the age of universal access is expected to come, where not only person-to-person information exchanges are possible, but everything trades data through the Internet.

Core technology of the IoT is wireless sensor networking, which establishes an autonomous network by arranging sensor nodes equipped with computing and wireless communication capabilities to the application environment, controlling and monitoring data wirelessly collected from sensor nodes. With little direct human intervention, it decisively contributes to an expansion of lifelogging by generating and reproducing personal information indefinitely.

2. Social Ramifications of Lifelogging Technology

Just as smart phone technology is now considered universal, not a special technology confined to specific sectors or users, so is lifelogging technology. As Larry Page, founder of Google, observed, "Invention itself is not really helping. If only the world finds it useful and people start to use it, it finally works" (Auletta, 2009). When it comes to universal technology, what really matters is not its technological capability or technical innovation, but how many people are using it. As assured by Gordon Bell and Jim Gemmel, who are predicting that lifelogging will become a daily practice before 2020, rejecting lifelogging in the future equals to refusing to use e-mail or a smart phone today. Some technologies tend to permeate into our daily lives unknowingly. Technology sociologist Sherry Turkle has conceptualized such a phenomenon as 'technological promiscuity' (Bell and Gemmell, 2009; Turkle, 2011).

Lifelogging exerts a grave influence on the way we think, feel and act by recording and measuring our daily lives with digital devices. It is true that this brand-new technology is considerably enhancing an individual's health, memories and restoration, security, work and inspection. Where there is gain, however, there is loss. Due to its heavy dependence on digital tools, lifelogging poses a serious challenge to individual privacy (Selke, 2014).

In digital society, privacy is bound to be invaded whether we like it or not. Our daily lives are exposed or open to others through various forms of data including GPS of a smart phone, a navigation system of an automobile, an ID card with a smart tag, or a credit card containing transactional details. With the rise of a lifelogging age, where details of a user's conscious or unconscious experiences, as well as his/her personal or daily information, are thoroughly recorded, invasion of privacy may take place more widely and more surreptitiously because documented personal data could be exploited as if it were a separate issue from privacy. In lifelogging, for instance, one's sleep, sex, workout, diet, productivity and emotion can all be measured, stored, utilized, evaluated and compared as variables, tremendously influencing an individual life (Selke, 2014).

Heed should be paid to the fact that potential effects of lifelogging are not identical with those of augmented reality or virtual world. Augmented reality and the world of lifelogging are common in that they complement the real world, but the former promotes its presence by reinforcing the virtuality of a real environment, while the latter substantiates life by thickening information. They share similarity in that they are an integrated system of recorded information, but they also show a difference: a genuine virtual reality is a sort of non-existent simulacre, while lifelogging intends to supplement and enrich the real world. Therefore, lifelogging exerts a greater impact on the real world than any other alternative realities as it basically shares the same trajectory as the actual world.

II. Changes of Self Through Lifelogging

1. Lifelogging, Body and Self

Warren Susman argues that the self came to be assembled and fabricated for impression formation and management around the early 20th century for the first time in human history. Such a phenomenon is in line with 'the dramaturgical theory of self' presented by sociologist Erving Goffman, which is considered a prototype of a post-modern self featuring flexibility, dispersibility, and fragmentariness(Illouz, 2006).

In recent years, discussions on self have been within boundaries of the theory of digital society, which presupposes periodical conditions since the modern era. Consequently, self has been perceived more flexible, variable, fragmented and complex compared with self in the past. In this sense, it is noted that a new theory of self is being proposed. Theories of self in the digital age, which have often been discussed under such themes as cyber self or virtual self, tend to mostly take issue with mental aspects excluding physical existence. Yet, on-line self can be easily represented by a wide range of symbols. As our body and looks are publicly displayed in the on-line world, we get extremely conscious of the way we look and often compete using the body as a main source of social and economic values (Kim, 2011).

As mentioned before, self in the lifelogging world, unlike that of virtual reality or augmented reality, is close to an existential self accompanying an individual's physical and emotional sentiment because lifelogging is a record of an existent being. In the theory of information technology society, emphases have mostly been placed on instrumental functions such as recording a user's life experiences in various ways, or letting relevant information known to the external world by interacting with a user's body: there has been little discussion regarding the user's existential characteristics unlike in lifelogging. In this sense, self in the lifelogging world is rather comparable with 'ontic self,' which Heidegger once observed.

Phenomenologist Edmund Husserl asserted that relations between different objects take place as a "perceiving and moving body" captures them. When interacting with the world, a lived body obtains a reflexive experience, which Husserl named sensation. In Phenomenologie de la perception, Maurice Merleau-Ponty defined a relation between individuals and their bodies as coexistence, arguing "the way a body exists in the world is identical with the way a heart exists within a body." He went further to distinguish concepts of perception and sensation: while the latter refers to experiencing active properties of an object, the former represents a perceptual recognition based on dead characteristics of its properties(Merleau-Ponty, 1962[1945]). It equals to a difference between watching a moving body and a non-moving body. Sociologist Pierre Bourdieu agrees with Merleau-Ponty, placing a body at the center of social interactions. Observing that a body can think on its own because social experiences are accumulated and displayed within itself, Bourdieu proposed habitus, an essential concept of cultural capitalism(Bourdieu and Wacquant, 1992).

In his writing, The Body and Society: Explorations in Social Theory, Bryan Turner introduced 'embodied self.' Criticizing that sociology has long dealt with self without the body, he considers the embodied self as a fundamental foundation of social interactions. As a substance supervising a process of making relations and interacting with others, the body becomes an object of reinforced self management, self regulation and self control. There lies a significance of body in the theory of self in the lifelogging age. Body is a bridge between the physical and mental worlds, and at the same time, a medium linking the actual world and the lifelogging world (Elliot, 2011; Turkle, 2011).

Thinking robots, which are witnessing a rapid progress in recent years, are also based upon the traditional monism emphasizing inseparability of mind and body. As Turkle maintains, it can later be used as grounds for an argument that a robot and a human being cannot possess equal intelligence. In this context, the theory of self in the lifelogging age is existential in that mind and body are not fundamentally inseparable, but it does not completely exclude a view of virtual self in the digital era. Therefore, self in the lifelogging age can be defined as a confluence of existential self and virtual self, and its convergent attributes will be examined from seven perspectives.

2. Seven Theses on Self in the Lifelogging Age

1) Quantified Self

First introduced by journalists Gary Wolf and Kevin Kelly, 'quantified self' includes health management data based on quantitative figures. According to Wolf's argument, in order to live an efficient life in the lifelogging age, we need to know about ourselves through diverse measurements (Wolf, 2009; Prince, 2014). Quantified self has become possible due to the advent of 'biometrics' with demands on accuracy and precision gradually rising. By measuring and examining body organs, it provides such information as sleeping hours, heart rates, caffeine intake, alcohol consumption, and self-attachment index (Selke, 2014; Lupton, 2016).

Quantified self pursues self optimization as well as self monitoring. Wearable devices offer a wide range of recommendations according to the principle of optimization: for instance, they might advise you to work out more and eat less for better health. Or, they might intervene with your life by setting up regulations like granting incentives if you follow their advice or giving penalties if you get lazy. In other words, with the help of wearable tools, a specific set of rules are internalized by enforcing or suppressing self-control. In quantified self, 'I' only exist in numbers: so far, height and weight were some of the few figures telling about an individual, but now, (s)he can be represented by many different figures detailing the oxygen level in blood, blood pressure, pulse, current index of self-attachment, or indicators of rage and other emotions.

As Wolf started using the concept of quantified self in 2009, researchers have expanded the theory to include 'quantified baby' or 'quantified car.' A quantified baby provides a diversity of data to parents. Devices attached to the baby sends signals via the parent's smart phone about when to change diapers or feed for the sake of the baby, who cannot speak. In this state, devices get to know much more about the baby than parents or the baby itself. Likewise, riding a quantified car equipped with smart sensors, a driver can perceive and deal with fatigue level, heart rate, speed control, traffic information, and anger and stress management behind the wheel (Swan, 2015).

Quantified self can evolve into a healthy being by enthusiastically checking body conditions and thus preventing deterioration in health. Consequently, quantified self and health care will inevitably interface with each other, and 'funny self-innovation' can be promoted by sharing and using lifelogging data as a means of friendly competition.

2) Recorded Self

Recorded self refers to a set of lifelogging data, in which journal keepers recount the details of their daily lives on Web log, Blogs or SNS in the digital age (Dijck, 2004). Conventionally, digital memories of the recorded self are accessed by the memories stored in the cloud: here, targets of inspection and supervision include me as a subject of a daily life, or me as a data footprint.

So-called digital memory, which remembers more than an individual's biological memory, represents "me, who knows more about me than myself" (Bell and Gemmell, 2009). Recorded self may become immortal: it is limitlessly accessible every day, and even after death, descendants can bring it up anytime they want. As it knows every little detail of my past, even the mistakes and memories I want to remove, me in the past can always haunt me in the present. If it is a good memory, then it is not a big problem, but if the memories I want to delete are haunting, they are not entitled to be forgotten. In other words, recorded self tend to persistently remind us of the memories we want to forget: such a side-effect is particularly overwhelming in influential figures and celebrities, whose past has greater social impacts.

Some researchers take the recorded self to the extremes. Marvin Minski, an artificial intelligence researcher, argues that human brain is a machine made of meat and his/her body is an organism of blood, which is completely replaceable by machines. According to their assertion that even human mind is like a program with a structure or a subroutine, human beings as a biological existence cannot be presumed any longer.

3) Connected Self

'Connected self' derives from an argument that a self is shaped depending on the way one makes relationships. Today's society separates social relations from places, employing dynamics of disembeddedness mechanism, which re-connects social relations with other relationships by isolating time and space. Such experiences linked by a new connection of time and space may overwhelm direct experiences.

As we can log on anytime anywhere, someone connected with us through a device is thought more important than a person right beside us. In the same context, a cessation of access may cause fear and anxiety, which means the ubiquitous accessibility amplifies angst from disconnection. High connectivity increases dependence on devices, reducing face-to-face communications: thus, depending on the way one makes relationships, an individual identity alters.

In War of the Worlds: Cyberspace and the High-tech Assault of Reality, Mark Slouka (1995) asserts that as cyberspace attacks human identity, what happens to a cyber self is equivalent to what occurs to me, and an on-line proxy challenges the identity of an original self. Self in lifelogging is similar. Proxies created by an individual are connected to the Internet: the higher the dependence on a connected self, the greater the tendency of mistaking a proxy for an original self.

4) Monitored Self

Abstract data elicited from a body through biometrics are driving away actual human beings. Today, a body as an ultimate source of information revealing a lot about an individual is being used to verify one's identity and predict behavioral patterns or circumstances. Accordingly, as with the omnidirectional digital surveillance, individuals in a physical sense are gradually disappearing in a physical surveillance under lifelogging conditions. For instance, passports have so far been used to verify identity, but in the future, physical data-based identification is expected to be prevalent, including fingerprints, rods and cone cells of retina, voice, facial shape, and DNA extracted from body fluids. Such data, however, may be handed to a government, the ultimate managing authority, gravely threatening individual autonomy (Lyon, 2001).

Since information regarding monitored self is highly likely to fall into someone else's hand or control, it is urgent to establish a social consensus or information protection policy concerning lifelogging devices. In other words, there is a concern that regardless of one's will, information on his/her physical status could be monopolized by device manufacturers or the government, or sensitive private information is likely to be abused by some specific groups. In fact, government authorities wielding public power have used CCTVs to monitor protestors, causing social issues (Whitaker, 1999). Furthermore, monitored self may bring about a 'post privacy' issue, which allows limitless surveillance and exposure under the name of a transparent society. It is partly the result of monitoring by others, but it is also a consequence of one's own disclosure or exposure. There lies a need to develop an in-depth discussion on it later.

5) Overloaded Self

'Technology overload' refers to an overflow of technology exceeding the need of consumers due to the interests of suppliers. It has promoted rapid development of new technology, but more and more people are having a hard time catching up. As Alvin Toffler observed earlier, advanced technology is oppressing, rather than liberating, human beings as it gets too difficult to use and too high-priced to afford, which rather results in limited choices and lost freedom (Ellul, 1997). Such a phenomenon has much in common with 'the paradox of choice' asserted by Barry Schwartz (2004), a presumption that with an increased range of choices, one's decision-making capability becomes weakened.

According to David Levy, a brain that is not capable of consistent thinking as it is excessively accustomed to convenient devices is named a 'popcorn brain,' which is the result of a reduction in the amount of gray matter of the brain caused by such information overload as ceaseless stimuli and rapid online processes. Information Fatigue Syndrome, which was conceptualized by British psychologist David Louis (1996), can also be considered part of side-effects of information overload. Back then, it was confined to a certain group of people, whose job was to deal with a massive amount of information for a long time, but today, it is not an exaggeration to say that most people are suffering this syndrome, which means information overload is generalized to such an extent (Han, 2012).

Lifelogging may contribute to diversifying one's interpersonal relationships or leisure activities, but it inevitably brings about information overload due to a constant connection with networks or devices. For instance, we have more Facebook friends than offline buddies. Asserting that "human minds are not made (by evolution) to be social with more than a limited number of people in the social world," Robin Dunbar proposed the Dunbar's number, according to which, human beings can only keep track of 150 meaningful relationships. Yet, most Facebook users have much more friends than that, which reveals an aspect of the overloaded self phenomenon (Bauman and Lyon, 2012).

6) Evaluated Self

Today, self is getting more narcissistic as the desire of recognition, i.e., being considered superior, grows stronger. In the SNS world, the number of user interactions is easily calculated, evaluating the degree of engagement or recognition by friends and acquaintances. According to Axel Honneth, a critical philosopher, decentering takes place in the subject of recognition, whose endowment of values to another subject provides a ground for legitimacy of being disconnected from self-love. In other words, a behavior of recognizing someone leads to social evaluation by causing a decentration from self-centered perspectives (Offe, 2010).

Characteristics of the evaluated self are like the intentions of the Calvinists, who aspired to assure a doctrine of predestination through diligence, abstinence and self-regulation. However, such an obsession with the pursuit of a perfect self may result in losing the essence of a self. Therefore a phenomenon dubbed 'Ripley's Syndrome' is prevalent in the lifelogging age. Ripley is a leading character of Patricia Highsmith's novel, who forged lies for an ascent of status and lived in a delusion that those lies were true, finally being dragged down to destruction. Every human has a desire of being looked up to by glamorizing him/herself, and such a tendency intensifies in modern society, where social competition grows fierce. If this desire goes overboard, the illusional self will be praised instead of seeing the true self. In this regard, the age of lifelogging is likely to produce a modern version of Ripley, who covets the benefits of the overrated data at the expense of his true self (Highsmith, 1970).

7) Separated Self

Lifelogging wearable tools are capable of recording and delivering images of mind as well as numbers and languages. According to Turkle, computers can render part of thoughts, pictures or feelings, if not all. She uses the term "computer programs as a replica of a mind" in a sense that human minds are changeable with devices.

As a result, 'the apathy generation,' a group of regressive digital natives, who tend to isolate themselves from the outside world, appear. Deriving from the Greek origin of 'apatheia,' the word 'apathy' refers to being free from sensible longings. The apathy generation born and raised surrounded by omnipresent smart devices are photographed even before they can control their body, and those photos are immediately posted on the SNS to be exposed to others. From the moment of birth, they make device-based contacts with society, instead of spending quality time with their parents. Hence, in the process of growing, they might lack in empathetic ability and social skills. Yet, they are not invulnerable to solitude and loneliness, which is affirmed by the current prevalence of diverse on-line communities, including dating sites for those who have hard time finding a date.

Accordingly, Turkle portrays them as 'connected but alone,' or 'alone together.' While the Internet is swamped with information overload, people in the real world are suffering from communication breakdown. Family members, who are living in a different time zone when working, relaxing or sleeping, tend to prefer interactions based on smart phones, Facebook and other lifelogging devices, rather than face-to-face contacts. In the age of lifelogging, such a contradictory pursuit of being "connected but alone" intensifies, which is expected to accelerate the generation of the separated self (Turkle, 2011).

III. On Lifelogging Self: Trends and Characteristics

In the previous section, it was discussed that the self in the age of lifelogging created by wearable devices and the IoT environment is quantified, recorded, connected, monitored, overloaded, evaluated and separated, meaning (1) it is quantified with diverse figures, (2) its every detail is recorded, (3) it is linked with many people and things, (4) it is monitored in a transparent data environment, (5) it is in an excessive status partly due to overflowing information, (6) it is constantly compared and assessed, and (7) it is connected but isolated.

Based upon qualitative similarities, such arguments come down to two main themes: segregation and exteriorization. In other words, the monitored, overloaded, evaluated and separated self can be condensed into the theme of segregation, in which the self is separated from an individual subject in a different space, while the recorded, quantified and connected self narrows down to the theme of exteriorization, which maintains that the self documented in various forms expands to the perimeters of an authentic self. Furthermore, themes of segregation and exteriorization can ultimately be unified into a theme of externalization. Then how is an externalized self different? Here, it will be examined relying on the life-world paradigm asserted by Peter Berger and Thomas Luckmann (1967), who used the concept of externalization in an analytical context for the first time.

Introduced by Husserl, 'life-world' is a concept that focuses on conscious experiences, rather than nature, in exploring objects. Husserl emphasized the ambivalent nature of consciousness--neither objective nor subjective--or "consciousness, neither an object nor an outcome of an object," asserting that it can be realized in a form of "natural attitude" accumulated throughout a daily life.

A sociologist, who played a leading role in disseminating the concept of life-world to social sciences, was Alfred Schutz, who tried to "examine subjective meanings in an objective way." Emphasizing the natural attitude asserted by Husserl, Schutz widely promoted the value of life-world in social sciences. His theory of life-world has been passed on to Berger and Luckmann, who proposed that "Reality is socially constructed." Arguing that the function of social science lies in investigating how daily knowledge is produced through dialectical interactions between objective and subjective realities, they focused on the analysis of life-world (Wagner, 1983). The legitimacy of their argument has been doubled by individualization that epitomizes modern society. In more and more individualized society, one's subjective consciousness and desires have an influence on shaping social orders (Beck and Beck-Gernsheim, 2002).

If the dynamics of self driven by lifelogging is traced to the real world, in which ubiquitous media is in wide use, by applying Berger and Luckmann's emphasis on the "social construction of reality," it can be concluded that the self in the age of lifelogging will become the objectified self.

The objectified self features aspects of 'de-subjective subject', also exerting variable expandability through lifelogging tools. In other words, humans and lifelogging devices are to take various forms of self in the process of objectification, which is in the same vein with an actant as non-human actor, or a delegation on non-human mentioned by Bruno Latour , a researcher of the actor-network theory (Latour, 2005).

Even before phenomenology appeared, psychoanalysis has conventionally treated human beings, as well as things, as an object depending on psychoanalysts' assumption that an individual takes losses of men and things in a similar way. For instance, Sigmund Freud argued that if someone loses a loved one or thing, a process of restoring begins internally, which helps an individual to grow into a human being. In this sense, for the objectified self in the lifelogging age to retain its fundamentally independent nature, it is urgent to make balanced interactions between subjective and objective worlds and secure a way to strike a techno-sociological equilibrium, where the former is not overwhelmed by the latter.

IV. Discussion

Critical arguments on the age of advanced technology has long been present based on the resistance against technology determinism or the anxiety about technology control. Also prevalent is an advocacy of technology that argues technological development is good for society with an emphasis on emancipatory potentials of technology. Today, however, instead of such extreme perspectives, an assertion for creating a desirable world by coping with issues caused by technological development in a balanced way is rather welcome.

In this study regarding the change of self in the lifelogging age, three issues can be posed: first, a paradoxical phenomenon of an objectification of a subject, which means an independent self loses its autonomy as it cannot bear the pressure of objectification inflicted through diverse channels; second, the issue of reification, in which individuals fall to become a zombie, who would mechanically respond to external stimuli and signals, as their physiological activities linked with technology become merely functional; and third, the issue of privacy newly raised in the age of post-privacy, where transparency is often lauded and glorified. These are generally in line with identity, helplessness and privacy issues, which Kieoron O'Hara, Mischa Tuffield and Nigel Shadbolt (2008) have presented as three challenges of lifelogging.

Lifelogging technology is often compared to a black box hiding internal motives or interests of its developers. Probably due to the past practice of being reluctant in opening the black box, however, we as an independent user have repeated bystander behavior staying outside the tool, instead of delving deeper into its internal mechanism (Brynjolfsson and MaAffee, 2014). To overcome such limits, efforts should be doubled to extensively and deeply understand the advent, expansion and development of lifelogging considering social interests and ideological differences with a focus on economic and political powers from the techno-sociological perspective based on interactions between social and technological systems.

Chapter 7

Avatars and the Formation of'Net Identity'

I. Problem

Just as there are mixed views regarding childhood socialization, there are both optimistic and pessimistic perspectives as to personality development in adolescence. "Anyone who seeks an adaptive strategy for the upcoming era has to look no further than our children," said Douglas Rushkoff (1996), convincingly arguing humanity can find a bright future in the world's adolescent population. To the contrary, some would predict a grim future on the ground of the reckless behavior of today's teens — particularly, their rebellious images represented by the 'enfants terrible'. Such skeptical views primarily come from Korean researchers who emphasize the hardships that regular Korean students are faced with: they are losing diverse opportunities of identity development and experimentation at home, school, and local community levels as a result of poor social interactions and examination pressures (The Commission on Youth Protection, 1999; The Korea Institute for Youth Development, 2000).

Amid current controversies, analysts are paying more interests in cyberspace, an alternative contact point where teens break down spatial barriers to build new relationships and familiarity, which are often missing at such conventional places as home, school and local community. By helping participants disguise or conceal themselves, online interactions in cyberspace, which ensure anonymity, autonomy and virtuality, are known to have special socialization effects rarely found in ordinary face-to-face interactions (Reid, 1991; Rheingold, 1993a, 1993b; Sachs, 1995).

With the emergence of cyberspace, today's living space is going through a radical transition. As young kids called the 'net generation,' have become highly dependent on the cyberspace where they work, play and interact, their socialization process defies limited boundaries of time, space and social norms, providing diverse and enriched values and interests. Therefore, today's youths tend to design their own independent views, rather than passively take in social concepts or life patterns inherited from previous generations. Though their influence may not be equal to that of adults in terms of politics and economy, they are obviously emerging as a powerful social leading force when it comes to cultural consciousness. To conceptualize such changes in cultural hegemony, Tapscott has referred to this as a 'generation lap' (Tapscott, 1999).

This chapter seeks to examine how cyberspace activities affect the adolescent culture and identity formation by focusing on rapidly increasing avatar usage. More specifically, it attempts to overview the current Internet access patterns employed by Korean youths; describe how adolescents present themselves in cyberspace and how technological advances have changed the means of self-identity presentation; examine avatar-mediated communications like games, chat, social interactions and self-expression; and analyze socio-cultural implications of avatar prevalence and its influence on adolescent identity development.

II. Methods

To obtain a better look at the avatar-mediated adolescent identity development in cyberspace, this analysis mainly relies on 'triangulation approach' including questionnaire surveys, in-depth interviews and online participation observations.

First, to grasp the behavioral and attitudinal trends of the adolescents and their cyber identity formation, the data of Korean Youth Consciousness Survey conducted on the younger generation under age 24 by The Korea Institute for Youth Development (KIYD) from July 28 to August 8, 2003 were analyzed. The socio-demographic characteristics of the sample are described as follows (see Table 7-1).

Table 7-1 **Socio-Demographic Characteristics of Survey Sample**

Socio-Demographic Characteristics		Freq	Ratio
Total		2,306	100.0
Sex	Male	1,160	50.3
	Female	1,146	49.7
Grade	Middle School	950	41.2
	High School	859	37.2
	College	497	21.6
Age	Mean	2,306	16.4

Area	Seoul	724	31.4
	Other City	717	31.1
	Rural	865	37.5

Next, in-depth interviews were conducted on adolescents to identify how they communicate and express themselves in cyberspace, how they confirm each other's identity, and whether and how they use avatars. Interviews were done both online and offline. Their sample characteristics are summarized in Table 7-2.

Table 7-2 **Socio-Demographic Characteristics of Interview Sample**

Socio-Demographic Characteristics		Freq	%
Total		32	100
Sex	Male	13	41
	Female	19	59
Grade	Elementary School	1	3
	Middle School	16	50
	High School	7	22
	College	6	19
	Working	2	6
Area	Metropolitan Seoul	23	72
	Others	9	28

In addition, online game sites, chat rooms and avatar service sites were regularly visited and examined as an extension of participant observation.

III. Internet Diffusion and Internet Use

With a rapid spread of personal computers and the Internet in the 1990s, Korean adolescents' ability to manipulate information equipment has dramatically increased. According to the 2003 KIYD survey, in comparison to the year 2000, there was a considerable rise in the number of people responding. "We have a personal computer at home and I mainly use it," and the number of adolescents who "use the Internet almost each and every day" also rose from 46.9% in 2000 to 69.8% in 2003. By gender, male adolescents tend to use the Internet more than their female counterparts, while by grade, university students were identified as the most frequent users followed by middle and high school students (KIYD, 2003).

The significant influence of the Internet revolution is not confined to the youth, who are dubbed as the N-generation. Yet, the younger generation is playing a central role in the information technology advancement and cyberspace expansion, and its influence gets more prominent in adolescents, who are highly sensitive to new technologies and social changes.

IV. Cyberspace and the Development of Self-Identity

Why are adolescents so zealous about the Internet? Primary reasons can be found in lack of proper leisure activities, stress from excessive work load, an adolescent desire to break away from the older generation, an irrepressible human urge for self-expression, and the search for identity. Among them, adolescents tend to pay more attention to the search for self-identity which represents their own existence (Erikson, 1968; Kroger, 1989; Mueller, 1998).

Generally, self-identity is perceived as a combination of personal qualities that distinguish a certain individual from others, helping to maintain his or her own image in a constantly changing social environment (Jenkins, 2014 Thoughts on self-identity lead to two questions: "who am I?" and "what kind of person am I?" The former pertains to one's existence in relation to others, while the latter is about one's identity, that is one's characteristics, personal qualities, values, aptitudes, and preferences.

As abstract reasoning develops and self-consciousness grows, adolescents tend to raise questions like "what kind of person I am" and "what can I do and how should I lead my life?" They also often experience ambivalent emotions like dependency and independence, indifference and passion, indulgence and abstinence, confidence and alienation, hope and despair, and self-centeredness and altruism and the like (Lieu, 1999).

The predominance of the Internet, however, has caused a significant rupture in the self-identity formation and development mechanism (Dibbell, 1998). In a traditional agrarian society, families and local communities were the primary source of defining a self-identity, while families and work places carried out that function in a modern industrial society. In an information society, however, an individual identity tends to be created, transformed and reconstructed in cyberspace: so does a considerable disparity between online and offline identities. Avatars are thought to be a response to such discrepancies.

V. Shifting the Means of Identification: From ID to Avatar

Earlier debates over cyberspace identity were mainly concerned about text-only communication environments. A cyberspace heavily relying on computer-mediated interactions (CMCs) is considered a type of a communicative system, where individual thoughts and emotions are freely exchanged beyond the physical limits of the offline world. This disembodiment of

CMCs causes a disjunction between mind and body: the latter is the ultimate tool of the physical world. That is because such communicative devices as facial expressions and gestures commonly used in everyday life are not working in cyberspace.

Therefore, the cyberspace can generate new personal identities free from physical limitations and create alternative online communities as well. As Internet-based MUD games clearly indicate, offline institutions and regulations do not readily apply to the online world, where users can go beyond the restraints of societal identities. It implies that online participants can create a new identity catering to their own will and desire (Jones, 1995). As a result, most netizens turn into a carrier of multiple identities, which combine a conventional status as a member of the offline society with a new set of identities representing distinctive ideas and emotions in cyberspace.

The problem, however, lies in how you can express 'yourself' and identify others in such a multiple-identity environment. Once you join an online community, you will be given an ID so that anonymity issues and identity mix-ups can be taken care of to some extent. Yet, as a regular log-in process normally requires identification, not authentication, it is still difficult to properly attain information regarding Internet users' real identity. Besides, online players can also have multiple IDs or easily change their user names to become a totally different person.

Members of a cyber community actively engaged in offline gatherings, whether they have multiple IDs or not, generally tend to create a distinctive personality within the group, and maintain a consistent identity, which leads them to form their own unique symbolic system. Depending on the user's preference, ability and circumstance, a diversity of nicknames, signatures and languages are in use (J. Kim, 2000).

With rapid development of IT and multimedia technologies, however, cyberspace interfaces have shifted its basis from text to graphic: and accordingly, patterns of identity formation and confirmation are following suit.

Amid this transformation, avatars are gaining popularity among the Korean youths. Internet sites particularly frequented by adolescents are packed with creative avatars adorned with fashionable accessories, hair styles, and clothes, almost comparable to those of downtown youngsters. When visiting a chat room or an online club, netizens now use a stylish avatar, instead of an ID. To those who used to have only a combination of numbers and letters to represent themselves, avatars have now become an alter ego, not merely an Internet character.

VI. Avatars and Presentation of Self in Cyberspace

Recently, avatars are experiencing a rapid evolution: some can not only write but also speak, while others can change their height and weight as well as clothes, and even create their own game rooms. In addition to clothes and props, they also have interesting background stories, pets and authentic motor skills.

In near future, avatar evolution is expected to occur more actively in mobile communications like cell phones or PDA than in personal computers. Since early 2003, a chat service providing wire and wireless Internet access has become available so that a PC user and a person on the move can initiate a one-to-one conversation, which will promote avatars to a larger extent.

1. Avatar Using Patterns of Korean Youths

Avatars are mostly in use for chats, games or message boards: 43.5% of Korean youths use them for chats, 39.9% for games, and 39.7% for writing on Internet bulletin boards (KIYD, 2003). When it comes to chatting, female adolescents use avatars more often than their male counterparts, while middle schoolers, followed by high school students and university students, are the most frequent users of avatars. In case of games, males make more use of avatars than females: by grade, middle school, high school and university students in the order named. When writing on bulletin boards, girls like to present their avatars more than boys: by grade, high school, middle school and university students in the order named.

Furthermore, the results of in-depth interviews have also shown great preference toward avatars among adolescents. Out of 30 respondents, 22 answered they had used avatars before, and there was little gender division. Their primary purpose of using avatars was for chats followed by games. The prominence of avatars in the chatting section may be related to the fact that the number of female interviewees was higher than that of male interviewees, and chatting service providers are competitively marketing a diversity of avatar characters. Over half of adolescents are known to have more than two avatars.

2. Avatar-Mediated Communications (AMCs)

Earlier, netizens used to hang around the cyberspace with readily changeable IDs and convenient anonymity. Even in those days, however, they tried to add more personal qualities to their ghostlike IDs with interesting nicknames or vitalize text-only chat rooms with emoticon symbols. Yet, there sure was a fundamental limit in what they could do with signs and letters. Despite obvious limitations of their own, avatars can realize young netizens' desire to express themselves with authentic gestures and freely move around the cyberspace in stylish outfits.

Adolescents who are longing for a new space and a new world use avatar to attempt a free transformation of their ego and recreate the cyberspace into 'their own world'. They are conducting an avatar-mediated experiment to restructure their multiple identities depending on circumstances, which has been impossible in real world.

VII. Types of Avatar

AMCs are available at most web sites popular among Korean youths. Users can dress up their avatars the way they want and then register them for some prices. The basic cost for adorning an avatar ranges from 5,000 to 8,000 won (5 to 8 USD) with additional expenses for fancy outfits, backdrops or accessories.

As in-depth interview results have shown, most respondents said they were expressing their tastes and preferences through personal avatar decoration, and even those who were not using avatars for this purpose claimed that they were willing to use avatars as a way of self-expression if free cash were given.

Interestingly, adolescent users go beyond abbreviations and emoticons to create their own language system, which is quite foreign to outsiders. It may be an effort made by adolescents to form a distinctively unique identity and cyber subculture distinguishable from those of adults, who are now increasingly joining the Internet society.

1. Game Avatar

To most Korean youths, online games are irreplaceable leisure activities, and even considered a rite of passage. According to the white paper "2004 The Rise of Korean Games," 96% of Korean adolescents are enjoying online games. The emergence of Internet games as a predominant cultural phenomenon is highly related to network services. Real-time communications with other gamers, add vigor and energy to a formerly monotonous and dry Internet games, consequently making them the most popular leisure-time activities among Korean adolescents. There may be many reasons for the recent popularity of online games, but one of the most fundamental reasons is that young kids enjoy Internet games simply because their friends do. This kind of peer culture makes more adolescents turn into digital gamers (Korean Game Development Institute, 2004).

Now in most online games, players are represented by their avatars. According to a survey on avatar presence in top 10 game portal sites (ranked by Rankey.com as of July 4, 2003), most online games are shown to involve certain forms of avatars with only a few exceptions.

There is no online game that provides users with a single avatar character. You may have a hunter and gatherer avatar at one time, and then a warrior at another. It may turn into a fairy that actively enjoys her social life. Success at online games depends on how well you present your avatars.

Game avatars have become prevalent partly because they are a central part of paying games. Originating from virtual games, avatars often make a lot of things possible, particularly those seemingly impossible in real life. Adolescents are considerably attracted to these omnipotent game characters that can gratify their desire to express themselves. By adding a sense of rivalry to this, avatars become an ultimate tool to satisfy a natural adolescent tendency toward self-expression and the search for fun.

With the onset of a game, participants introduce themselves through their avatars: for example, their physical features, personal qualities, and educational backgrounds. When it is a team play, they go through a pairing process. If you like a particular character, you accept him or her as your partner, and then a team play begins. During the game, penalties are given to losing avatars: to name some, water balloons, poisonous gases, and dungeons. Winners have a change to get basked in a spotlight with cheering applause and whistles.

2. Chatting Avatar

Formerly deemed exclusive to Internet portals, communities and game sites, avatars are currently expanding to what is called an avatar chat service. If earlier avatars helped users to present themselves by transforming their virtual ego's physical appearances, the second-generation avatars go further hanging around with new friends or even making their own rooms to establish many varying degrees of relationships. This is where avatar chatting services play an important role.

Unlike text-only chats, recent avatar chatting enables you to see others' facial expressions and gestures, and spontaneously react to them in various ways, which makes a more authentic communication possible. When elements of game and community are added to this, it becomes an irresistible entertainment to adolescent users.

There are about eight avatar chat service providers in Korea. Most noticeable among them may be "POPPLE," whose main theme is a fancy cruise boat. Users make new friends there and build their own cabin to enjoy life on board. On this virtual 7-story ferry, you can have a nice dinner at a restaurant, or enjoy the panoramic ocean view just like you are on a real cruise. Ferry nightclubs are always crowded with teens who are looking for virtual dating.

"Joy City," another provider of avatar chatting service which is much like an online game, offers a virtual village, where many things are closely connected with the real world. A TV set there, for example, broadcasts real-time programs, while personal computers give you an access to the Internet. Furthermore, if you pick up the phone which is connected to the Internet, you can make an actual phone call.

Some sites offer more interesting services through which a diversity of emotions and actions can be presented. In "Noritel" mostly visited by young kids who are looking for cyber families or friends, users can play rock/scissors/paper, cry, laugh, kiss, dance, blush their face, kick and even sweat (see Figure 7-1).

Figure 7-1 **Chatting in 'Noritel'**

3. Networking Avatar

In most cases, avatars carry a self-introductory message, which serves as a useful tool for young netizens to initiate new relationships. Popular Internet sites often hold an avatar PR contest. A winner gets a tremendous number of visitors and reply memos. Those memos usually ask for a return visit, through which netizens can develop what could be a single-time contact into cyber norms of reciprocity.

Formation of avatar-mediated ties does not stop here. In the previously mentioned POPPLE site, users can have their own rooms, where several avatars live together. Frequently found there are ads like "Roommate Wanted." Moreover, adolescent users like to decorate their living quarters with many household appliances and furniture.

As avatars have been able to demonstrate more authentic feelings and actions, many adolescents experience what is called cyber hallucination, in which Internet users identify themselves with their avatars and start to perceive them as real. In fact, avatar couples often fall in love with each other, or even groups of avatars establish a blood relationship to make an extended family, which is called a cyberfam.

Cyberfam is a coined word combining cyberspace and family. Despite little age gap, they establish a family hierarchy by playing roles as father, mother, uncle or aunt. Sometimes, they have 'family' gatherings outside the cyberspace. Many adolescents find it hard to communicate with their real family. Sometimes, they don't even have a chance to sit down and talk to their parents. In contrast, cyberfam members are very easy to bond with because they are a peer group about the same age sharing common concerns. Within the community, they call each other Dad, Grandpa or Darling, and they even use the same family name. Unlike in real-world families, cyberfam adolescents tend to readily overcome differences in age and views and establish intimate relations.

VIII. How to Interpret the Avatar Boom?

As societal tendencies shift from industrial capitalism to information capitalism, commercialization of culture has been ever accelerated. For this reason, some sociologists expect the 21st century to be an era of culture. Obviously, one of the main driving forces behind this cultural commercialization is the limits of mass production based on Fordism. More noteworthy, however, is that the consumption of culture is more focused on non-material symbols and meanings than on materialistic values: consequently, consumer behavior comes to be conducted based on complex implications and interpretations, not just a simple functional judgment.

Consumption of culture as a product tends to be more active and subjective than that of material products. Since material products in a traditional sense mostly involve 'necessity consumption,' consumption is mostly subject to production. In case of cultural products characterized by 'surplus consumption,' on the other hand, consumption defines production, not the other way around. Rapid expansion of avatar services is caused by multiple factors: primarily, a new capitalist profit model commercializing game characters, and adolescent preoccupation with the cyberspace and their predisposition to cultural consumption.

1. Avatar as a New Cultural Commodity

It is indisputable that valorization is the goal of capitalism, but as society diversifies, so do methods and objects of profit realization. Currently, cultural products have become attractive to capitalists in many respects. Most of all, cultural products are known to have a high potential as a replacement for conventional commodities in a time of recession by adding symbolic values. Whereas values of material commodities are rather objective and fixed, cultural products generate varied effects depending on consumer tastes and societal trends. For this reason, the world witnesses a diversity of symbolic manipulation on cultural products.

Today's avatar boom is inextricably related to this symbolic mechanism. Increasingly organized and corporatized avatar producers now create, diffuse and reproduce symbols by employing more thorough strategies. As evidence indicates, the latest avatar enthusiasm has been initiated by 'dotcom companies,' which see a lucrative chance in the avatar industry. Adolescent netizens zealously respond when those companies put out fresh ideas and attractive digital products in the market.

2. Avatar as an Object of Consumption Behavior

Today's consumers are no longer satisfied with simply functional consumption. They have broken a new ground in consumption by putting more emphasis on images, personal preferences, and moods. Of course, to most consumers, the primary goal of consumption is to sustain their survival and livelihood. Yet, a latent function, which is very important but not readily apparent, is inherent in ordinary consumer behavior. As Veblen and Simmel observed, consuming behavior usually involves a social mechanism of indicating status differences. Conspicuous consumption conducted by a social group makes a clear statement about their existence within the social fabric, setting up an exclusive boundary.

Prosperity of the cultural contents industry and recent popularity of avatar products have resulted in making adolescents a new leading group of online consumers. Rushkoff (1997) perceives adolescents in cyberspace as main consumers of collective illusion and images. Primary objects they fantasize about are online characters appearing in cultural contents. Now as a central part of the avatar industry, those characters are constantly stimulating adolescent consumption in cyberspace. Young netizens try to verify their existence and differentiate themselves from other groups by empowering a special set of symbols. In other words, an adolescent desire to secure a distinctively different identity partly contributes to the emergence of the avatar phenomenon.

3. Avatar as Something to See or a Sort of Spectacle

Today's adolescents are overwhelmingly a multimedia generation. Compared to previous generations of narration and print, this multimedia generation demands stronger and more sensitive stimulations, so that they can satisfy both audio and visual needs. In the past, information used to be obtained mostly by listening and reading, but now, visual images offering instant information are gaining predominance. If the past was "the age of reflection," the present and future will be "the age of intuition," where visual images outrun printed letters (J. Kim, 2002).

Thus, it is not surprising that most people feel bored or restless when there is nothing interesting to see around them. Amid abundance of intriguing spectacles, more and more people try harder to present themselves in an attractive way. Adolescents, a major consumer group in information society, are producing their own way of self-expression through Internet-based fashion items. A good example is facial painting, which was in vogue during the 2002 FIFA World Cup. An online facial painting community offers a diversity of relevant information, along with part-time job tips.

Because of adolescent netizens' cultural needs, there has been a remarkable advancement in avatar technology. Recently in the market are actual avatars, which are totally different from previous avatars with the same physical shape. Unlike cartoon characters, these actual avatars can reflect real images of users or famous models through digital manipulation. Users can design their own style with various fashion items from department stores or designer shops. They also choose whatever hair style and outfits they want, and they can even tailor a jaw line to their taste.

4. Avatar as a Part of Virtual Body

With the growth of digital networks and expansion of the cyberspace, it is often argued that humanity can transcend such physical limitations as time and space. Today, we can do the online shopping without even going to a shop or appreciate art pieces without visiting a museum. Thus, it is no wonder that some say your body has been rendered useless. With considerable development of the multimedia, indirect experiences have taken up a large portion of our knowledge, and sometimes, experiences in the virtual world tend to be more vivid and vibrant. Some people enjoy playing an Internet soccer game instead of going out to a field or watching a ball game on TV rather than visiting a ball park. As opportunities for substitute gratification increase through such indirect life experiences, the significance of our physical body starts to diminish.

Ironically, however, such de-incarnation turns into a fundamental source for re-incarnation, which emphasizes physical experiences. We can easily spot a group of adolescents dancing on the street, or men, not just women, who are working out to show their nice body to others. Furthermore, an increasing number of adolescents long for physical contacts to fill the void coming from non-materialistic online experiences. A case in point was the 2002 FIFA World Cup games, where hundreds of thousands of netizens took out to the street to root for their country and feel the heat themselves.

Yet, Korean adolescents' desire to have more hands-on experiences is hard to be fulfilled in the offline space. Their life is rather defined by the absence of their own territory, while always rushed around under the examination pressure. Avatars serve as a convenient alternative to resolve the discrepancy between adolescent desires and reality. They provide adolescent netizens with a familiar medium to satisfy their longings, which are often frustrated in real world for many reasons. In this regard, an avatar can be perceived as a virtual body that represents its owner in image-oriented cyber society.

In sum, as netizens previously attracted to the anonymity of cyberspace have become more aware of personal needs to be seen and heard, avatars have begun to draw attention as a useful tool to gratify an ambivalent desire toward their wishful hyperreality. Straddling in the middle of anonymity and authenticity, avatars play a significant role as a mediator bridging the offline world and cyberspace.

5. Avatar as a Tool for Identity Experiment

In the offline world, we can draw a clear line between appearances and reality, and such distinction plays an important role in grasping an object's identity. There, an identity is considered as something with real substance, relatively unchangeable, or uniquely produced by a set of roles and norms. Because of cyberspace expansion, however, assumptions of such a single individual identity do not hold water any more. In cyberspace, appearances are often deemed equal to reality (Baudrillard, 1983).

Avatars offer an effective means to deconstruct one's actual individuality, and at the same time, experiment with multiple layers of identity (Schroeder, 2002). Since the cyberspace is a world of non-materialistic information, our physical body is not actually admitted to that territory: we instead participate in it through our keyboard-controlled representative. Avatars pacify a basic human desire for self-expression and peer recognition by making full use of online anonymity. The reason why avatars are particularly popular in dating and chat sites can be traced to their function as a tool for self-statement and substitute experiences. With proper means in hand, netizens actively pursue an identity transformation in diverse ways: from presenting themselves just the way they are to try something eccentric which they wouldn't do in reality.

Avatars help you to show who you are, who you want to be, or even what you don't have or what is not easily revealed outside. In this respect, avatars are an essential device for identity experimentation. Through various modes of identity experimentation, you can experience different lines of living, which are not possible in real world. It is a sort of self-reparation process. An avatar-mediated self-identity is multi-dimensional because it is not confined to a single entity, and fluid because it is not fixed or unchangeable.

IX. Discussion

In a traditional industrial society, adolescent identity development occurred through conventional socialization mechanism like family and school, primarily in a top-down, gradual, and sequential way. But in today's complex, multi-layered, and consolidated cyber environment, such development model does not hold good any more.

As evidence shows, Internet sites most popular among the adolescents involve chats, games, learning, consumer items, debates, news and information, and communities. Thanks to technological features of the cyberspace, such activities are interconnected in the form of hypertext, and boundaries are crossed with mere a click or two. Therefore, an immersion in a activity does not necessarily exclude a participation in other activities: it rather helps make them all happen simultaneously. In cyberspace, a considerable amount of socialization occurs in a very condensed or reversed version, with a complete gender equality, or in a hypertext-based multi-linear form. It is highly possible that such experiences produce unprecedented multiple identities, and consequently shape a new cultural consciousness.

It may be considered positive, on the one hand, that adolescents are able to practice many different characters in cyberspace through identity experimentation. On the other hand, however, it may cause a serious problem to the adolescents who are going through a crucial period of identity formation. During identity experiments, they could experience a chaotic confusion with realities. Moreover, if they use the cyberspace as a hideout, it could adversely influence their social skills in the offline world. Such negative effects include an addiction to the Internet, escapism, social avoidance, obsession with cyber families, and several juvenile crimes mostly caused by identifying themselves with game characters.

Apart from debates over positive and negative influences, identity experimentation in cyberspace is expected to be established as a dominant model for adolescent identity development in the upcoming information society. For this reason, there need to be thorough theoretical explorations and empirical observations on the dynamics and transformations occurring between the cyberculture and identity.

Section IV

Topics in Risk Management

Chapter 8

Surveillance Technology, Privacy and Social Control

I. Overview

One of the important sociological questions about technology and society is how, and to what extent, technology affects our society. This may be a critical issue, since every technology gains its value in terms of its effect upon other parts of the social system.

Despite popular enthusiasm for the recent accomplishments of new information technology (IT), many researchers have expressed skepticism concerning the perfect image of the information society and pointed out the potential dangers that are expected to result from this 'information revolution'. The problem of privacy being impinged by various surveillance technologies is one of the oft-cited concerns about the current 'IT-led social transformation.'

Most studies dealing with the privacy problem caused by advanced surveillance technology have focused on the interpersonal or intrapersonal adjustments to the changing conditions of a life existing with increasing surveillance, relevant practices or strategies and required institutional arrangements. Early studies, like Politics of Privacy (Rule et. al., 1984), Protecting Privacy in Surveillance Societies (Flaherty, 1989), and The Rise of Computer State (Burnham, 1983), tried to trace the development of social surveillance systems and subsequent legal-political issues (Kling et. al., 1996). More recently, research interest tends to encompass a wide array of societal consequences caused by advanced surveillance technology and their feedback effects.

This study attempts to analyze the dynamic relationship between surveillance technology and social control. As elucidated in James Beniger's book Control Revolution: Technological and Economic Origins of the Information Society (1986), technology has been playing a significant role in shaping the level of social control. The social effect of surveillance technology that contributes to what he calls 'control revolution' can be outlined as follows (Figure 8-1).

Figure 8-1 **Social Effect of Surveillance Technology**

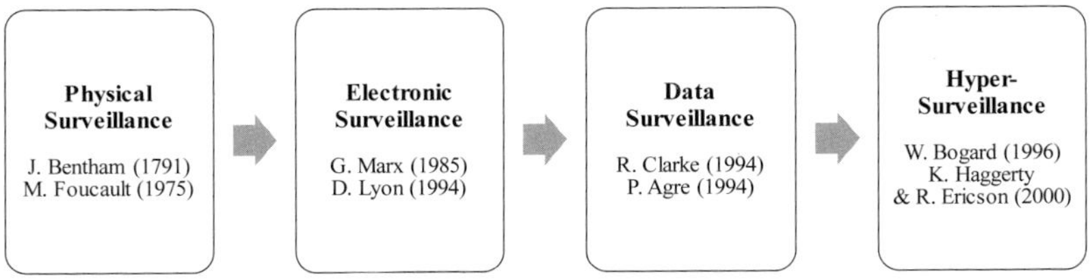

Also, the trajectory of social control can be traced in terms of the development of surveillance technology. Before examining this evolutionary process, basic ideas such as surveillance, privacy and social control will be discussed. Next, the dynamics of technological and social systems will be examined under the titles of "Development of Surveillance Technology" and "Shaping of Advanced Surveillance Society," respectively. Then, the changing concept of privacy will be explored from a dialectical perspective casting an interaction between technology and society. A brief discussion of the dispute over the Electronic National Identification Card in South Korea will follow. Based on these considerations, the changing patterns of social control that reflect the life-world of ever increasing surveillance power will be investigated. Finally, relevant attempts to cope with such surveillant ways of life will be explored (Figure 8-2).

Figure 8-2 **Outline of Overall Discussion**

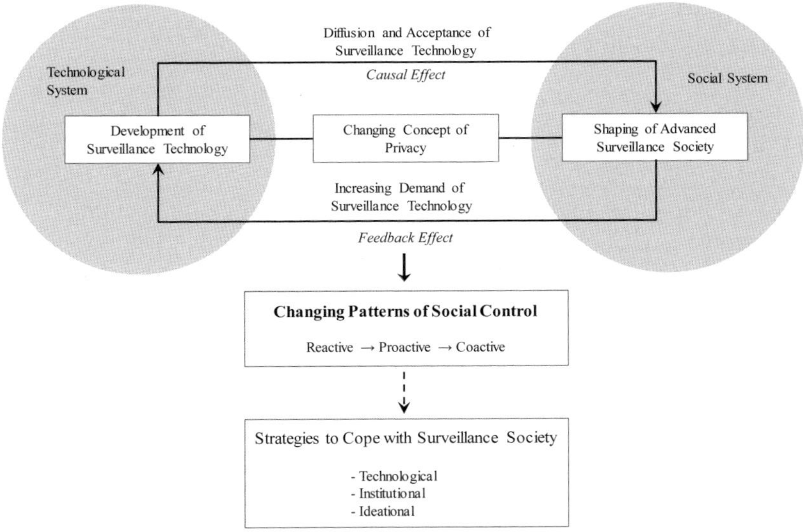

II. Surveillance, Privacy and Social Control: A Conceptual Review

Jeremy Bentham's idea of panopticon has remained a dominant metaphor in the discourse of surveillance and social control. This 'all-seeing' prison design is comprised of an annular building full of individual cells facing a certain 'watch' tower. Light and architecture, zigzag openings and Venetian blinds display the inmate and conceal the onlooker, thus creating the illusion of total, omniscient surveillance. The panopticon's magic lies in its ability to "see without being seen" (Green, 1999).

It is Michel Foucault who recasts Bentham's concept of panopticon and characterizes the nature of modern social control. Foucault identifies Bentham's panopticon as the architectural expression of the modern desire to observe, control and rule. The observed 'subject', through the internalization of the relentlessness of observation, finally assumes the responsibility for self-surveillance and allows the surveillance to be increasingly disembodied and not corporal (Foucault, 1975). As such, panopticon can be regarded as a model that initiates the transition from traditional to modern control, moving from overt, external and punitive to covert, internal and preventive one which can be subsumed under the thesis "from reactive to proactive social control." This transformation coincides with the ideal of modern liberalism that emphasizes personal freedom, respect for individual right, overthrow of ascribed roles, and self-determination or autonomy.

While admitting some positive aspects, Foucault recognizes the repressive element underlying the modern social control and labels it as 'disciplinary' control. For Foucault, discipline is an effective means to reduce the body as a political entity as cheaply as possible while maximizing individual 'utility' (Foucault, 1975). This Foucauldian idea of disciplinary control is different from Bentham's panoptic control in the sense that the former stresses more refined, spiritual correction while the latter lays greater emphasis on bodily sanction like physical isolation. However, they are the same in upholding the effect of regulatory techniques relying on visual monitoring.

Oscar Gandy recollects Foucault's idea of disciplinary control in the context of the political economy of personal information (privacy). For him, the panoptic sort is a kind of "high-tech, cybernetic triage" that depends on digital technologies and technical rationalization to collect, evaluate, store and retrieve personal information and to control human behavior. Gandy continues by saying that he describes it further as a "discriminatory process that classifies individuals based on their estimated value or worth" (Gandy, 1993). For many IT researchers with a critical mind, new IT developments are taken to be a practical application and an intensification of Bentham's panoptic gaze.

Currently the panoptic gaze is becoming more widespread and omnipresent, in the "shopping mall, bank, subway, sometimes even a bathroom" (Marx, 1985). Thus, "not just the prison or factory, but the societal totality comes to be part of the hierarchical and disciplinary panoptic machine" (Webster and Robins, 1986). Poster, in his post-structural analysis of personal 'data images,' also employs the same metaphor, equating new technologies with a 'super-panopticon,' a system of surveillance without walls, windows, towers or even guards (Poster, 1990).

Most of these analyses seem to be rightfully concerned about trends of increasing surveillance and increasing external control thereafter. However, in the present paper questions are raised about whether and how individual autonomy, subjectivity or personal liberty will cope with the increasing surveillance power of new IT.

In discussing the way that the panoptic system works, Oscar Gandy argues that classification does not emerge naturally from some intrinsic characteristics of persons or things but rather from culturally defined perspectives that are often associated with economic and political power (Doty, 2001). This is the point where the issue of privacy is highlighted as an antithetical counterpart of surveillance.

Privacy is a complex and multifaceted phenomenon that has many connotations and has become a catchphrase to signify diverse issues (Kling, 1996). However, in western societies it usually means the physical seclusion or solitude that an individual may seek. In a different context, privacy is defined in terms of interactions with others: the right of individuals to determine for themselves when, how and to what extent to release personal information to others or to receive information from others (Turn, 1985).

Turn points out that it is not feasible to implement privacy as the "right to be left alone" or as the "right to unilaterally control information about oneself" in the modern world. For an individual must surrender a part of his(her) personal information to society to receive the available services and benefits and a society must protect its members against the erroneous or irrelevant use of personal information in return. Therefore, Turn claims the merits of his following definition of privacy, "the right of individuals regarding the collection, storage, processing, dissemination and use of personal information about themselves" (Turn, 1977: 242).

More recently, Philip Doty has tried to renovate the concept of privacy since it has been mistakenly assumed to accrue to individuals. He argues "While there is often some mention of the need to conceive of privacy as a broader conceptual category, far too many privacy discussions have limited their definition of privacy to individual concerns" (Doty, 2001: 127). This kind of atomism, he argues, fails to reflect the phenomenological reality that people experience as human being and has a few negative effects on our ability to conceptualize privacy, especially in the digital environment.

Doty (2001) claims that without the rejection of such an ideological legacy of classical liberalism, no productive research would be expected since the constitutive nature of human relationships are ignored. Insisting that the simple public/private dichotomy must be avoided because privacy builds and results not from a simple atomistic individualism but from human interaction, Doty attempts to clarify and specify the link between information privacy and privacy to act, phrased as 'freedom of surveillance' and 'freedom of self-determination' or simply as 'freedom from' and 'freedom to' (Etzioni, 1999; Thompson, 1990).

In sum, underscoring the weaknesses in many previous conceptions of privacy, some researchers have been searching for a wider, more comprehensive and more complex view of privacy that is applicable to the current digital environment where networked information is more common and has become an integral part of our social life. With this alternative concept of privacy designated as 'act privacy', problems concerning self-regulation or self-determination that belong to the general theme of autonomy or social control can be better clarified.

III. Development of Surveillance Technology

In his 1985 article, "I'll Be Watching You: Reflection on the New Surveillance," Gary Marx illustrates how computer technologies of the past 100 years "cross a critical threshold as a result of broad changes in technology and social organization" (Marx, 1985: 26). He identifies nine characteristics of newer surveillance technologies that mark them as different from more traditional, coercive, penal surveillance technologies (Marx, 1985: 30-31):

- Able to overcome distance, lack of light, and other physical barriers.
- Able to transcend time.
- Capital- rather than labor-intensive.
- Focus on all possible wrongdoers, not on particular suspects.
- Focus on the prevention of violations rather than simply pursuing violations.
- Decentralized and thereby encourage self-policing and inhibition.
- Actually and nearly invisible.
- Attempt to delve into personality and self, not simply the body.
- Deepen and widen surveillance to new areas.

Besides describing the benefits and limitations of new surveillance technologies, Marx emphasizes how they tend to undermine an essential feature of social life and individual well-being. In 1990, Marx adds the following rationales to explain why such stifling and invasive surveillance technologies have diffused so fast to all aspects of our world: for security, well-being, competitiveness, efficiency, management, amusement, justice, quality of life, etc.

The development of surveillance technology has continued. Philip Agre (1997) provides a comprehensive list of major changes in the socio-technical environment that gave rise to more dangerous, but less obtrusive and less controllable surveillance technology in the 1970s and 1980s. Most noteworthy among those are: (1) new digital media that facilitate new or new kinds of social relationships, (2) the emergence of global digital communication networks, (3) the intimate ways in which users have woven digital technologies into their lives to the extent that any possible harm is largely invisible, (4) increasing erosion between the public and the private, especially by joining together spaces that were once disparate, and (6) the somewhat paradoxical mismatch between the relatively high level of moral concern with privacy and the low level of ordinary concern of it (Doty, 2001; 156-157).

The underlying factor that encompasses all these new environmental changes is information networking. The marriage of computing and high-tech telecommunications brought us networks. This led to connections among networks, most importantly the Internet. With the Internet has come a new life space, popularly called the 'net', 'cyberspace' or 'matrix.'

In the special issue of Communications of the ACM on email and privacy, Suzanne Weisband and Bruce Reinig (1995) point out the vulnerability of email communication to interception, examination and retransmission and insist that the belief in email privacy is ill-founded. They contend that the seemingly isolated, online communication setting leads the user to disregard the monitoring behavior.

Voice mail is also being integrated into computer networks and can be retrieved, forwarded, archived, sold or transformed. As cellular phones become more like computers, sound may turn into paper messages that are available if the host computer exists (Hawkins and Mannix, 2000). However, given the expansion of online networks and the incorporation of digital technologies and information into many phases of contemporary activities, data surveillance (often abbreviated to dataveillance), which can be differentiated from conventional forms of physical surveillance, is gaining significance. Dataveillance is the systematic use of personal data systems in the investigation or monitoring of the actions or communications of one or more persons (Clarke, 1994).

In recent times many advanced forms of physical surveillance have been available, such as the telescope, camera, telephoto lens, auto recording and directional microphone. In addition, electronic surveillance has emerged in such forms as telephone bugging devices and the interception and analysis of telex traffic. However, dataveillance differs from physical and conventional electronic surveillance in that it involves the monitoring not of individuals and their actions, but of data about them(Bogard, 1996).

Compared to conventional physical or electronic surveillance, dataveillance is inexpensive and moreover, is getting cheaper all the time thanks to IT progress. Furthermore, dataveillance is now favored by its limitless application once the relevant raw data are available. However, the cost is not the only factor in the growing use of dataveillance; it is also an inevitable outcome of the current situation of 'information overflow'. Thus far, only particular populations have been the object of dataveillance, not because of technical limitations but rather the absence of any substantial data set. Therefore, physical surveillance is to be progressively replaced by dataveillance to the extent allowed by supporting database.

IV. Shaping of Advanced Surveillance Society

Advances in surveillance technology have led to ever more pervasive intrusion into our private lives; hidden cameras in bathrooms, the explosion of random urinalysis by companies and schools, and parents and spouses installing surveillance tools at home to monitor family members. Meanwhile, developing technologies such as wireless tracking devices, biometric identifiers, 'spy TV' and 'super ears' are creating a new set of privacy worries (Hawkins and Mannix, 2000). Yet, this may not represent the whole story due to the increasing difficulty in keeping things private because our ordinary activities are increasingly mediated by and incorporated into computerized network systems.

Throughout its development, surveillance technology has exerted a great influence upon the external world. In its early stage, the impact, by and large, seems to have remained within our external life condition. With the advent of dataveillance, however, a substantial change is occurring in our internal world. Based upon the dual classificatory scheme of physical surveillance vs. dataveillance, I will succinctly compare the differential social impact of old and new surveillance technologies.

The discussions on the impact of new surveillance technologies conveyed by pioneering scholars in the 1970s like Gary Marx and Mark Poster are generally conceived as emphasizing the increasing power of newly developed surveillance technologies. Whether wired or not, new surveillance technologies up to the 1970s basically aimed to enhance the surveillance functioning such as intensifying the responsiveness, expanding its coverage, and integrating various aspects of activities. Nevertheless, dataveillance engenders unique consequences quite dissimilar to those caused by the conventional surveillance technologies.

Agre compares these in light of two models of privacy: surveillance and capture models. The surveillance model, still the most prevalent in current surveillance literature, concerns information being used for unintended purposes. However, Agre introduces what he calls the 'capture model' that maintains a great affinity with dataveillance. The characteristics of the surveillance and capture models are summarized in Table 8-1 (Agre, 1997: 105-107).

Table 8-1 **Comparing Surveillance and Capture Models of Privacy**

Arena	Surveillance Model	Capture Model
Metaphor	Visual	Linguistic
Purpose	Unnoticed Watching	Intervention in Human Activity
Emphasis	Territoriality	Structural Aspect
Dossiers	Centralized	Decentralized
Ideal Image	Repressive State	Mathematical Formalism

Agre notes that although the capture model is less familiar than the surveillance model, it has deep roots in the practical application of computer networks and he emphasizes its heavy reliance on building systematic models of activities, using what he describes as grammars of action. These grammars are imposed on human action through five stages: (1) analysis of components and their interrelationships; (2) articulation in sensible combinations; (3) imposition of the grammar using normative power; (4) instrumentation to measure the activity, especially as actors adjust their activities to the imposed grammar and capture; and (5) elaboration of the records of the captured activity through storage, combination, processing, error detection, and quality control (Agre, 1997: 107-113).

In addition, Agre enumerates eight ways in which the imposition and instrumentation phases reorganize and redefine an activity, from the introduction of new technologies, and the self-adjustment of actors to meet the expectations of capture, to the formation of new intra-organizational relationships, and the rearrangement of activities. Appreciation of the elements of the capture model is, in Agre's view, essential to understanding the current surveillance situation (Doty, 2001).

There lies a significant difference in the social impact between the conventional form of surveillance technology and the recently developed new surveillance technology supported by efficient computer network systems. The general function of conventional electronic technology may be regarded as the enhancement of surveillance capability, thereby increasing or augmenting surveillance competence. A resulting phenomenon is the rise of a highly transparent society where everyone can watch everyone else. However, traditional surveillance tools and conventional electronic surveillance of the 1970s do not differ significantly with respect to their nature of social impact. Their effect is basically a matter of degree, i.e., to what extent we will be able to reach the state of non-disruptive data collection and thus be able to see, hear or feel without serious surveillance disturbance. A subsequent consequence is the ubiquity of surveillance as implied in the well-known phrase, "surveillance in everyday life" (Lyon, 1994).

If we turn our attention to the matter of dataveillance, the situation looks quite different. The impact of surveillance is far beyond the external change in our objective world. Owing to the operation of dataveillance that abstracts human bodies from their territorial setting which has been called 'surveillance assemblage' (Haggerty and Ericson, 2000).

Communicators in times past would speak of the 'information mosaic' built by aggregating information about someone from originally disparate information sources. Originally, the concept referred to a profile built on an individual that combined both print and electronic information. Now, however, the concept of the information mosaic has been supplemented by the formation of a more conspicuous idea; that of the 'digital persona' (Forester and Morrison, 1994; Doty, 2001). The digital persona is a model of an individual's public personality based on data and maintained by transactions and is intended for use as a proxy for the individual. It is a useful and even necessary concept for the understanding of human behavior in the new, networked world (Clarke, 1994). Furthermore, it indicates how people nowadays tend to use many digital technologies to perform various ordinary activities in their life.

While the information mosaic has been widely regarded as a threat to individual and group privacy, it is said that the digital persona offers benefits as well as costs. On the contrary, as with the discussion regarding dataveillance, Roger Clark insists that the threats to social and individual liberty and autonomy surpass its merits.

> The ability to create a persona may be vested in the individual, in other people or organizations, or in both. The individual has some degree of control over a projected persona, but it is generally harder to influence imposed persona created by others. Each observer is likely to gather a different set of data about each individual, and hence to have a different gestalt impression of that person. Frequently, individuals who are aware of the use of data may be in better position to project data selectively in order to influence the imposed digital persona that is formed (Clarke, 1994: 78).

Clarke's argument also focuses on the problems with erroneously attaching particular actions to particular digital persona. Since there can be many ways for actions to be mislabeled, he argues, mistakes are becoming more common and are having serious real-world consequences (Clarke, 1994).

Max Kilger(1994), who seeks an answer to the question of how individuals construct themselves and form images of these constructions, focuses on the individual and threats to individual privacy. He identifies a form of social being called 'virtual self'. This socially recognized and used entity is a "composite of multiple digital information sources". Although Kilger enumerates several costs and advantages for the existence and use of virtual selves, he also warns that the ubiquity and multi-dimensionality of the virtual self poses greater threats to personal freedom and social security.

V. Changing Patterns of Social Control

As computer network systems have become pervasive, citizens of technological societies have found that their ordinary activities are increasingly mediated by computerized representations of themselves. Some of these activities, such as chatting on computer bulletin boards, are wholly voluntary and thus give individuals great freedom. Overall, however, individuals tend to feel captive in many activities, such as driving, receiving medical care, and using credit cards, etc. because they are exposed to the new network environment connecting to computerized surveillance systems.

Under the claim, "During the last thirty years, people have lost control over their records," Kling offers an explanation on privacy invasion in the contemporary United States. He contextualizes the privacy issue in the following five major value orientations: (1) the search for profitability by private firms (the enterprise model); (2) the influence of government institutions (statist model); (3) the protection of civil liberties (libertarian model); (4) the clarity and responsiveness of public and private enterprises (neo-populist model); and (5) the efficient and reliable organization of financial systems (system model). What he eventually emphasizes is 'information entrepreneurialism,' the institutional arrangements that encourage organizations to develop information services, products, and work patterns that use IT to threaten privacy (Kling, et al., 1996).

Castells calls this new form of techno-economic system 'information capitalism', wherein the rationale, assumptions and methods of capitalism are adapted and changed by informationalism. He identifies four important constituent elements of this form of capitalism: business networks, technological tools, competition on a global scale, and the state (Castells, 1996).

Kling adds that the widespread geographic reach of large organizations, the massive post-World War II population mobility and the tenets of information entrepreneurialism and information capitalism all feed into the culture, control and rationalization of indirect social relationships that characterize the large organizations of modern societies. The resulting surveillance is made up of a cult of risk-averse information systems full of highly detailed records of individuals' and groups' actions, characteristics, preferences, and beliefs.

The drive to reduce risks has stimulated increasingly sophisticated analysis and integration of personally identifiable information. Managers seek to know more about current and potential customers, clients, employees and partners. These represent cases of the 'micro-practices' of information capitalism, the pursuit of which is deemed to be acceptable despite any social ill effects of having, collecting or otherwise using such knowledge (Doty, 2001).

The ideas of information entrepreneurialism and information capitalism all address the institutionalization of information as a private property and a source of profit, and thus imply that it may form a strong driving force for valorization through a commoditizing process. In The Mode of Information: Postmodernism and Social Context, Mark Poster clarifies how information has become the privileged category today in his discussion on how databases maintained by credit companies, health insurance agents, municipal police, bureau of motor vehicles, federal agencies, banks, utilities, and so on, allow the reconstruction of most of the daily activities of individuals (Poster, 1990). Such knowledge lends itself, in his estimate, to an almost inexorable push toward commoditizing the most intimate and confidential information.

All these writers on information entrepreneurialism and information capitalism also indicate how such an institutional arrangement has contributed to the internal state of human psychology. However, these techno-psychological discussions have not yet been explored in enough detail to understand the overall effect of the new surveillance technology.

With technological advances in data-manipulation, the increased 'inforability' of our daily lives and the potential for social arrangement, surveillance has become an indispensable part of our daily life. Although the ubiquity of surveillance raises many criticisms and objections, it should be noted that it has also contributed a lot to reinforcing positive attitudes toward surveillance.

Based upon Peter Berger's dialectical framework on the construction of social reality, it may be possible to draw out a model that helps to explain the emergence of a new 'digital life-world.' Here, the emergence of the digital life-world is considered as the result of reciprocal processes of objectification and subjectification (Berger and Luckmann, 1990).

In the newly constituted life-world where surveillance is a taken-for-granted aspect of everyday life, people will be so accustomed to a monitored life as to feel afraid of not being protected by the silicon cage of digital networks. The construction of the digital life-world out of the dialectical interaction between objective and subjective worlds is illustrated in Figure 8-3.

Figure 8-3 **Construction of the Digital Life-world**

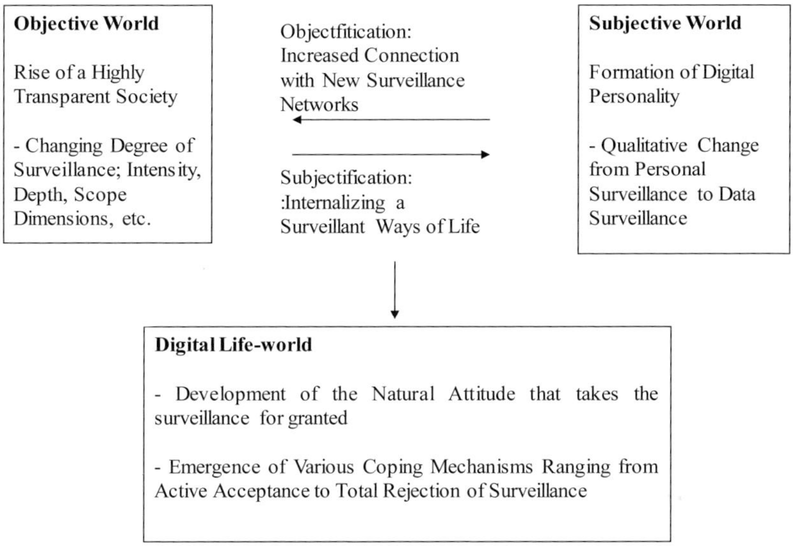

In the past, there used to be a strong, spatial, institutional, normative boundary awareness between public and private spheres. However, as the concept of privacy defined on this boundary is gradually losing salience, most cultural or moral taboos that inhibit entering the private sphere are becoming a plausible repertoire of action. For example, a hidden camera installed in a lady's restroom would not carry particular value as a news item or a topic of social dispute because of the argument that if surveillance is everywhere, why not in restroom (Hankuk-Ilbo, 07/19/1997). As even war becomes the target of surveillance, soldiers are now no longer allowed to express their fear of death in a highly transparent battleground as clearly demonstrated in the recent Anaconda Operation in Afghanistan. Given such tightly captive circumstances, many people feel the pressure to remain good citizens in a surveillance society by complying with the demands of the omnipresent 'snitch culture' (Redden, 2000), where surveillance is far more insidious and pervasive than anything George Orwell ever imagined. Recently, Lyon argues that surveillance tends to be more intensified in the aftermath of September 11 and diverse surveillance techniques or systems are being adopted on behalf of personal or national security (2003).

VI. An Empirical Case: Dispute over Electronic National Identification Card in South Korea

1. Governmental Initiative

In 1996 the Korean government launched an ambitious electronic ID card plan on behalf of the more effective administration of personal data. Forty-two items of personal data from 6 different database sources were to be recorded on a single electronic ID card. The expected structure and contents of the electronic ID card are summarized in Table 8-2 (Department of Domestic Affairs, 1996; 1997).

Table 8-2 **Elements of Electronic National Identification Card Plan in South Korea**

Element	Written Item	IC Input Item
Residential Registration	Name/Resident Registration Number/ Address/Picture/Date of Issue/Authority	Name/Picture/Seal/Resident Registration Number/Personal Record/ Address Change/Military Service/ Household/ Family Member/Household Address/Career/Others (Blood Type, etc.)/Confirmation
Driver's License	License Type / License Condition/License Number/ Aptitude Test	License Type/License Number/ Authority/License Condition/ Aptitude Test/Date of Issue/Violation Score/ Pending or Cancellation Record
Medical Insurance		Code and Title/Type/Registration Number/Contractor/Dependent/Entry and Expiry Date/Region/Term of Validity
National Pension		Entry Date/Entry Type/Amount Paid/ Membership Period/Relationship/ Registration Number/Type of Allowance/Reason of Payment/Payment Serial Number/Date of Final Revision
Finger Print	Finger Print	Finger Print Trait
Other	Special Notes of Medical Insurance	Authority of All Certificates
Total	12 Items	42 Items

This new electronic ID card was neither a substitute nor a simple extension of the current paper ID card. It was designed as a smart card installed with an IC chip that could contain a large amount of personal data and be easily connected to other main databases. The government proclaimed the merits of the new ID card in being the most advanced version introduced anywhere in the world.

2. Reactions from Citizen Groups

There were no immediate reactions to the ambitious governmental proposal. Some analysts pointed out the following technological, cultural, political, economic and social factors to explain these insensitive responses: (1) strong technological and industrial background supporting the electronic ID card policy, (2) lack of privacy concern stemming from a collectivist tradition, (3) awareness of national security due to the sharp military confrontation between North and South Korea, (4) neglect of social justice due to intensified economic competitiveness, and (5) apathy to conventional top-down policy practices (Koh, 1997; Kim, 1997).

However, critical voices began to flourish when the utopian image of a digital society began to falter with the apparent negative consequences of ever-developing surveillance technologies. Against the naïve perspective of the proponents who reiterated the positive aspects such as cost reduction, administrative efficiency and better social service, critics tried to highlight the issues of privacy invasion, abuse of personal data, and degrading informational human rights. Nevertheless, they did not seem to advance their argument to the point where human dignity was threatened by the intensification of external control.

Opposition was raised from many sectors of society, including the Union of Science and Technology Workers, Coalition for Labor Informatization, Lawyer's Association for Democratic Society, Confederate of Intellectuals for Democracy and Progress, Forum for Human Rights Movement, YMCA, Progress Network, National Union of the Press, Citizen's Action Group for Democracy, Human Rights Committee of the Korean Coalition for Abolition of Electronic National ID Card, Catholic Church, Youth Action Group for Information Culture, National Christian Coalition, Coalition for Abolition of Electronic National ID Card (Coalition for Abolition of Electronic National ID Card, 1997). Among these groups, the activities of the Progress Network, Human Rights Committee of the Korean Catholic Church, Lawyer's Association for Democratic Society and Coalition for Abolition of Electronic National ID Card appeared the most remarkable. Progress Network published a newsletter and a series of compact booklets and contributed much to publicizing the expected negative effects of the electronic ID card. In a sourcebook, Progress Network described the struggle against the governmental proposal of the national ID card called 'Australian Card' in 1987-88 and praised the Australian citizens who smashed the attempt as "great people" (Progress Network, 1997). The Human Rights Committee of the Korean Catholic Church and the Lawyer's Association for Democratic Society held a special symposium on human rights issues and a workshop on the legal and social problems. They played significant roles in calling public attention to the risk of the electronic ID card concerning the matter of privacy invasion. Coalition for Abolition of Electronic National ID Card, an ad hoc council organization, collected resources of diverse action groups and guided the anti-card movement successfully.

3. Results

Faced with diverse critical voices from civilian sector, the government tried to improve the public opinion by making a series of significant revisions. However, the anti-card campaign shattered all those governmental attempts. Owing to increasing pressure from action groups and worsening public attitudes, the government decided in 1998 to defer the introduction of the electronic ID card to 2000, and eventually abandoned the whole project on February 22, 1999. It may be noted as one of the few special cases where civil power won a sweeping victory over almighty state power.

In 1993, the Korean government completed the installation of a national database composed of a selection of personal information of the whole population, including colored photographs and fingerprints. The electronic ID card plan was presumably a consecutive arrangement to allow for more effective inspection by way of a more advanced digital network system. Since the electronic ID card was designed to be mandatory and thereby tended to facilitate dataveillance, the risks of the new electronic ID card seemed to be quite serious compared to its expected gains.

By now, the national electronic ID card plan is totally scrapped. Especially, due to the concern over the privacy invasion intensified by a series of informational crimes like hacking or illegal data circulation, the governmental proposal is widely thought to be an official 'tagging' and public attitude towards the national ID card is getting aggravated. Therefore, the national ID card proposal will not reappear in the near future. This can be considered as a result of the claim for the citizen's right which has been growing insistently throughout the democratization process from late 1980s.

Nevertheless, the current situation appears quite exceptional since the Korean government has implemented very systematic and comprehensive informatization policies over the last two decades and has gained a strong confidence both in and outside the country. Thus, it should not be regarded simply as governmental or policy failure. More than anything else, current political atmosphere characterized as "a series of slander and debunking" and the reaction of the civil society obsessed with perfect privacy protection may be the most crucial factors that can explain the "revolt of the mass" against the ambitious governmental drive toward a 'digital leading country' in Korea.

VII. Discussion

Computer networks and associated technologies are elements of the medium that is changing our social order. These developments are changing how people live and define their boundaries, not only physical ones but also institutional, political and even moral. This has led us to a highly transparent world of no secret whatsoever as appeared in the movie "Truman Show."

Claiming that there are formidable dangers in a society dominated by centralized surveillance and widespread sharing of medical, financial, insurance, vehicle, property, legal location, retail, and other information, Rob Kling (1996: 625) states, "What is at stake is the extent to which the resulting social order enables people to live dignified lives; that they can participate in diverse social and economic relationships that they can adequately comprehend and control; and that people are not thrust into cries because of errors or sublime idiosyncrasies of personal record systems."

Just as there are different images of the information society, so reaction can be raised from different angles. From an examination into the electronic ID card struggle in Korea, three different reaction frameworks can be identified. The types of reaction framework and their key issues are summarized in Table 8-3.

Table 8-3 **Types and Issues of Reaction to Surveillance**

Reaction Framework	Key Issue
Benefit Framework	Convenience vs. Hazard
Protection Framework	Public Welfare vs. Privacy
Control Framework	Internal vs. External Control

When the government proclaimed the new electronic ID card plan, a mood of acceptance seemed to predominate. While those who were involved in or supported the state policy publicized the potential advantages of the integrated electronic ID card, the opponents who regarded all the proclaimed merits as merely pseudo-benefits tried to highlight the negative side effects that were expected to be introduced by the intensive online network system.

During the discourse, the problem of privacy invasion resulting from illegitimate data management gained public attention and the strength of the claim for individual privacy tended to outgrow that of the need for information dissemination for public well-being. However, the problem of 'act privacy' that centers on the control issue leading to the autonomous vs. coercive image of society, would not turn out to be a matter of great concern.

Observing the transition from benefit to protection framework, many people who were afraid of privacy invasion reserved their support for the governmental initiative. Such a tendency is obvious from an examination of the pamphlets, manuals and articles published during the whole campaign period from the time of official announcement to the point of final withdrawal. Yet, it is very interesting that only scant attention has been paid to the control issue.

The same thing is happening in the current debate on the National Educational Information System (NEIS). NEIS is known to be superior to the existing online database for students and teachers in most aspects including workability, efficiency, parsimony and connectivity. However, the president of the National Human Rights Commission called for NEIS to be abandoned in light of the security problem.

Despite a growing concern held by many school teachers who are afraid of being constantly monitored on a real-time basis, the current debate on NEIS is still lingering around the protection of personal information, far from the issue of self-determination or 'freedom to.' In short, there appears to be no clear evidence indicating a shift toward 'control framework' yet (JoongAng Daily, 06/12/2003). Several interpretations can be suggested to account for such a lack of concern for personal autonomy: legacy of Confucian patrimonial tradition, effect of authoritative military rule over the past several decades, prevalence of rigid bureaucratic culture, etc. Yet none of these seems to adequately explain such a widespread acceptance of surveillant ways of life. Considering the concept of a new digital life-world emerging from the interplay of the objective world of increasing transparency and the subjective world of the digital persona, we can understand the willingness of so many people to render their personal freedom to surveillance systems or agencies. Under these circumstances, the Foucauldian idea of disciplinary control that proclaims the shift from reactive to proactive control needs to be extrapolated to a form of control that may be designated as 'coactive', implying the preference for symbiotic cohabitation with empowering surveillance technologies by the process of "manufacturing consent."

With increasing surveillance, however, diverse coping mechanisms ranging from active acceptance to total rejection are expected to emerge. Basically, two ideal-typical reaction patterns may be identified to cope with ever-increasing external control: technological and social.

The technological solution to the problem of privacy is based on the use of privacy-enhancing technologies (PETs) that allow data subjects, information collectors and users to express their subjective expectations of privacy (Walters, 2001). PETs may aid societal transparency as well as reconstruct interpersonal trust in the networked environment. Therefore, they hold out new possibilities for the protection and promotion of privacy or privacy rights. Using such technologies and from the consequences of their use for transparency and trust, good privacy practices can be expected. Nevertheless, from the political and economic points of view, an expectation for the introduction of such technological solutions turns out to be very naive since it fails to acknowledge the drive for dominance or exploitation.

The social solution may be subdivided into two components; liberal versus Luddite (Lyon, 1995). While the Luddite solution is correct in identifying the hidden interest of the dominant group underlying the neutrality assumption of technology and criticizing the technical determinism of the technophile, it will nevertheless lead to another one-sided view of economic determinism as it attributes all the previous technological accomplishments to the manipulation of the ruling class.

As for the liberal solution, in so far as it stresses the importance of choice and then emphasizes democratic decision making, it seems to be the most valid solution by far. Such an emphasis is a vital antidote both to any technological determinism which forecasts that future society will be determined by new technologies and to any economic determinism that sticks to class relation in any analysis concerning techno-social phenomena. Thus, a critical liberal stance must be the most sensible and practical way to close the credibility gap between optimistic futurist fantasies and the totally negative Luddite view.

However, considering the formation of the aforementioned 'naturalization effect' (the display of a natural attitude that takes surveillant ways of life for granted) in the new digitalized life-world, we conclude that the critical liberal attitudes cannot be automatically constituted without serious reflections upon the present subjective life-world that is consistently in danger of being colonized by empowering digital ideology. That is why a new pedagogy is required; one that enables us to identify various negative latent functions hidden behind the proclaimed benefits of the transparent 'Brave New Digital World'.

Chapter 9

Dialectics of Risk, Security and Surveillance in a High-Tech Society

I. Introduction

Whatever we choose from train accident to dam rupture, from factory explosion to chemical intoxication, from SARS (Severe Acute Respiratory Syndromes) to global warming, 'risk' appears to be one of the most urgent issues producing a high degree of anxiety. Risk is described as the potential damage caused by a single event or series of events. More technically, risk is defined as the product of the probability of a harmful event and expected losses caused by the event (Stern and Fineberg, 1996).

Risks come in many forms. At one end of the spectrum there are risks that threaten the market functioning, political stability or social integration. These are not the concern of this study. It is the other end of the spectrum that is of interest here, physical threats to human life, property or environment.

Despite growing concern about risk, characterization of risk is still far from a consensual state. Nature and mechanism of risk has not been satisfactorily explored. Coping with risk situation makes the problem more perplexing and controversial. Although government and industry have devoted themselves much to developing strategies or techniques of risk management to make better decisions about hazard to human welfare and environment, they are not likely to meet the expectation of the population yet. The failure may portray the limit of administrative or technological means of risk management. Or it may be the result of unscientific, unorganized decision makings on risk situation. But more than anything else, the greatest failure seems to stem from a lack of comprehensive understanding of risk characterization (Stern and Fineberg, 1996).

To capture a broader perspective on risk, I begin by a brief chronological review of the changing pattern of disaster, i.e., the objective source of risk. Next, based upon an interactive model that postulates the dialectical interface between perceived risk (risk awareness) and perceived security (security need), the current paradox of high risk situation amidst growing public concern for security are explored. Here, the process wherein surveillance have been socially approved and institutionalized as a legitimate means of risk management is examined. Finally, the interplay of safety need, risk awareness and surveillance culture under the context of a high-tech social formation is analyzed and alternative means to cope with current technological disaster are discussed.

II. A Chronological Review

In the past, the most threatening factor to human survival was natural disaster. Natural disaster is concerned with the threat caused by hazardous geological or atmospheric phenomena. Avalanches, forest fires, floods, earth movements, cyclones, storms, earthquakes and volcanic eruptions are considered major natural risks when they cause important damage to men, goods or the environment.

But disaster tends to be evolved in accordance with the advancement of human society. As various technological means of production are infiltrated into the world of work since the Industrial Revolution, more attention was paid to the human-made disaster called "industrial disaster." As the rate of technological advancement accelerated, another type of disaster named "technological disaster" including the threat of nuclear war, ecological catastrophe or side effect of GMOs has become a major public concern in many societies (Table 9-1). Therefore, those who live in a high-tech society would not appreciate their quality of life any more (APRI, 2012).

Table 9-1 **Chronology of Disasters and Responses**

Stage of Society	Pre-Industrial	Industrial	Post-Industrial
Type of Disaster	Natural	Industrial	Technological
Coping Strategy	Magic	Recovery	Recovery/ Precaution

In accordance with changing types of disaster, significant shift has occurred in recent years in the dominant pattern of risks. Nowadays technological risks are the most threatening factor that causes more casualties than traditional risks shown a long-term trend report of disaster shows (OECD, 2003).

II. Technological Risk

John Eldridge (1999) has shown that founding fathers of sociology were, in their own ways, concerned with questions related to risk. While Karl Marx drew attention to the instabilities and misery created by the capitalist mode of production, Emile Durkheim was concerned with the danger of society disintegrating as an over-emphasis on economic development led to the breakdown of moral regulation. Max Weber analyzed risks that were associated with the growth of bureaucratic organizations which emerged as because of industrialization (Denney, 2005).

But it is Charles Perrow who first raised the technological risk as a topic of intellectual discourse. His seminal work, *Normal Accidents: Living with High-Risk Technologies* in 1984, provided a useful starting point from which to understand the nature and dynamics of technological risk.

Ulrich Beck is another important figure in the field of technological risk study in the sense that he has successfully disseminated the idea of technological risk both in and outside the academia. After the publication of Beck's bestselling book Risikogesellschaft: Auf dem Weg in ein andere Moderne, risk has been the buzzword that heralds current social condition of high modernity. According to Beck, modernization has eroded industrial society and given birth to another kind of society, a society that is connoted by the social distribution of risks. The social distribution of wealth goes together more and more with the distribution of risks. Moreover, in late modernity risks tend to be global. As Toxic waste from a factory in one place may bring damages in another place far from its origin, risks are getting delocalized. More than anything else, nowadays risks come from the excess of technology. They are thus taken to be the negative latent function of technological development (Beck, 1992[1986]).

In a more recent book entitled *Risk: A Sociological Theory*, Niklas Luhmann (1993) defines risk as a potential harm that is based on decisions made by individuals. Given the statement, Luhmann makes a distinction between risk and danger; the latter defined as a potential harm to which an individual is passively exposed like natural disasters such as flood, tornado or earthquake, while the former is basically cased by the individual decisions. In the case of danger, he explains, "the possible loss is caused externally, it is attributed to the external sources. Instead, modern ecological problems are regarded as risk because, like deciding whether or where to build a nuclear plant or locate the site to dispose nuclear materials, is the result of personal judgment.

In the same vein, Anthony Giddens (1999) suggests considering two kinds of risks: external and manufactured risk. External risks are risks coming from "outside", while manufactured risks are the products of impact of human knowledge and capacities on the world. External risks, that dominated the industrial society, are concerned with the possibility of individuals to be involved in unexpected event, even if in some ways such events could be anticipated. On the other hand, manufactured risks, that are product of late modern society, arise form technological or scientific development and cause unanticipated consequences (Maturo, 2004).

III. Conceptual Status of Risk and Security

While risk has been promoted to an analytical term through a series of intellectual endeavor mentioned above as is clearly assured by the concept of "technological risk", security has long been regarded as an ordinary term simply describing the state of physical, material, institutional or psychological wellbeing. Probably, national security may be an exceptional case since it has been included in the agenda for the academic debate on the matter of security.

As far as security kept playing such a denotative role devoid of any analytical functioning, it remained as a residual category simply describing the state of a risk-free or "riskless" condition. Given the pragmatic disparity, no progressive dialectical interaction between risk and security is to be expected. Only when this disparity is eliminated, security and risk will be able to constitute mutual-reinforcing chain reactions of positive feedback and produce a strong confluent effect of exponential growth.

Risk and security occupy the different side of the same coin. Due to the conceptual lag between the two, they have not constituted an effective explanatory model for long. Owing to its conceptual development, risk has been gaining a potential to explicate contemporary casualties or concomitant malaise in its own tongue. It may not be the case with security concept though.

There is an immense literature on the analysis and categorization of security; physical security, financial security, information security, social security, emotional security, etc. Part of the reason for such ramification is that, in most security systems, the "weakest link in the chain" is the most important. It is analogous to such an asymmetrical situation as the defenders must cover all points of attack while the attackers can simply identify a single weak point upon which to concentrate their efforts (Burton, 2007). For all those classification attempts, however, security remained as a fuzzy concept until late 1990s. There had been no such things as natural security, industrial security or technological security that enables us to figure out the transformations of our social landscape.

Although Beck coined and began to disseminate the term 'risk society,' it was Giddens who attempted to link the concept of risk closely to that of security. Giddens argues that new risks arise from the nature of modern social organization: there is risk stemming from the created environment or socialized nature that is gradually becoming insecure. Particularly, he added that there has been a huge historical transformation of the nature of risk and security. Preoccupation with risk in modern social life has nothing to do with the actual prevalence of life-threatening dangers. On the level of the individual life-span, in terms of life expectation and degree of freedom from serious disease, people in the developed societies are in a much more secure position than those who were in most previous ages. The physical security of human beings has been enhanced in industrial societies, but it is balanced by a list of new risks: war, motor accidents, drugs, environmental pollution, etc. Therefore, Giddens concludes, "the risk-reducing elements seem substantially to outweigh the new array of risks" (see Show, 1995).

From a series of recent case studies on fierce risk disputes happened in South Korea over the last few years (Kim and Kim, 2006), a strong tendency can be identified concerning the dynamics of risk and security on a perceptual level. Calling for more advanced or more efficient means of surveillance turned out to be the most pervasive response from stakeholders and their allies, mediators who oversee risk management or conflict resolution and spectators who have nothing to do with the controversies as well.

IV. Aftermath of September 11

A year later after the September 11th Terrorist attack, Beck raised a following question, "Does 11th September stand for something new in history?"

It was a not a war, not a crime, and not even terrorism in a conventional sense. It was not a little bit of each of them and it was not all of them as well. No one has yet offered a satisfying answer to the simple question of what really happened. Beck's thrust is the 9/11 expresses our fundamental situation in the 21st century, of living in what he calls 'world risk society', because typical characteristics of current technological risk, that is 'de-bounding' of uncontrollable risks, are manifested in the event on a global level (Beck 2002).

Repeating his previous argument that uncontrollable risk is now irredeemable and deeply engineering into all the aspects of human life in advanced societies, Beck suggests two forms of state models to sustain national security: surveillance state model and cosmopolitan state model. Although Beck himself strongly prefers the latter to the former, the reactions to the 9/11 turn out to be quite opposite. The general tendency was the intensity of surveillance is increasing dramatically as the result the 9/11. Owing to the massive influx of new high-tech driven surveillance facilities, our everyday life is turning to a "contested terrain of surveillance."

The most visible sign of changes after the 9/11 is surveillance is legally favored and technically supported. The USA and several other countries have passed legislation intended to tighten security, to give police and intelligent services greater power, and to permit faster political response to terrorist attack. Technical responses to the 9/11 have also proliferated. Seeing the 9/11 providing the platform they exactly needed, high-tech companies spurred themselves to launch new surveillance products. Ironically, while terrorists relied upon relatively aged technologies like bombs, knives or aircrafts, seeking superior technologies such as electronic scanners, CCTV cameras, smart cards, biometers of various kinds appears as a primary social goal (Lyon, 2001).

David Lyon (2001) summarizes all these current transformations of surveillance process as follows.

- Range of surveillance extends beyond existing level, aiming to reach the state of "ubiquitous surveillance."
- Tendency to rely on technological enhancement to surveillance systems increases.
- Centralized, exclusionary, hierarchical surveillance practices are shifting to decentralized, intrusive, rhizomic ones.

V. Dialectics on Work

Thanks to the diffusion of handy, powerful, invisible, smart surveillance devices having a powerful discrimination function, surveillance becomes more unnoticeable, discretional, simulated, and preemptive and technologically dependent.

For all the changes in this 'surveillance-scape,' most people are likely to be more insensitive to the evils of surveillance. They are not only permissive to overt inspection, inquiries, tapping or the other forms of privacy invasion, they also seem to have more embracing attitude toward surveillance. Undoubtedly, the destruction of the World Trade Center located in the heartland of the US made surveillance even more acceptable. In the airport, the government building, the stadium, the suburban high school, the queue at the ATM machine, the local convenient store, video surveillance is now rather welcomed as an undeniable good. Almost everywhere, people are repeatedly confronted by the message "You are being watched" and comforted (Pecora, 2002). How is it happen?

In principle, it is taken to be an outcome of successful socialization of

Figure 9-1 **Dialectics of Risk Awareness and Security Need**

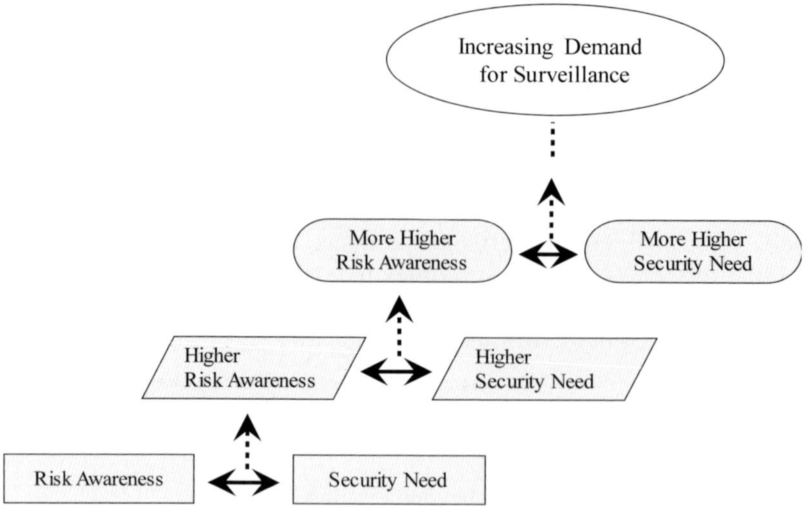

surveillance subculture. Due to massive diffusion of advanced surveillance technology, increasing 'inforability' of our daily lives and its growing potential for social arrangement, surveillance has become an indispensable part of our daily life. In this newly constituted life-world where surveillance is a taken-for-granted aspect of everyday life, people are getting so accustomed to a monitored life as to feel rather afraid of not being protected by the silicon cage of digital network. But, it is the 9/11 that stimulated the latent collective consciousness of security need.

Shortly after the September 11, Jean Baudrillard (2004), who had kept complaining that the contemporary era was an era of "weak events" in which nothing significant has changed claimed that the assaults on the World Trade Center and Pentagon constituted a "strong event", in the sense that they were "the ultimate event, the mother of all events, the pure event uniting within itself all the events that have never taken place." (Kellner, 2004).

How could September 11th terrorist attacks be differentiated from tie other disaster like Chernobyl accident, mad cow disease or global warming? During the last decade, the international stage and its main players have changed significantly. With the collapse of the Soviet empire, they gladly welcomed the end of the cold war, its hateful propaganda, and the lingering threat of a third world war. Citizens of Western nations could enjoy security during a long-lasting period of peace in their home territories. But the September 11 activated their dormant security need and initiated a series of subsequent interactions between security need and risk awareness elevating the demand for surveillance. The formation of favorable attitudes toward surveillance after the September 11 is thus interpreted as an unintended and unseen side-effect of continual chain relations between risk and security on a perceptual level (Figure 9-1).

VI. Future Prospect

What will be the consequence of the consecutive interplays of risk awareness, security need and demand for surveillance? As indicated in the well-known claims of "Liberty or Surveillance", there had been dual scenarios emphasizing autonomy and control, respectively. While the former is the ideal most libertarians such as Alexis de Tocqueville and proponents of "reflexive modernity" favor, the latter represents Orwellian and Foucauldian perspectives that depend on highly centralized surveillance systems. Although the controversies between the two have not been fully settled, it looks rather clear by now that the surveillance paradigm dominates the libertarian paradigm, which can trace back to Immaunel Kant's idea of republican freedom.

In his philosophical essay Perpetual Peace, Kant states "Fundamental rights are never guaranteed by the individual, but always by the law-based state and its institutions of power, which in turn threaten those rights. State power and the individuals are born as twins. Without the state there is no individualization. More individuality means more of the state. But this also means that state power is both in one: a source of security and of danger to individual rights and freedoms." However, in a footnote he adds, "Freedom should be defined as a warrant to obey no external laws except those to which I have been able to give my own consent" (Kant, 1991).

After the September 11 in the US and subsequent terrorist attacks elsewhere, the libertarian logic has given way to the disciplinary logic that are strongly supported by technocratic or commercial visionary. Especially, the two terrorist strikes that hit London in July 2004 contributed much to reinforcing the disciplinary logic. They transcended ethical lines, national causes, blended ideological fervor with criminology and were rooted to a large extent inside the target country. There was no centrally controlled Al Qaeda of the 9/11 anymore. As a law enforcement official confesses, "We are seeing a terrorist threat that keep changing," The terrorist groups are not homogeneous, but a variety of blends, and their networks are much structures that they used to be. That makes it much more difficult to identify terrorists and uproot them (Sciolino, 2005). Given the circumstance, who dares to criticize the tyranny of surveillance?

However, out of the chasms of seemingly seamless fabric of Brave New World, we may be able to detect a gist of alternative scenario that would not converge to neither liberal nor surveillance paradigm. What is it? (Figure 9-2).

Figure 9-2 **Exploring an Alternative Scenario**

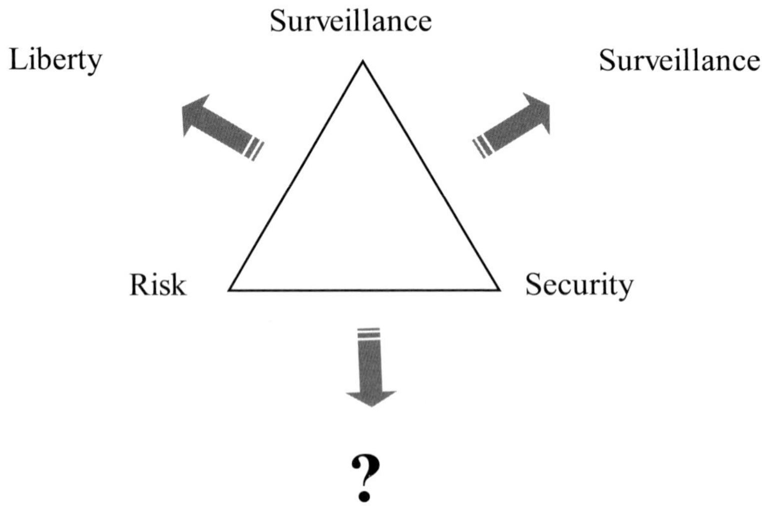

It is 'sousveillance' which refers to "watchful vigilance from underneath" including inverse surveillance and the recordings of an activity from the perspective of participants in the activity in a multimedia setting (Mann et. al., 2003). 'Sous-veiller' is French for Under-Watch. Classy's Kitchen describes sousveillance as "another way to add further introspection to the commons that keeps society open but still makes the world smaller and safer." In this way, we might regard sousveillance as a possible replacement for surveillance.

As the technologies get smaller, smarter and easier to use, the capture, recording, and playback of everyday life get much easier and thus tend to proliferate a variety of personal sousveillance. Recently, some industries and corporations are interested in sousveillance too. Microsoft is exploring cyborglog, as Hewlett Packard, Nokia and many others. Using camera phone, Joi Ito is trying to get the idea of a cyborglog, in the sense that his images are sent often, with little conscious thought or effort (Ganascia, 2010).

The proceedings of the Association of Computing Machinery (ACM) Multimedia 2004 succinctly summarizes the characteristics of surveillance and sousveillnace as follows (Table 9-2).

Table 9-2 **Comparing Surveillance and Sousveillance**

Surveillance	Sousveillance
God's Eye View from Above	Peer's Eye View from Below
Architecture-Centered	Human-Centered
Recordings Made by Authorities	Recordings Made by Participants
Usually Kept in Secret	Often Made Public
Panoptic Origin	Community Origin
Illegal in Most States	Legal in Most States
Losing Locus of Control	Equalizing Locus of Control
Affinity with Ubiqcomp	Affinity with Wearcomp

Some recent studies seek to make an equilibrium between surveillance and sousveillance. So called "equiveillance theory" holds that sourveillance, to some extent, often reduces or eliminates the need for surveillance. In this sense, it is possible to predict some replacement of Panoptic eye model of surveillance with a more community-based model of sousveillance, that can lead to a mutual–reliant 'coveillance' by way of active working of 'equiveillance' in the near future.

Section V

New Media and Society

Chapter 10

New Media and the Social Reconstruction of Reality

I. Problems

Before the advent of the mass media, public attention to the media was scant. While messages conveying the joy and sorrow of life were deemed a representation of reality, the media as a medium was merely regarded as a means of mediation. A social interest in the media has soared, however, as thoughts and experiences, which were once communicated through narrations or manuscripts, can now spread through books with the invention of printing, and the media effects are being amplified by newspapers and broadcasting.

As social anthropologist Edmund Carpenter once remarked, “All the media are new languages in that they independently encode reality (Carpenter, 1982).” Yet, the attention to the media, not just as an instrument, has begun to escalate since Mashall McLuhan's assertion, “Medium is a message,” was widely disseminated (McLuhan, 1968). His theory of media, which puts the media as a medium of communications in the same context with messages as contents, can be replaced with the dictum, “Media is life”. Neil Postman's statement, “Medium is a metaphor for the way we think,” also reflects the view of media as life (Postman, 1985).

The socio-constructive capacity of the media, which creates the world, is dramatically grown as the age of new media based on digital technology unfolds. The web-based space of information and communications goes beyond a forum of information exchanges, creating a connected life-world, where people gather to promote knowledge, life and dreams. Likewise, the app-based space of information and communications reinforced by connectivity, mobility and portability encourages the convergence between the actual reality and the virtual reality. Therefore, the media is now growing into a life-world, or life itself, not merely an instrument of our lives.

II. Methodology: A Life-world Approach

"Life-world" is a concept developed by philosopher Edmund Husserl, a phenomenologist who emphasized a perceived world of experiences, rather than substances, in studying objects. Stressing "consciousness, not an object itself nor an outcome of an object," and dual properties of consciousness, neither objective nor subjective, Husserl has argued that it is generally embodied in the form of "natural attitudes". Criticizing philosophers pursuing fundamental, inexorable truth and a weak epistemological foundation of philosophy in his days, he proposed "philosophy as a rigorous science". Through phenomenological reduction, or epoché, Husserl asserted, "natural attitudes" surrounding pure consciousness should be bracketed (Mayer, 2008).

Life-world, which is often compatible with the term 'social world,' can be applied to natural attitudes, which Husserl argued should be bracketed. Since it is a way of life commonly used in our daily lives, it is called "everyday knowledge," "common-sense knowledge," or "taken-for-granted knowledge." Also, as repeated patterns of life day after day, it is referred to as a "paramount reality."

In his later writings, however, Husserl defines the "life-world as a realm, where our senses are directly manifested for the first time prior to every theory and every logic," asserting the significance of the life-world, which was the very target of phenomenological reduction (Husserl, 1954). Therefore, his later thoughts are called "a philosophy of life-world." Yet, it is Alfred Schutz who has made a decisive contribution to enrooting the concept of life-word in social science by applying Husserl's phenomenological philosophy, which developed an objective investigation of a subjective meaning, to social science. By noticing and systematically studying the importance of the natural attitude, which Husserl tried to reject through a transcendental approach, Schutz has disseminated social scientific values of the life-world, which was shunned by many rationalist philosophers as doxa(Schutz, 1970).

Schutz's philosophy of the life-world was passed down to phenomenological sociologists Peter Berger and Thomas Luckmann, who maintained, "Reality is socially constructed (Berger and Luckmann, 1967)." Arguing that the core of social scientific investigation is to figure out how everyday common knowledge, which is constructed through a dialectical interaction between subjective reality and objective reality, is produced, they focus on analyzing ordinary everyday reality including religion and the marriage institution (Berger, 1967; Berger and Kellner, 1964).

Relevance of the life-world approach has now doubled by individualization - trend that characterizes contemporary society. Since amid mounting individualization, subjective consciousness or drives of an individual are exerting more influence on the constitution of social order (Beck and

Beck-Gernsheim, 2002). By applying Berger and Luckmann's proposition, the "social construction of reality" to modern society, where ubiquitous media such as SNS are in wide use, this study is going to shed a theoretical light on the changes in the life-world caused by the expansion of the new media using digital technology under the theme of "social reconstruction of reality." Also, by analyzing the survey data of happiness conducted on a 1,027 netizen sample, I will try to compare reality construction mechanisms of offline and online life-worlds as well.

III. Background: The Age of New Media

By literal definition, new media is a generic term for all the media that have not existed before. Therefore, letters or printing must have been considered new media at the point of their invention. This article, however, confines the range of new media to the communication tools or systems, which have emerged since Internet came into wide use in the 1990s. Due to the spread of the Internet, "the network of networks," a new social system of network society has been established, and at the core of that change lies digital technology.

Digital technology executes distinct functions of entering, converting, processing and outputting every information and data with a binary system using only two numerals, 0 and 1. Along with network technology, sweeping innovation in patterns of life can be attributed to this digital technology, which receives, manages and transmits a vast amount of audio-visual and other types of information converted into digital forms, and also makes unlimited duplication possible. Through the web-like digital network, a new media world has arrived where unrestricted communications with the unspecific majority is possible beyond the limit of time and space.

Characteristics of new media, which is leading a new revolution of communications, are often said to involve connectivity, anonymity, multiplicity, and time-space transformation. These features can be briefly described as follows (Kim, 2013).

1. Connectivity

With the rise of new media, users can select any medium they want more easily, faster and more arbitrarily. Mass media of the past provided the general public with homogeneous messages through broadcasting. Unlike the unilateral and passive mass media, new media guarantees individual users free and active choices, optimizing effects of connectivity (Rifkin, 2000).

2. Anonymity

Digital communications do not technologically guarantee anonymity since they function only if an address identifying an individual node exists. By using different IDs and nicknames, however, new media assures complete anonymity. People tend to enjoy anonymous existence through new media, which make it possible for them to attempt diverse identity experiments.

3. Multiplicity

As one of the distinctive features of new media, through which many different functions and contents can be managed in a complicated way, multiplicity is effectively accomplished by compressing, dividing and transmitting information with digital technology. Along with functional convergence, new media's multiplicity accompanies portability. Beyond a mere function as a telephone, smart devices are equipped with a wide range of functions as a camera, a game machine, an MP3 player, a digital dictionary, the Internet, and many other useful applications, epitomizing multiplicity of communications.

4. Time-Space Transformation

Earlier, McLuhan described a situation, where a physical distance was overcome with electronic media, as "global village." Harvey also portrayed a phenomenon, where time and space were shortened by information and communications technology, as "time-space compression (McLuhan, 1994; Harvey, 1989)." New media's transformative capacity, which enables expansion as well as contraction, can promote inter-cultural communications and collaborations by bridging gaps in not only physical time and space but also cultural differences. Such tendency is being accelerated by now prevalent SNS, in particular, net-based media such as Twitter or Facebook.

IV. Rise of "Digital Everyday Life"

Social expansion of new media featuring a series of characteristics like connectivity, anonymity, multiplicity and time-space transformation is dramatically changing modern daily lives. Such changes are yet to be in full swing due to the limit of time and sphere of Internet applications, but through a mixed reality, which mingles the online world and the offline world, or an augmented reality, which applies characteristics and mechanisms of the online world to the offline world, our daily life is poised to leap into digital everyday life, which shows following attributes.

1. Accessibility

Combined with advanced information technology, the relational structure of modern society has radically changed, and the Internet has played a decisive role throughout that process. "It is not an object, nor a substance, or an organization. It does not belong to anyone. It connects everything with everything else, and that is the Internet." As this definition reflects, links, rather than elements, are considered more important on the Internet.

At the early stage of the development of the Internet, a private communications network was not directly linked to a computer, and the Internet access was only possible through a modem or a telephone line like communications between personal computers, which means users needed additional preparations for web surfing. With the development of such web browsers as Netscape or Internet Explorer and the doubled speed of access due to the enhancement of services accompanied by mobile and portable functions, media accessibility in our daily lives is reaching the stage of completion.

2. Boundlessness

A desire to break away from rules and conventions are widely observed in recreational activities to escape a workplace or a downtown in leisure time; fashion items with a short period of circulation as they are easily thrown away or changed; text messages, which are instantly checked and deleted; and a flash mob, who suddenly assembles and disperses. This desire for boundlessness is easily gratified by utilizing the space of information and communications with just a click, a screen touch, or voice information.

Noting that the dissemination of new media is being led by young adolescents, who are well known for their high adaptability of technology, Maunel Castells (2009) asserts that there is a high correlation between their post-conventional behavior and new technology. Yet, this tendency of boundlessness is gradually expanding to other age brackets, entirely diminishing physical, cognitive or moral constraints as well as limits of time and space.

3. Nomadism

In the digital age, a new breed of nomads has emerged. "digital nomads," a concept introduced by Jacques Attali in Dictionnaire du XXIe siecle, refer to those who live a flexible life transcending the constraints of time and space via digital devices (Attali, 1998).

Nomadism in the digital age can be found in a new concept of space called "mobile space." With a wide range of portable information and communication devices including cell phones being utilized in this mobile space, nomadism has become one of the hallmarks of the contemporary life. A recent "Velvet Revolution" in the Middle East can be interpreted as a manifestation of nomadic traits via SNS, and such digital nomadism is expected to spread throughout the globe owing to the expansion of mobile media.

4. Ubiquity

Deriving from "ubiquitous computing," a term introduced by Mark Weiser of the Xerox Parc Institute in 1988, the concept of ubiquity is now being realized in reality as the Internet-based new media percolate into every aspect of our daily lives.

One of the important features of the ubiquitous media is that users are not mostly aware of their presence. Though surrounded by cell phones, MP3 players, smart phones and many other media devices, not to mention such traditional mass media as newspapers, TV, and radio, we tend to take their presence for granted. In other words, due to the increase of media interface in real life, people consider the ubiquitous media environment, where they can freely exchange any message with anybody anytime and anywhere, as a natural part of everyday life.

V. Implications of Digital Everyday Life in Life-world

While everyday life epitomized by repetitiveness, normality and familiarity represents a boundary of standard activities ensuring a stable life, non-everyday life characterized by unpredictability, exceptionality and eccentricity is considered a category of uncustomary actions outside normalcy. As seen in an expression "stuck in a rut," The value of everyday life with usual routines has been diminished as a state of uneventful boredom as opposed to spectacular and exciting occasions or festivals.

In contrast, digital everyday life which has reinforced connectivity, boundlessness, mobility and ubiquity due to the proliferation of new media equipped with such new features as accessibility, anonymity, multiplicity and time-space transformation, offers a wide range of events and spectacles, transforming an arid daily life into a stage of vigor and exuberance. Also, as digitization progresses through (1) the technological development stage (technical level), (2) the social utilization stage (social level), (3) the life innovation stage (cultural level), (4) the metal transition stage (intrapersonal level) and (5) the body transformation stage (biological level), digital everyday life is being shifted into a space of possibilities, where people can freely think, feel, act, dream and change.

As far as the time of appearance goes, the digital everyday life in the space of information and communications must be a successor of the pre-existing everyday life. And up until recently, it has been underrated as a mere illusion of virtual reality, which lacks any physical substance whatsoever. As a new space of activities, where independent thoughts, feelings, actions, wishes and changes are allowed, however, digital everyday life overwhelms its traditional counterpart in terms of the degree of freedom, briskness and dynamism. Therefore, a hypothesis can be posed that digital everyday life may retain 'neo-routines' distinctively different from offline daily life.

Before the Internet-based space of information and communications appeared, there was only one world given to us. Of course, there were always a world of art to writers or artists, a world of faith to the clergy or devotees, a world of academics to scholars, and a world of power to politicians, but since they only dealt with an existing social reality of their age, they should be seen as different viewers of the shared world. Therefore, the fundamental proposition of sociology of knowledge, "Existence determines consciousness," was able to remain.

Yet, since the Internet came into wide use in the early 1990s, another world of virtual reality has emerged, reinforcing its daily influence with functions, contents and usages doubled by the advancement of digital technology. Earlier, due to technological limits and lack of contents, virtual reality was looked down upon as fake, nothing more than a coarse imitation of a real world. Owing to the advanced simulation technology, however, it is getting harder to distinguish virtual reality from actual reality, and its capacity for reality construction has been more than doubled as 'hyper-reality' which is more real than actual reality, and augmented reality or mixed reality that converges with actual reality have emerged one after another (Gibson, 1984).

Such a circumstance raises a need for the ontological life-world theory to replace the "epistemological life-world theory," which has postulated diverse views on the one and only material world. In other words, as the space of information and communications utilizing new media is establishing a new form of everyday life, which is hard to explain with real-world principles, mechanisms of online and offline worlds need to be understood from different ontological views, and relations between the two worlds should also be investigated with a new perspective that postulates the dual-world image.

VI. Comparison of the Determinants of Happiness in Offline and Online Worlds

As tools of measurement to comprehensively diagnose individual thoughts and attitudes toward daily lives, life satisfaction or quality of life indexes have been widely used. In recent years, however, as independence and subjectivity of different life styles or goals are more emphasized, an index of happiness, which is considered to more actively reflect an individual's internal desire, has come into attention. Therefore, this section will investigate dual properties of the everyday world by comparing determining factors of happiness in offline and online daily lives, which have been found in the "Happiness Survey" conducted in South Korea on 1,027 netizen samples nationwide from October 24th to 31st, 2011.

1. Research Model

The "Happiness Survey" model designed to examine factors and mechanisms of happiness in the digital era will focus on inspecting how a netizen's happiness is affected by personality, self-clarity and self-disclosure, which are thought to represent the deep, intermediate and surface layers of the subjective life-world respectively. To study the media effects, this article will delve into how such mass media as newspapers, TV and radio as well as new media like the Internet, online games and SNS both directly and indirectly affect happiness.

Yet, subjective happiness may include not only an individual's inherent nature mentioned earlier but also the influence of social capital, which defines a relationship with others. That is because, as many researches prove, trust from others tends to enhance an individual's happiness. There are also research outcomes showing that social capital affects happiness both directly and indirectly through health variables, and that the use of Facebook interacts with preexisting factors of happiness by increasing social capital (Helliwell and Putnam, 2004; Ellison et al., 2007).

Therefore, based on online and offline inquiries conducted on the same samples, this article intends to analyze how happiness is affected by the use of media, variables of subjective life-world and types of interpersonal relations generalized as "social capital." Respondents' gender, age, educational background, household income, standard of living and the number of SNS friends are added as background parameters.

In short, this study attempts to construct causal models by setting such attributes of the subjective life-world as personality, self-clarity and self-disclosure as independent variables of happiness; social capital encompassing both strong and weak interpersonal ties as an intervening variable that bridges variables of life-world and happiness; and patterns of media usage and socio-demographic characteristics of respondents as background variables.

2. Variables

1) Dependent Variable: Happiness

Happiness is a broad concept, which encloses an individual's emotional gratification, self-fulfillment on his/her actions and the overall contentment in life. As leading researchers in this realm, Edward Diener, Daniel Kahneman and Nobert Schwatz have defined an individual's general evaluation on his/her life as subjective well-being (SWB) and have developed measuring methods for it (Kanemann, Diener and Schwartz, 1999; Diener, 2000).

Thanks to their devotion, an assumption that happiness cannot be measured has been dissolved, and with reinforced elaboration and operationalization of the concept of happiness, empirical researches in psychology, sociology, journalism and behavioral economics have been promoted. In this regard, the article will use Diener's criteria to measure happiness, the final explained variable.

2) Independent Variables: Personality, Self-Clarity and Self-Disclosure

In the process of measuring personality, which is a deep layer of life-world, this article has consulted the "Big Five Personalities": openness, conscientiousness, extraversion, agreeableness and neuroticism. Openness represents a trait, which focuses on diverse experiences and ideas, and a character tendency associated with curiosity and tolerance toward experiences, feelings and thoughts of other people. Conscientiousness, a tendency to carry out well-organized and planned actions, means a character trait, which is good at fulfilling obligations, strong in self-control, achievement-orientated and systematic. Extraversion, a tendency to get along with other people, refers to an enthusiastic, vigorous and positive trait. Agreeableness, a tendency to be sympathetic and cooperative with others, means a harmonious and empathetic trait. Last, neuroticism represents a tendency to get easily agitated, dispirited and vulnerable to emotional unrest (John and Srivastara, 1999).

When it comes to self-clarity, which is an intermediate layer of the subjective life-world, Jenifer Campbell's measurement index has been used to assess whether a respondent has a clear and consistent perception of his/her ego. Regarding self-disclosure, which, as a surface layer of life-world, represents a predisposition to share his/her personal information or emotions with others, this survey has used a modified version of GDS (General Disclosiveness Scale) developed by Whealess (Whealess, 1978).

3) Intervening Variable: Social Capital

As a concept initiated by Pierre Bourdieu and James Coleman and passed down to Ronald Burt, Robert Putnam and Nan Lin, social capital implies "an aggregate of actual or potential resources linked with a continuous network among acquaintances (Bourdieu, 1984)." As Putnam argues, social capital can be divided into bonding and bridging types (Putnam, 2000). The former is associated with such strong ties as emotional support, physical help or other large benefits, while the latter mainly involves assets attainable from light relationships such as exchanges of new information and small talks, which can be acquired from weak ties.

Social capital as an intervening variable will be measured based on the ISCS (Internet Social Capital Scales) of Williams, who separated online social relations from their offline counterparts (Williams, 2006). These criteria are designed to evaluate social relations by dividing them into the aforementioned bonding and bridging relationships epitomized by familiarity and accessibility.

In recent years, a group of scholars have conducted a research on the relation between social media and social capital. Nicole Ellison and her associates proved that the use of Facebook was related with bonding, bridging and maintaining social capital all at the same time, asserting that bridging social capital showed the greatest relevance of all. Charles Steinfield, who emphasized the significance of social capital, also maintained that the degree of using Facebook in the first year had an enormous influence on bridging social capital in the following year (Ellison et al., 2007; Steinfield et al., 2008). Researches mentioned above correspond with Mark Granovetter's proposition, "strong effects of weak ties (Granovetta, 1973)." Sebastiań Valenzuela also validated that the use of Facebook by adolescents had a positive correlation with their life satisfaction, social trust and political participation (Valenzuela et al., 2009). One of the most essential factors in weak ties is the number of friends that one casually hangs out with. Therefore, this survey has studied interpersonal relationships in social media by identifying them as "followers" in Twitter, "ilchon" (roughly translated, closest relative) in Cyworld, "friends" in Facebook, "michin" (meaning, friends in Metoday) in Metoday, and "neighbors" in Naver blogs.

4) Background Variables: Patterns of Media Usage and Socio-demographic Characteristics of Respondents

Patterns of media usage were assessed based on the degree of use of newspapers, TV, radio, Internet, online games, and SNS. SNS, in particular, was examined by categorizing it into five types: a microblog type like Twitter or Metoday; homepage type like Facebook or Cyworld; location-based service type like Foursquareor I'm IN; blog type like Naver or Daum; and messenger type like Kakaotalk or Mypeople.

In addition to gender and age, family income and class standing are also included as background variables of respondents. The number of friends interacting through the five types of SNS mentioned above is added to online background variables.

5) Overall Conceptual Framework

Figure 10-1 **Conceptual Framework**

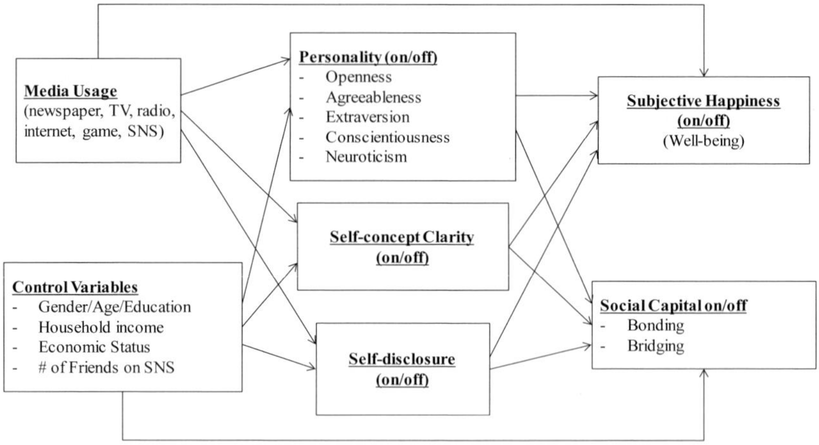

3. Procedures of Analysis

Through a series of following procedures, this article will verify how subjective happiness is affected by an identical online/offline respondent's sociodemographic characteristics, patterns of media usage, subjective life-world as deep, intermediate and surface systems of consciousness, and social capital as types of interpersonal relationships. Effects of offline factors on happiness in the actual everyday life will first be examined, and then effects of online factors on happiness in the digital everyday life, and lastly, how both online and offline factors influence happiness in both actual and digital everyday lives will be assessed and compared.

In other words, with other variables controlled, how the usage of media impacts an individual's personality, self-clarity and self-disclosure will first be investigated, and then how they, along with social capital, affect subjective happiness of an individual will be comparatively analyzed in separate cases of offline and online everyday lives.

4. Results

1) Regression Analysis(A): Factors Leading to Offline Happiness

Table 10-1 **Regression Analysis (1): Determinants of Offline Happiness**

Variable	Model 1 (Offline well-being)	Model 2 (Offline well-being)
Social Capital		
Online Bonding		.012
Bridging		.046
Offline Bonding	.135***	.132***
Bridging	.025	.017
Personality		
Online Openness		-.007*
Agreeableness/Extraversion		.008
Conscientiousness		.027
Neuroticism		.035
Offline Openness	-.002	.046
Agreeableness/Extraversion	-.027	-.028
Conscientiousness	-.002	-.018
Neuroticism	-.124***	-.151***
Self Identity		
Online Self-Concept Clarity		.040
Offline Self-concept Clarity	.085**	.069*
Self Disclosure		
Online Self-disclosure	.162***	.085*
Offline Self-disclosure		.111**
Media Use		
Newspaper	.113***	.112**
TV	-.041	-.034
Radio	.052	.049
Internet	-.082**	-.071*
SNS	.052	.037
Online Games	-.027	-.026
SNS Use		
Twitter	.001	-.001
Facebook	.029	.024
Im-in	.083*	.077*
Blog	-.042	-.048
Kakao-Talk	-.010	-.006
SNS Friends number		
Twitter	-.031	-.038
Facebook	-.039	-.026
Im-in	.049	.042
Blog	.021	.034
Kakao-Talk	-.047	-.044
Control General		
Gender(Male=1)	.004	-.001
Age	-.114**	-.126***
Education	.075*	.079**
Monthly Income	-.036	-.036
Economic Status	.333***	.326***
N	1026	1026
R-Square	.300	.312

2) Regression Analysis(B): Factors Leading to Online Happiness

Table 10-2 **Regression Analysis (2): Determinants of Online Happiness**

Variable	Model 1 (Online well-being)	Model 2 (Online well-being)
Social Capital		
Online Bonding	.096	.095
Bridging	.293***	.289***
Offline Bonding		-.024
Bridging		.012
Personality		
Online Openness	-.040	-.008
Agreeableness/Extraversion	.084*	.105**
Conscientiousness	-.003	.009
Neuroticism	.022	.013
Offline Openness		-.029
Agreeableness/Extraversion		-.063
Conscientiousness		-.022
Neuroticism		-.005
Self Identity		
Online Self-Concept Clarity	-.040	-.023
Offline Self-concept Clarity		-.017
Self Disclosure		
Online Self-disclosure	.132***	.138***
Offline Self-disclosure		-.001
Media Use		
Newspaper	-.016	-.014
TV	-.002	.004
Radio	.014	.021
Internet	-.066*	-.069*
SNS	.040	.038
Online Games	.081**	.082**
SNS Use		
Twitter	.041	.035
Facebook	-.003	.006
Im-in	-.017	-.016
Blog	.054	.049
Kakao-Talk	-.071*	-.063
SNS Friends number		
Twitter	-.038	-.035
Facebook	-.055	-.058
Im-in	.037	.036
Blog	.015	.019
Kakao-Talk	-.004	.007
Control General		
Gender(Male=1)	-.003	-.013
Age	-.026	-.019
Education	.075*	.073*
Monthly Income	-.011	-.004
Economic Status	.075*	.076*
N	1026	1026
R-Square	.325	.331

3) Major Determinants of Personal Happiness, Offline and Online

Figure 10-2 **Overall Results: Two Faces of Happiness, Offline & Online**

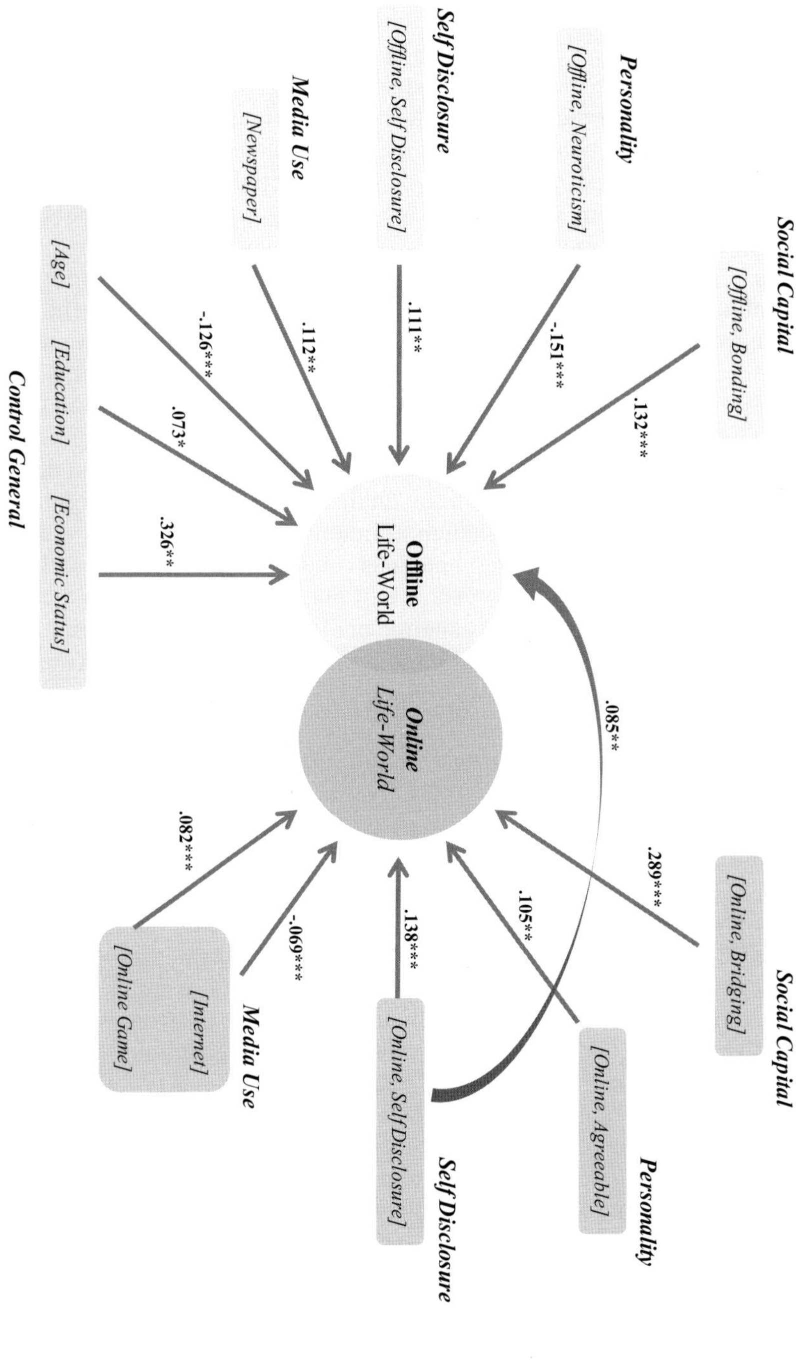

VII. Interpretations and Implications

1. Dualization of Life-world

The outcome of analysis shows that variables, which have a significant influence on offline and online happiness, are generally divided formulating separate path models. Except that self-disclosure in the online world has a significant effect on offline happiness, it is all the online variables that influence online happiness or bonding social capital, while it is all the offline variables that affect online happiness or bridging social capital. This indicates that life-world duality is being established, where online and offline worlds do not exchange cross-sectional influences with each other.

This dualization of life-world connotes a probability that people living in the online world can be disconnected with those who largely depend on the offline world. In addition, as those with dual personalities, who live as totally different people in online and offline worlds, have emerged, it is highly probable that falsification of identity may be commonly conducted. Also, an excessive obsession with the online world may generate anti-social behaviors that go against established social order or values and norms. On the other hand, there is a positive view on the dualization of life-world, arguing that those who are not satisfied with their offline lives can endure or overcome the grueling life-world by enjoying happiness in the online world. As seen in the cases of Internet addicts, however, an extreme preoccupation with the online world may trigger a new type of anomie or alienation by reducing motivation or affinity toward the real life, and this pessimistic view is gaining more momentum.

2. Comparing the Properties of Online and Offline Life-worlds

As the digital age is getting into full swing, the online life-world has emerged as an alternative life-space, a counterpart to the offline life-world that holds substantiality. A life of a citizen, the main agent of action in the offline life-world, is generally ruled by reality principles, and when it comes to explaining or understanding circumstances, causality is deemed more important. On the other hand, netizens' behavior in the online life-world is governed by fantasy principles going beyond realistic limits, and more emphasis is placed on narrativity rather than on causality. In addition, the offline world is mainly based on working and writing is prevalent as a way of communication, while the offline world is more focused on playing and talking is preferred not only in colloquialism but in written language.

In sum, with the transition to the digital age, our everyday life-world has been divided into analogue world and digital world, which coexist sometimes complementarily and sometimes competitively. Thus, contemporary men and women in this digital age live with dual citizenship: as a citizen in the offline world and a netizen in the online world.

If a common expression of netizens is used to distinctively describe these two life worlds, the offline world can be dubbed a "Real World" and its online counterpart can be called a "Real (as in Spanish) World." This implies that the two worlds are oriented toward different principles and properties by perceiving and interpreting the word "Real" in distinctive ways though they share the same spelling.

VIII. Discussion

From the early 1990s, when the Internet came into wide use, to recent years, the online life-world has exerted an influence within the limited range of constitutive principles of its predecessor, the offline world. However, the digital everyday life-world, which can cross the boundaries of time and space and even the routine-non-routine borderline, is gaining more power as a mighty black hole, which stimulates and concentrates users' attention, as SNS is getting prevalent with reinforced mobility and applicability.

Via the SNS, communications between one and many, many and one, and many and many are all possible, not to mention the one-on-one correspondence, and in this respect, it has become a highly effective way of making a relationship. Earlier, Beck asserted the "individualization thesis" to point out that an individual tended to plan and design his/her own life in modern society, where collective bonding was getting weaker. Such a tendency is most prevalent among the new generation of netizens, but they as Homo Socius also want to mingle with other people. The SNS offers an excellent means of communication, which properly satisfies twofold contemporary desires to be left alone and yet associate with others as well. Sherry Turkle, a new media researcher, has been actively involved in informing this contemporary inclination to "connect if they want and disconnect if they don't" under the title of "Alone Together" (Turkle, 2011).

Accordingly, netizens in the SNS era are prone to amorphous herding, unlike binding behaviors of netizens in the Internet age. These people with a strong tendency for individualism focus on their own thoughts or decisions, and yet, they are also sensitive to their surrounding circumstances. Antonio Negri and Michael Hardt have defined a group of people with this ambivalent predisposition as 'multitude' distinguished from the uncivilized mass from the age of mass media or the enlightened public. Able to exert a powerful influence with an instant unity, they are connected with a loose tie, lacking a strong sense of solidarity, as a hypersensitive collective, whose arbitrary behavior is hard to predict when and where to bounce or rush (Hardt and Negri, 2004).

In terms of the time of appearance, it is evident that the digital everyday life-world is a subsequent form of the preexisting everyday life-world. For a while, the digital everyday life-world in the space of information and communications based on the new media was disregarded as a fake reality lacking material foundations. With technological development, however, it is overwhelming the conventional everyday life-world in terms of degree of freedom as a new space of activities, where thinking, feeling, doing, wishing and transmorphosis can be arbitrarily realized. Thus, a dismal outlook may be proposed that if the hypersensitive multitude gets actively engaged in this online everyday life-world, the digital life-world may colonize the offline everyday life-world by incorporating and dominating it with mighty digital power.

Then will hypersensitive drives produce only negative results exacerbating social disorder? While noting creative properties of desires, Gilles Deleuze and Felix Guattari, post-modern psychoanalysts who advocate micropolitics of desires have proposed "de-territorialization of desire," which rejects any repressive mechanism that obstructs a productive energy of desires, as an alternative life strategy (Deleuze and Guattari, 1999). In this context, smart netizens versed in the SNS, which is oriented towards openness, participation, sharing, collaboration and empathy, are expected to play a pioneering role in establishing "an alternative brave new-world." For this, mind cultivation, which can properly manage excessive impulses or behavior, is anticipated to become a decisive factor. That is because whether a creative hacker, who may contribute to human welfare, descends to become a malignant cracker or not ultimately depends on what kind of character he or she possesses.

Chapter 11

Policy Measures in the Age of New Media

I. Overview of Past Media Policies in Korea

Like many other policies, media policy is a result of political, economic, social, cultural, and technological conditions of the time. Korea's media policy has also developed in tandem with diverse changes of complex circumstances including the shift of central media from newspapers through broadcasting to the Internet.

It is not an exaggeration to say that Korean media policy in the early period — when the influence of political power was enormous — used to be swayed by the ruling intentions of the government. Newspapers that had been under the control of Japanese imperialism and the U.S. military were not free from political restraints even after the establishment of an independent administration. Administrations of Lee Seung-man and Park Jeong-hui divided newspapers into pro-governmental and anti-governmental to impose restrictions on those critical toward the regime, and sometimes used them as a means for political promotions and propaganda. The same applied to the broadcasting, the next mainstream media following newspapers: it is evidently proven by a series of repressive measures like Coercive Media Merging and Closing, which was implemented in 1980 by the Fifth Republic to establish its political legitimacy (Kim, 2002: 561-562).

Around the mid 1980s, the age of democratization, Korea's broadcasting policy changed its regulatory directions to focusing on realizing publicity and public interests based upon the frequency scarcity principle and an argument thrusting that airwaves are a public resource. Furthermore, to the broadcasting having an immense direct appeal, the principle of public interests was more strictly applied, and regulations of entry, possession and contents were imposed. This principle of publicity and public interests was also emphasized in telecommunications media. Thus, instead of providing the telecommunications industry with monopoly rights, entry regulation, monopoly protection, and fees and charges regulation for the achievement of universal service were implemented.

As seen above, Korea's media policy in the past was regulatory in essence. The advent of Internet-based new media, however, demands a change in this regulatory media policy. It is hard to uniformly impose regulatory principles and standards upon the new media which is characterized by diversity, multiplicity, and unpredictability, and it is not easy to access the plausibility or effects of regulations as well. In addition, due to accelerating technological innovation and growing competence of new media users, the gap between the regulatory system and the reality has been radically widened. This "policy-lag" phenomenon is expected to be more aggravated in tandem with the trend of media convergence. In a word, policy innovation is urgently demanded as the relevance of previous media policy is getting obsolete along with socio-technological changes.

Countries with the advanced media industry have been quick to cope with such circumstances. Despite different policy focuses, they all have been seeking for easing regulations. Britain, which has responded to the convergence of broadcasting and telecommunications more promptly than any other country in the world, enacted the "Communications Act" in 2003, which combined the acts regarding broadcasting and telecommunications, and launched the Office of Communications by merging regulatory bodies of relevance. Declaring the "Light Tough Regulation" as an ultimate version of deregulation to cope with the digitalization and integration of media and communications, the Communications Act intended to promote a market environment, where all the players could compete on the level ground, by switching to autonomous regulations. Yet, even under such autonomous regulations, Britain has underscored the importance of the government's active role at the same time. America also established the Federal Communications Commission, the key regulatory agency, and organized a legal system corresponding to media convergence through the enactment of telecommunications act in 1996. Special features of this act were "competition and market opening": in other words, it was designed to reinforce a competitive system in every market within the pro-competition and less regulatory framework of national policy. Accordingly, the U.S. has been promoting competition through the reduction of regulations, eagerly encouraging the industry's adoption of autonomous regulations and minimizing governmental interventions. Taking this global trend into account, it has been constantly maintained that government should attempt changes in its regulatory policy framework in Korea.

So far, Korea's media policy has been centered around media suppliers.

In other words, there has been a tendency that media users are regarded as mere consumers, rather than independent agents of media action, or passive recipients unilaterally taking what media suppliers deliver. That is a vestige of an outmoded belief from the past, when uni-directional mass media such as newspapers, magazines, radios or televisions were predominant. The so-called media-scape is radically changing, however, due to the emergence of top-notch new media featuring multi-convergence functions and the advancement of prosuming one-person media that can execute the production, delivery and possession of information all at the same time. In addition, the tsunami of convergence is expanding well beyond the world of media to the structural, institutional, cultural and conscious level of the social system. Therefore, it is urgent to reestablish the goals and action strategies of media policy.

II. New Directions in Media Policy

Shifts in the communicative order due to media convergence and the accompanying changes in social environment and awareness have formed a wide consensus for the need of new media policy, generating useful ideas for action strategies and directions. A typical case in point includes popular discussion over the issues of defining new forms of media like smart TV and integrating regulatory bodies, and entry and possession regulations. In this process, the establishment of alternative policy goals and strategies is deemed a task that should be given priority.

Society of media convergence tends to augment the opportunity structure of media usage, but at the same time, it accompanies a risk of causing information overflow, which usually aggravates the difficulty of choosing information. Therefore, some regulations are inevitable to overcome uncertainty and confusion. Yet, new policies should not only reflect such fundamental characteristics of the new media as openness, sharing and participation, but they should also aim for an expanded communicativeness to embrace many other areas beyond the logical level. Thereby, the theory of autonomous regulation should be the basis of new media policy.

Under the autonomous regulation, individuals, enterprises and private organizations, not the government, become the subjects of regulation, which is considered a part of changes in governing patterns resulting from the expansion of informatization and globalization (Swise, 1997). Informatization, in particular, transforms the relational structure among the principal agents of governmence — state, corporations, and civil society — and gets to be a driving force behind the collaborative mode of regulation, or the so-called cyber-governance, by transcending the government-centered ruling mechanism that used to be prevalent in the industrial society. Under cyber-governance, while roles of state and corporations diminish, the significance of civil society rises to prominence. Autonomous regulation is conceptually different from deregulation, which is intended to alleviate or remove excessive state regulation that weakens market factors, and different from un-regulation, which means avoidance from or confrontation with the state. Autonomous regulation rather seeks for improving the agents or methods of regulation than rejecting or demolishing state regulation itself—thus, it is desirable to maintain a complementary relationship with governmental regulation.

Korea's media policy in the past was centered around governmental regulations on the media market. Even discussions over regulation in society of convergence have been mostly about the existing media industry or new-coming media enterprises. Unlike in the past when a dualistic view of nation and market was the mainstream perspective, a tripartite model involving state, market, and civil society has come into the spotlight both in and outside the academic realm due to the rapidly increasing influence of civil society (Cohen and Arato, 1992). Therefore, civil society should be given equal significance along with the state and the market in drawing up a new media policy. As a major player in the world of media, citizens in the age of convergence actively participate in autonomous regulation within the significantly transforming media environment and reinforce their role as a monitor to make sure that the regulation is properly implemented. Therefore, the government should recognize them as an active agent of media activities, not a mere object of public regulation or protection, and it should concentrate its efforts on working out policies that can promote an autonomous regulatory environment.

Emerging as independent agents of communicative activities in the age of media convergence, citizens are no longer passive as they used to be in the past. As technology and knowledge concerning media have become common and the borderline between information production and consumption has blurred, citizens are now doubling their communicative competence by taking part in the tasks that once used to be occupied only by media professionals. Through blogs, personal Internet broadcasts or a variety of social networking systems, citizens are exerting a tremendous influence by spreading the information they have either created or selected throughout the globe and making exchanges with world-wide users: more surprisingly, they do this with simple communication tools such as private terminals or mobile telecommunication devices, not with some huge, complex technologies.

Heightened social standing of citizens implies that the nation as a policy maker needs to view them from a different perspective. In case of labor policy, for instance, a grand three-party compromise among labor, management and government was considered important, but when it comes to media policy in the age of convergence, "persuasion" and "alignment," beyond negotiation, compromise and reconciliation, among principal agents, are given more significance. Therefore, citizens should play a role as more than an object of negotiation and be a partner of persuasion and alignment. Alignment signifies a progressive action, through which actors independently respond to policy issues in accordance with their own principles and standards, not unilaterally manipulated by the state power.

In a word, as a transition to the society of convergence renders the existing regulatory policy unsuitable, an alternative paradigm for communications policy tuned into autonomous regulation must be established. This new policy paradigm should not only meet the needs of rapid technology development, it should also reflect the capacity of civil society as a newly emerging agent of media activities. In addition, it needs to reinforce its policy flexibility so as to properly respond to such trends of a new age as sensibility, mobility and rapidity through mid-to long-term prospects.

A centralized regulatory system represented by "Big Brother" is no longer suitable for new communications policy. Instead, an expansion of new media awareness based upon a mature sense of citizenship is in urgent demand. In short, the rationality of communications is expected to improve throughout the whole society by minimizing forced regulations mostly consisted of monitoring and punishment and strengthening the civil society's capability of autonomous discernment. And that should be achieved in accordance with autonomous regulation apparatus based on mutual trust.

III. Growing Accountability of Citizens: Every Individual is a Gatekeeper in Communication Pathways

A gatekeeper of communications refers to a doorman (or woman), who guards pathways, through which each and every message comes and goes. Yet, the meaning of a gatekeeper, who used to select and edit articles and reports in conventional forms of media such as newspapers and broadcasting, has enormously changed in the society of convergence. In the age of convergence, the role of a gatekeeper is extending from professional journalists to ordinary citizens: this shift grants legitimacy to the principle of autonomous regulation, a basis of a new paradigm for communications policy.

Due to the advancement of digital technology, a new media environment, where every member of society can play a role as a journalist if they want, is being promoted. The advent of the Internet helps ordinary people create news through their blogs, which means that they are now fully able to accomplish the tasks that used to be only executed by such professionals as reporters and broadcasters (Castells, 2009). As Dan Gillmor, author of We, the Media, predicts, grassroots journalism will be prevalent in the future. He argues that the current lecture-type method of message delivery has been indifferent to the recipient's feedback, but in grassroots journalism based upon blogs, voices of individual bloggers will gain much more influence than opinions of the press (Gillmor, 2004). In a word, we are entering an age where every individual can be a journalist. In fact, bloggers now have open debates on a regular basis by posting their thoughts on both personal issues and such big social agendas like the 9.11 terrorist attack or the war in Iraq. This trend is expected to be more expanded and diversified along with media convergence. As old and new media forms meet — the former provides news within the set time and form and the latter features mobility, realtimeness and interactivity — stories circulating on the web can be delivered to a great majority of people via old mass media, and likewise, the information that the old forms of media do not deal with is eagerly dissipated through the Internet: the whole process is expected to double the ripple effects of messages.

It cannot be denied that ordinary people are now enjoying access to diverse and abundant information, which was previously inaccessible, as they play a role as a journalist in a new space of communications forged by media convergence. Yet, in this new media environment totally different from its predecessor, the process of selecting, verifying and filtering useful information has yet to be institutionalized. Therefore, every individual can work as a gatekeeper. Now ordinary citizens think that it is inappropriate that only such gatekeepers as some government officials, entrepreneurs and professionals can control the access to the circulating information. They rather seek to participate as a gatekeeper in accordance with new ethics and values suitable for the age of media convergence, and thus, secure an independent status in this new communicative space characterized by participation, sharing, and openness. Individual users as a gatekeeper can choose subject matters from more varied perspectives than existing media professionals and filter false information by enhancing information accuracy through ongoing verification. Moreover, the whole process is not decided by a few people behind the scenes, but by a majority transparently in an open space: therefore, it is less likely that the prejudice and high-handedness of a few men in power can intervene (Jenkins, 2008).

In fact, there is always a risk that citizens may degenerate into an onlooking consumer amid information overflow and confusion, not a progressive and self-regulating gatekeeper. Furthermore, ominous attempts by private corporations to dominate the Internet or the world of convergent media well beyond the press and broadcasting are being detected across the globe. Hence, the government should concentrate on developing a media policy to deter such harmful circumstances, and at the same time, media users should focus on nourishing their communicative capability by making wise use of both old and new forms of media.

IV. Alternative Models in Media Policy

A series of changes in the field of information and telecommunications harbor both potentials and drawbacks. Particularly in recent years, media convergence from the technological perspective and the expansion of communicability from the socio-cultural perspective have become the axis of transition, thereby ever more increasing the amplitude of changes. Accordingly, the existing policy of broadcasting and telecommunications needs to be innovated into a fresh form suitable for a new age. For that, reform measures must be explored to meet the new needs of civil society, and as described above, the principle of autonomous regulation can provide a basis. In short, emphasis should be placed upon the principle of autonomous regulation, which can expand the sphere of communications and gratify the communicative desires of most citizens, who want freer expression and exchange of their opinions.

In this section, I would like to present a "media engagement model" as a new paradigm of media policy. This policy model has been devised for citizens to actively participate in media activities and cultivate their competence in making right decisions: in the course of conception, the "Public Understanding of Science (PUS)" model for socializing science and technology information was consulted (Wynne, 1991, 2006; Lewinstein, 1992).

1. PUS (Public Understanding of Science) Model

Due to the transition to modern society, people came to consider science, which pursues objective truth, as a prototype of rational thinking. As science was thought to belong to the scientists who were professionally trained to explore, ordinary people were generally excluded from science discourse. Yet, sustainable development of science was impossible without the correspondence of the general public, the eventual recipients of scientific activities: for that reason, plenty of policy measures were created across the world to improve their knowledge and awareness of science. Britain's policy of science known as the popularization of science can be one of the most classic and typical cases in point.

Earlier on, the Royal Academy exerted efforts to disseminate scientific knowledge outside the academic circle through lectures for laymen. The 19th-century Britain intended to pave the way for the popularization of science through the Mechanics Institute movement, which helped the general public understand scientific knowledge more easily. Yet, it was not originally designed for the public to actively participate in science discourse. Its real purpose was to help them acquire the minimum knowledge of science and promote their understanding of scientific development (The Royal Society 1985). In short, as for science, the general public was considered an object of enlightenment, not an independent agent, who was supposed to support the development of science by receiving and understanding the given knowledge.

The earlier PUS model was basically a byproduct of this logic. Beyond the necessity of public understanding of science as required by national development, it also stressed that the popularization of science was important for the "understanding of science in everyday life" or the "management of technological risks." However, it regarded the general public mostly ignorant of science as a party that had to acquire and accept the knowledge of science, and in that point, the PUS model can be seen as an extension of the 19th-century popularization of science.

While lasting to recent years, the PUS model went through a big changeover in the 1999s. The previous PUS model supposed that the general public were passive actors and ignorant beings in a "state of cognitive deficiency" when it comes to science. Here lies a reason why the conventional PUS model is also called a "Public Acceptance Model" or a "Deficit Model."

The traditional PUS model did not cause any problem in terms of knowledge because there was little difference of opinions on the argument that professional scientists with intellectual privileges should unilaterally deliver and impart knowledge to the unprivileged general public. However, the next-generation PUS researchers attempted to transcend the previous model by criticizing the limit inherent in the conventional popularization of science, which presumed the public as passive actors. As an alternative, they presented the constructive PUS which weighed in the relationship between society and science or the constructive Public Understanding of Science and Technology (PUST) which additionally involved the issues of technology. One of the most notable researchers is Wiebe Bijker, a technology sociologist from the Netherlands, who introduced the methodology of the constructive PUST in The Social Construction of Technological Systems: New Directions in the Sociology and History of Technology co-edited with Trevor Pinch and Thomas Hughes, and other books (Bijker, 1993, 1995). While sociology of scientific knowledge in the early 1970s focused on the interpretive flexibility of scientific knowledge, the constructive PUST in the 1980s contemplated beyond the limits of knowledge. It criticized technological determinism and rejected linear and instrumental academic trends, adhering to the viewpoint that the construction of knowledge largely depended on social circumstances and conflicting interests among social groups (Fuglsang, 2001; Wajcman, 2004; Kim, 2006). In other words, revolted against the purity and absoluteness of science and intended to involve the public in the broad network of science.

2. PUM (Public Understanding of Media) Model and Its Derivatives

An overview on the PUS and PUST models can be a good starting point to elaborate the Media Engagement Model. In order to develop a Public Understanding diagram into an Engagement diagram, a proper apprehension on basic characteristics and limits of the public access model must come first. The purpose of the Media Engagement Model is to define the relationship between the media and citizens as an agent of action, and it can be largely divided into three categories: the Public Understanding of Media model that shares the basic premise with the traditional PUS model, the Public Apprehension of Media model which has similar features as the constructive PUST model, and the Public Participation of Media model. They can be diagramed as in Figure 11-1.

Figure 11-1 **PUS (Public Understanding of Media) Model and Its Derivatives**

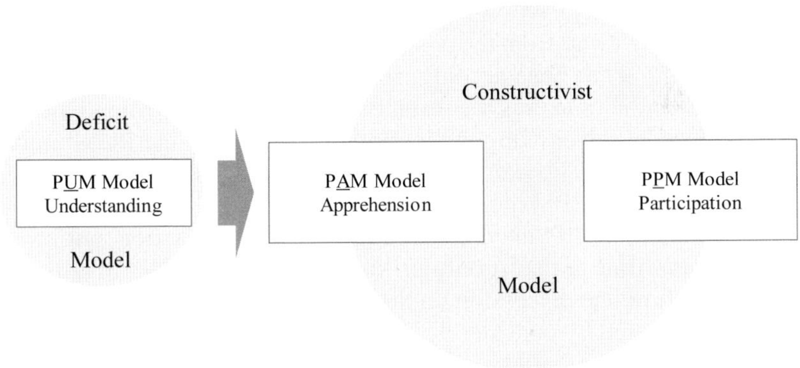

It would be most desirable that the general public learn the relevant knowledge provided by professionals, and support and champion the media industry with acquired insights. Yet, this desirable development is only possible on the premise that independent agents of media activities, who can monitor and criticize the tyranny of media professionals or media powers, should be organized first. Therefore, the Understanding model that stressed cognitive aspects centered around knowledge acquisition needs to be expanded to the PAM model which implies keen discernment in a broader sense, and ultimately to the PPM model which signifies active involvement of the public in media activities.

Of course, it is true that there lies a little gap between the PUS and PUM models. It took long to acknowledge the argument that science was socially constructed, but in case of media largely deemed part of a daily routine, its relevance with society is so obvious that there is no need for an explanation. It is a quite well-known fact that the media obtains content materials and organize stories from diverse factors such as society, culture, politics and economy, and in return, it exerts an enormous influence on many visible aspects of social life. Despite this difference, the PUM model can offer a meaningful starting point in discussing a media policy because the relation between the public and science, which the PUS model proposed, is considerably similar to that of the public and the media in the past. In the Mass Society Theory that used to be prevalent along with the Mass Communication Theory, the relation between the media and the public was described asymmetrical and one-directional, and thus, in order to understand the media, particularly the mass media, which has a powerful influence on the general public, agents of media discourse should be magnified first. There lies an original value of the PUM model.

3. From Media Understanding to Media Engagement

General users in today's world of media are now playing an active and leading role, breaking away from the position as a mere consumer or a passive recipient. This trend has been accomplished at the demand of the general public, and at the same time, it is the result of the changes occurring in the world of media. Hence, the existing media policy based upon the PUM model is in lack of relevance. This can be partly overcome by introducing the aforementioned PAM and PPM models. This series of model shifts from the PUM to the PAM and the PPM may retain validity in terms of action, but it shows a fundamental limit in that it only presumes a single subject of action, the public. Therefore, the discussion on the theory of media engagement should be further promoted by considering actors, not just the action itself (Wynne, 2006).

From an extended perspective, the media engagement model can be divided into a total of nine categories (3x3): in terms of action, understanding, awareness and participation; and in terms of actor, the masses, the multitude and the enlightened public. Here comes a brief account of different models, which present diverse interpretations on the media engagement mainly around the two standards of classification — action and actor.

1) Action: From Understanding through Apprehension to Participation

In the world of media radically changing due to the evolution of digital technology and the advent of the age of convergence, the civil society is increasing its influence on media day by day. More than just cognitively understanding media information, they display varied patterns of behavior like comprehensively apprehending the knowledge and putting it into practice. Therefore, just as the PUS model shifted its main issue "from fact to opinion" and "from scientific to social debate," it is desirable that the PUM model expands the range of issues "from knowledge to system debate" and "from thinking to doing debate." Régis Debray argues that the process, through which the media carries thoughts, necessarily involves material, technological, social and organizational conditions. He asserts that "no message can pass through time and space by itself," which signifies the social nature of the media—namely, its connectivity with the general society. Furthermore, if the same issue is viewed from the perspective of the Actor Network Theory, both the media and the public within the media network are equally independent actants connectable in a wide range of ways.

In the PUM model, the prototype of the theory of media popularization, "understanding (U)" denotes an improvement of cognitive competence via the media. The public acquires knowledge through various forms of education or the process of media usage. In the PAM model, "apprehension (A)" signifies a perception in a broad sense, which embraces normative, emotional, and aesthetic aspects (Michael, 2002). In the "Understanding" model, the purpose of policy makers and media professionals was to make the public realize the effective value of the media as an intermediator, but in the "Awareness" model, the public who can experience and communicate with the media contextually and comprehensively depending on given circumstances and affiliated groups are deemed ideal beings. Meanwhile, in the PPM model, "participation (P)" means the citizen's participatory activities toward the media. Participation can be achieved in varied ways: individuals can pursue their own goals through the media or create new social orders and norms, while restraining the private interest for the sake of public good (Rowe and Frewer, 2005).

In some respect, it may seem unreasonable to understand the behavior patterns of the public in this simple, uniform way as in the theory of media popularization, but the classification diagram of media activities, which involves understanding in a narrow sense, awareness in a broader meaning, and participation in a practical perspective, may retain typological values for developing a media policy.

2) Actor: From the Masses to the Multitude or the Enlightened Public

The expansion of the media popularization model can be distinguished in terms of actors as well as actions. It would be oversimplifying the characteristics of a collectivity to assign all members of today's society to a single category, the public. Depending on ways of thinking and behavior patterns, collectivities can be conceptualized into the masses, the multitude, and the enlightened public.

Mass According to H. Gans (1974), author of Popular Culture and High Culture, the term masses derives from a German word "masse": here, the masses mean the non-aristocratic and uneducated class in modern Europe.

Compared with the upper class, the masses were considered incapable of actively coping with any issue. Such elite theorists as Vilfredo Pareto, Gaetano Mosca, Robert Michels, and C. Wright Mills also grant similar attributes to the masses by understanding them as an opposite category to a handful of governing elite. The elite theory presumes that there is a minority ruling group in a society that carries out important decision-making tasks. Isolated from the majority, this elite group governs the masses. According to a conservative elite model, a social system is basically maintained through competition among the elite: there are also legitimate processes like an election, which sustains a society democratically (Kourvetaris, 1998). That is because the masses are not reliable, not capable of leading substantial changes, and thus not self-governing.

Mills, portrays the masses of mass society not only as social "lower class," but also powerless beings, who are politically fragmented and passively manipulated by the mass media with little will to resist. Moreover, the mass media in modern society makes a depoliticization effect of making unbearable conditions bearable by shutting down the existential meaning of the masses and controlling their desire with a deep involvement in the process of socialization. Therefore, a reasonable and free communication comes to be blocked in a society, where the masses are manipulated by mass media.

Multitude According to Paolo Virno's argument, choosing between the two concepts—a populaces and a multitude—was one of the most essential issues in the 17th century. Those two concepts were respectively presented by Thomas Hobbes and Baruch Spinoza: they used to be in acute conflict in modern society, but as the populace prevailed, the concept of multitude came to vanish temporarily (Virno, 2004). In *De Cive*, Hobbes (1642) stated that "a populace is something homogeneous. In other words, they possess and belong to a unitary will": his argument is often cited to emphasize the existential indispensability of a populace and a nation. On the other hand, Spinoza defined a multitude as "a dynamic being, who cannot acquire a status of a legal personality because they avoid political unity, reject obedience, refuse to make a sustainable agreement, and never hand over their own rights to the sovereign." The multitude whom Spinoza deemed as an existential plurality with "a perpetual form" and "a cornerstone of civil freedom" was seen as a threat by Hobbes that could undermine the existence of the populace and the nation. Virno points out, however, that the concept of a multitude is "much more useful than a populace in reflecting on the public sphere in contemporary society" (Virno, 2004). In short, groups that had lasted in liberal nations of modern society were close to a populace in nature, but it would be more appropriate to understand most collectivities in contemporary society within the conceptual framework of a multitude.

The multitude is more intellectual than the masses and more emotional than the enlightened public. They can collect information regarding a certain phenomenon or a fact through a wide range of media forms and expressing their opinions based upon it. Yet, their views mostly derive from emotion and sensitivity, rather than reason or debate. As both Hobbes and Spinoza mutually indicate, a multitude pursues individual freedom in the private, rather than public, sphere, refusing to be a gigantic homogeneous collectivity (Hardt and Negri, 2004; Shirky, 2008). Namely, the multitude's behavior can be better explained with ever changing emotions including opportunism, cynicism, fear, curiosity, and chitchat than with universal reason: here, we can discern both potentials and limits of a multitude at the same time. Recent collective spectacles like a street cheering in the 2002 Seoul World Cup, volunteer works for the oil spill in Taean, and a candlelight vigil against U.S. beef imports are cases in point showing unique mobilization patterns and attributes of a multitude.

Enlightened Public As Jürgen Habermas contends, human rationality is inherent in the intersubjective competence of communicative actions based upon the creativity of lifeworld through discourse. Focusing on basic forms of a successful intersubjective communication, he has set forth the "universal pragmatics," a precondition for promoting communicative competence. For a successful language-mediated communication, both speakers and hearers are required to have a capability to coordinate mutual expectations concerning the power of an action that arises in the process of speech acts. Here, the speaker carries out a speech act bearing validity claims, which are realized by such standards as "truth," "normative appropriateness," and "sincerity (Roderick, 1986)"

Those who can conduct a rational communication through this procedure are the enlightened public, who, unlike the masses or the multitude, can be defined as a social collectivity armed with modern rationality. The enlightened public is often defined as a group of scattered people with mutual interests and concerns. In other words, they are not a group of people organized with a sense of belonging, but they still interact both directly and indirectly through a diversity of media and form public opinions. Yet, Mills (1956) maintains that they are those who have a political competence of sustaining democratic balance of power through free discussions. The enlightened public, who set to act with judging the sincerity and legitimacy on their own, are generally considered more rational than the masses or the multitude.

3) Matrix of Media Engagement

Table 11-1 below explains the media engagement in a form of matrix crossing patterns of action and actor. The vertical columns feature the categories of action, while the horizontal lines classify types of actors, or the subjects of action. Thereby, this dualistic approach shows who acts how through the intersections of the vertical and horizontal lines.

Table 11-1 **Classification by Actor and Action Types**

Actor / Action	(M; Mass)	(T; mulTitude)	(P; Public)
(U; Understanding)	MUM	TUM	PUM
(A; Apprehension)	MAM	TAM	PAM
(P; Participation)	MPM	TPM	PPM

Among those above, most typical cases are the MUM Model, the intersection of the masses and understanding, the TAM Model, the contact point of the multitude and awareness, and the PPM Model, the junction of the enlightened public and participation. As shown in the table, there indeed are other models as a result of coordinating actions and actors of media activities, but the MUM, TAM, and PPM models are realistically most probable. In addition, taking into account the complex nature of contemporary society, we cannot stick to the unilinear course proceeding from the MUM through the TAM to the PPM, but there will be little disagreement on the argument that a democratic society should ultimately aspire toward the PPM model.

V. Discussion

So far, the media engagement model has been analyzed by types of media action and actor. Table 11-2 below infers media policy orientations in the age of convergence by including the categories regarding types of media, the object of engagement, and leading factors.

Table 11-2 **Comparing MUM, TAM and PPM Models and Their Policy Orientations**

Model	Agent	Action	Mode of Mediation	Policy Orientations
MUM	Knowledge Recipient	Cognitive	Broadcasting	Intellectual Persuasion
TAM	Meaning Transmitter	Perceptive	Narrow-Casting	Empathic Association
PPM	*Action Practitioner*	*Behavioral*	*Free-Casting*	*Collaborative Alignment*

Table 11-2 compares the MUM, TAM, and PPM models by types of the subject and object of media engagement and patterns of action, also presenting respective policy orientations. The subject of the MUM model is the masses as a recipient of knowledge, or the objective facts. Here, their action is confined to acquiring knowledge at the cognitive level and the major form of media used is the generally acknowledged broadcasting. Mass media such as newspapers, televisions, or radios unilaterally impart information into the masses via fixed forms and channels. In this context, the media policy seeks to cultivate knowledgeable citizens based upon the media knowledge.

In the TAM model, the subject of engagement is the multitude. They play a role as a subjective and arbitrary expositor or messenger because they show different perceptual responses toward certain situations or circumstances they confront. A case in point here is user created contents (UCC), which individuals produce and distribute through personal channels. In this case, policy orientation aims for establishing a collective trust.

Finally, the subject of action in the PPM model is participatory actors, who progressively access the media and voluntarily act in the world of media. Here, the media becomes a space of collaboration founded upon communication and mutual consent. Therefore, the media policy under the PPM model should be oriented toward harmoniously aligning independent acts of individual social members.

While the masses, the multitude and the enlightened public are analytical categories of collectivities based upon the styles of existence that the civil society has maintained so far, blind citizens or wise citizens do not belong to the academic terminology, but they are sort of "sensitizing concepts" with a sense of realism (Blumer, 1954). Blind citizens refer to a reckless collectivity, who indiscreetly respond to the outside world without rational judgment. On the other hand, wise citizens signify an evolutionary collectivity, who build up their discernment and power of execution through critical discourses. All the three forms of collectivity — the masses, the multitude, and the enlightened public — have potentials to become either blind or wise citizens: both attributes are inherent in them. In this regard, those two terms do not stop short at merely describing characteristics of a certain collectivity: they can be utilized to infer the progress, through which the masses, the multitude, and the enlightened public transform.

Figure 11-2 **Bifurcation of Citizens**

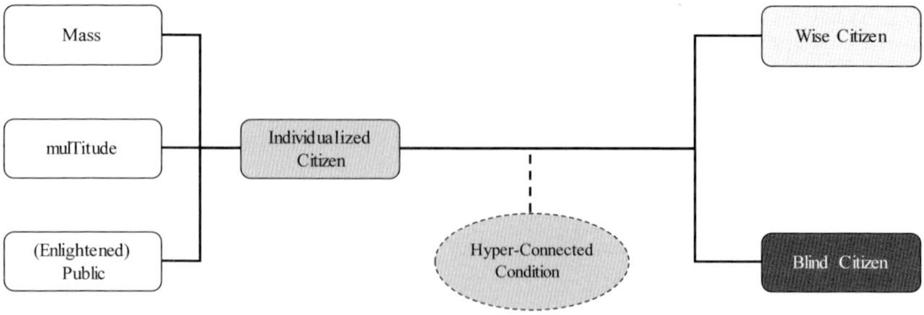

The figure above intends to show how blind citizens and wise citizens are formed. The masses, the multitude, and the enlightened public are the terms to name each collectivity of individuals: they are all basically made up of individuals. In this respect, those three terms can be generalized with a comprehensive concept, the individualized citizens. If interacting at the occurrence of a certain situation, these individualized citizens can become either blind or wise citizens. Thus, the two terms can be used as ideological concepts describing the resulting aspects that a collectivity pursues.

Today's individualized citizens have attributes of the masses, the multitude, and the enlightened public all at the same time. With reasonable communications and rational judgment based upon tolerance, they will be transformed into wise citizens: straying without discernment or judgment, they will fall to become blind citizens (Prior, 2007). Therefore, the process of developing media policy in the age of convergence based on the principle of autonomy should be devoted to establishing the media engagement model and relevant action strategies, which can lead individualized citizens, who are at the risk of degenerating into blind citizens, to become wise citizens through free and equal communications.

Chapter 12

Closing

Toward a Convergence Civilization

By seeing human society from an extremely long-term perspective, the entire history of mankind until the twentieth century can be described as "the process of differentiation" moving from undifferentiated differentiated or highly specialized state. Such argument can be illustrated in the works of modern great thinkers including Immanuel Kant's series of critiques on truth, virtue and beauty, Herbert Spenser's idea of sociocultural evolution from simple, undifferentiated homogeneity to complex, differentiated heterogeneity, Emile Durkheim's argument on the changing types of social solidarity from mechanical to organic one, Marx Weber's dictum of "age of polytheism" which indicates the multiple goals of life to pursue in a modern society (Spencer, 1885[1874]; Durkheim, 1947[1893]; Weber, 1973[1919]; Guyer, 1992).

In the beginning of the second millennium period, however, we are witnessing a signal of epochal reversal, in that the centrifugal force of differentiation is substituted by the centripetal force of convergence. The professional knowledge, professional certificate or professional expertise was an object of respect or trust until a decade ago. Yet, instead of the declining authority of professionalism, convergence which emphasizes the border-crossing, consilience, fusion or hybrid comes to be the goals or means of social achievement.

This convergent turn is inspired by digital technology that enables us to deal with a great amount of data on the basis of binary classification system of 0 and 1. Functions of digital technology such as receiving, managing and emitting diverse forms of data, coupled with those of advanced telecommunication technologies that help to exchange messages irrespective of temporal or special boundaries, have contributed much to converging the world of media. In addition, as convergence effects diffuse into the economic, political, social, cultural and mental dimensions, radical transformations in industrial arrangement, power structure, interpersonal relations, lifestyles and social consciousness have followed.

In the past decade, "discourse on difference" has proliferated. It reflects the skepticism about modernity led by the logic of casuality, dualistic mode of thinking and mechanical worldview. As to the impetus of modernity, Alvin Toffler coined the word 'wedging' to describe the situation where a social reality is forcibly decomposed in various ways. As a result, separation between cognition and affection, mind and body, rationality and irrationality, civilization and savagery, development and un-development, West and Non-West are carried out, so that one part is ascribed as normal and the other part as abnormal (Toffler, 1980). However, the spirit of modernity related with such ideas as progress, rationality, dualism, standardization, universalism, and synchronism have engendered ironical dysfunctions like "civilized violence," "rationalized irrationality," "inclusive exclusion." Such paradoxical conditions tend to stimulate the discourse concerning difference.

In "History and Social Sciences: Long Duration," Fernand Braudel, a leading scholar of the French Annales School, criticizes many historians for using the time as one specie and thus spoiling their historical insights. He classified the time-span into three; short-term, mid-term, and long-term durations, and matched these with three types of history: event history, conjuncture history and structural history (Braudel, 1960). As such, Braudel tried to highlight the poly-layered characters of human history.

Stating that "The event is like a dust," Braudel evokes the importance of long-wave history. He stresses out deep structural dynamics underlying the series of affairs happening in our ordinary life. Extrapolating Braudel's argument emphasizing long-term societal transition, I will first construct an extra-long-term diachronic framework that helps to articulate the stages of transitions in our civilization. Next, based on this conceptual scheme, the recent megatrend towards convergence is to be examined. Finally, nature, mechanism and the prospect of convergence civilization will be explored.

I. Feature of Civilization

The concept of civilization implies the desire of human beings to search for a better life by enhancing objective and subjective living conditions. Thus, the discourse on civilization encompasses all material and spiritual dimensions including political, economic, social, cultural, religious, moral and technological spectrum. Such an idea of civilization is not far from what many evolution theorists have maintained (Morgan, 1877; Spencer, 1885).

Another implication rooted in the civilization concept is the notion of continuity. Civilization is regarded as a continuous process connecting the past and present to the future (Elias, 2000). The continuity theme exists not only in most orthodox evolution theories, but in some influential social theories as well. Examples are Marx Weber's rationalization theory and Gilles Deleuze and Félix Guattari's territorialization thesis (Bendix, 1960; Deleuze and Guattari, 1983).

Given the circumstances, civilization has been investigated in many ways. Thus, before we start the discussion of convergence civilization per se, it may be worthy to construct a comprehensive model to diagnose the current megatrend of convergence with the main thrusts of past approaches to civilization.

1. Civilization as Progress

Most civilization researchers having enlightenment minds are inclined to conceive civilization as a sign of progress. They believe that the human societies have been evolving from barbaric to civilized forms through the improvement of our mode of existence. The basic idea is quite similar to that of classical evolutionism since both believe in the physical and mental abilities of human beings to transform nature at their own will.

This progressive view of civilization is regarded to be Occidental in the sense that it is preoccupied with the idea that promotes the division between the civilized West and the non-civilized rest. For example, Edward Said's conceptualization of Orientalism, Samuel Huntington's critique of universal civilization and James Blaut's criticism of historical Eurocentrism point out the provenance of Westcentrism and how it has been generalized into civilization research in general (Said, 1995; Huntington, 1996; Blaut, 2000). Even Marx Weber, who considers the modern social transformation as the process of rationalization, is not likely an exception of this ideological bias. Because he claimed that the disenchantment of the world that brought about the modern Western society is the consequence of the sense of calling stemming from Calvinist creed of predestination (Weber, 1959).

2. Civilization as Deterioration

One of the most remarkable criticisms of civilization is found in the works of Jean-Jacques Rousseau. He warned about the negative effects of civilization in the sense that civilization tends to destroy nature. In Discourse on the Arts and Sciences, Rousseau highlighted the moral degradation in our civilized society by saying "All arts and sciences are results of moral corruption." His skeptic view of civilization was found in his later work Discourse on the Origin and Basis of Inequality among Men and The Social Contract as well. To overcome the restraint or suppression of civilization, he claims "Return to nature" (Wokler, 1995).

In a similar vein, Sigmund Freud and other Freudian scholars argued against civilization suppressing the human instinct (Freud, 2002[1930]; Marcuse, 1987). Freud stated that unregulated satisfaction of an individual's natural desire cannot be compatible with civilized societies. Since the control of Libido in accordance with "reality principle," is the measure of civilization, abstinence or deferment of gratification would be the necessary condition for civilization development. Individuals are considered to be civilized when they accept the conventional norms and values of the society they belong to.

The idea of civilization as deterioration is shown in Michel Foucault's discussion of the development of modern total institutions. According to him, the clinic aiming to prohibit madness was the origin of modern civilization. Afterwards, similar institutions that depended on physical punishments have been replaced by disciplinary ones. This deteriorative conception of civilization is also found in the works of recent Post-Freudians like Jacque Lacan, Gilles Deleuze, Félix Guattari and Slavoj Žižek. They criticize the reinforcement of socialization for the purpose of cultural refinement, that produces 'over-socialized man (woman),' because it is quite opposite to the manifestation of natural desires of a human being.

3. Civilization as Process

Norbert Elias underscores the relationships between social forces, social structure and individual actors and their consequences in The Civilization Process. Elias says society and the individual are inseparable parts of the civilization process. Also, he adds that both the individual and society share dual aspects, process and structure. He suggests 'theory of figuration' as a conceptual tool to understand the dynamic relations between society and the individual. The interdependence of human beings constitutes a microscopic world of personal interactions. Interpersonal relations are its outcome. But they are integrated and constitute a macroscopic world of social structure (Morrow, 2009).

Elias believes that there lies a consistent trend in a long-term civilization process; from external control to autonomous self-control, from natural instinct to conforming to the norms or values of a society, and from egocentric consciousness to elaborated and stable superego (Elias, 2000). Consequently, civilization is shown as seamless continuum in Elias's conception of civilization process.

II. Paradigmatic Approach to Civilization

The radical transitions in civilization are known to be the consequences of technological innovations. The impact of technology upon human society has been so great that it has played a significant role throughout human history. It is best illustrated by Marx's theory of 'historical materialism' stating societal transition (progression) in terms of mode of production (Marx, 2007); Alvin Toffler's classification of the history human civilization as: agricultural, industrial and information revolution (Toffler, 1980); Maunel Castell's conception of 'development form' which defines the transition of the human civilization into following three stages: agricultural, industrial and information (Castells, 2000). They all share the idea of stepwise paradigmatic social transition in their development models.

Fritjof Capra defines social paradigm as the sum of knowledge, values and behaviors of society. It constitutes the perspective regulating the ways in term of which the society organizes itself (Capra,1996). Accordingly, social paradigm is not just a static concept, Instead, it contains a dynamic property to presuppose transitions to next stage. Manuel Castells defines the paradigm as a frame of reference that sets the standards of entire social practices. Then, he regards the social paradigm as a self-organizing coherent system searching for a new social order that is substantively different from the previous one (Castells, 2009). This paradigmatic approach to civilization provides a double-edged viewpoint to understand the continual aspect of civilization process and its transitional aspect.

As convergence across all sectors of society is emerging as the megatrend, there is a need for a new paradigmatic framework that expands beyond the existing civilization argument. This new paradigm should highlight the process of civilization as a continuum proposed by Elias, accepting the idea of transition suggested by progressive and deteriorative approaches to civilization. In sum, paradigmatic approach to civilization provides a mean to explicate the paradoxical phenomena of "continuous transitions" or "transitional continuity" that enables to understand the macro dynamics of civilization. Given the considerations, a three stage of civilization process is delineated and explicated as follows.

1. Stage of Undifferentiated Civilization: Agricultural Civilization

Agricultural civilization, the initial stage of the civilization process, started with sedentary settlements. It is the successor of nomadic society depending upon hunting, gathering, fishery and herding of livestock. It is the sedentary lifestyle established by the agricultural revolution that created agricultural civilization. Cultivation, land, villages, joint family, patriarchy and patrimonialism are core components that comprise the undifferentiated agricultural civilization. At this point, it should be noted that cultivation is identified as the key factor which ended the nomadic lifestyle. The agricultural civilization converted from a nomadic to sedentary lifestyle largely through the development of new efficient means of production which in turn allowed people to secure land and settlements to colonize villages (Morgan, 1877).

The age of agricultural civilization is recorded as an initial stage of social differentiation, because the agricultural revolution could then activate vertical social differentiation owing to propagation of surplus. Despite the fact, most people went to and from between home and farm areas and dedicated themselves to the homogeneous activity of farming. Therefore, the age of agricultural civilization can be defined as the stage of undifferentiated civilization.

2. Stage of Differentiated Civilization: Industrial Civilization

Industrial civilization may be the result of association between modern spirit requiring efficiency and rationality and fossil energy. Compared with previous undifferentiated civilization, emerging civilization is so unique that it is taken to be the consequence of the first paradigmatic turn of civilization in human history.

Toffler who named industrial civilization as "the second wave" tried to analyze it based on the effect of industrial revolution. Castells who thought that the rise of new social system was related to a new mode of development put industrial mode of development as a core idea.

During the fifteen to seventeenth centuries, enlightenment ideology and scientific revolution have consolidated the confidence in reason, progress, and mechanistic world-view. But subsequent events that helped to reinforce division of labor or role differentiation such as Industrial Revolution, development of capitalism and Scientific-Technological Revolution spurred the movement toward industrial civilization (Toffler, 1980). But it is Fordism that completed Industrial civilization with a new civilization paradigm.

3. Stage of De-Differentiated Civilization: Convergence Civilization

Near the end of the twentieth century, discourses on new revolution began to proliferate. This discursive has surged since 1980s when matured industrial civilization symbolized by steel mill, machinofacture, oil refinery plant, car factory, assembly-lines and factory workers merged with ICTs (information & communication technologies). Diverse labels such as post-industrial society, age of post-Fordism, information society, consumer society or postmodern society were suggested to figure out the essentials of the new civilization paradigm.

Industrial civilization characterized by such ideas as principle of causality, instrumental use of science and technology, measurable and calculable image of the world, predictable future, distinct institutional divisions started to transform itself into a new form represented by hybridity, morphogenesis, uncertainty, unpredictability and high contingency (Wallerstein, 1991). As a result, a new civilization associated with uncertainty principle, time-space transformation, consilience of knowledge, cross-sectional interpenetration, etc. is emerging. From a socio-economic point of view, this recent civilization transformation described as the shift from differentiation civilization paradigm to de-differentiation paradigm of convergence, is conceived as the result of the capitalist restructuring to cope with the accumulation crisis of Fordism (Amin, 1994).

But we have to mention another factor that has contributed much to the birth of convergence civilization, Thanks to advanced technological revolution, we are now entering a new stage of human history, where information and knowledge that maintain high exchange value due to their universal applicability are regarded as the most valuable social resources. In market language, it means the transition where values of commodity are assessed not in terms of amount of labor time but in terms of the amount or quality of information invested in the production activities (Bell, 1973).

Convergence civilization is not the chaotic state where heterogeneous civilization units are messed up as a state of confusion. Instead, a variety of civilization units can coexist maintaining a harmonious unity. Henry Jenkins who examines the sociocultural consequences of media convergence emphasizes that convergence does not mean the state of simple integration. Although continuous confluence movement must be the universal characteristic of a convergence civilization, it always maintains a dynamic state due to the counteracting movement of diversification like ramification, separation and disruption. In this regard, with relation to convergence, it means a series of condivergence (convergence+divergence) processes based on the dialectic interplay of differentiation and integration (Kim, 2008).

III. Convergence Society: Its Nature and Implications

Convergence is defined as the process of merging, mixing, changing, dividing, reproducing or creating new products or phenomena (Hwang, 2009). Due to this dynamic process of high complexity, convergent society is seen as the prototype of complexity system of the highest degree (Forrester, 1968). However, as a high complexity system, convergence society not only contains interpersonal associations between people, it also includes the interactions between human and non-human that used to be out of consideration in the discussion of complexity system. That is why new definitions, roles, functions or meanings have to be conferred to non-living things. Accordingly, the asymmetry between human and other organisms or human and non-human, which have been strictly divided as subject and object before tends to break down and give rise to a radical change in conventional anthropocentric ways of thinking. If reinforced by new epistemology that takes time-space transformation for granted, it is expected that a totally new worldview will emerge, which is based upon the "the conviction of universal convergence," that is, anything in the universe is able to be a part of a universal movement toward conjunction.

It is true that an increasing degree of freedom reinforced by a series of 'condivergence' tends to amplify social uncertainty. Given the state of excessive chaos, it is expected that 'convergence system' that is substantively different from conventional complexity system will emerge through the process of reconstructing a new social order. The characteristics of convergence systems can be summarized as follows.

1. Hyper-Openness

A hyper-open system is a system that postulates free interactions between the subsystems or unobstructed interchange between system and environment. While the conventional open system theory lays a stress on personal, material, and informational exchanges between system and its environment, the hyper-open system claims unbounded interactions of all kinds disallowing any form of internal or external boundaries.

Consequently, convergence under hyper-open system tends to substitute the concept of "link-centered network" that resembles the image of thread ball or rhizome for that of "node-centered network." As long as convergence emphasizes system structures, it highlights the relations of elements or their alliances (Latour, 1997). Furthermore, in a hyper-open system, where all conceptual boundaries are imploding, intercourses of any direction, forward or backward, right-hand or left-hand, upward or downward, inside and outside or whatsoever would be allowed. As a result, it is expected that the image of the world of free association where everything can combine with everything else is going to prevail.

2. Multiplicity

A convergence system consisting0 of diverse structured social factors is likely to structure a multi-layered world arranged with variety of overlapped realities. In other words, it implies that the world exists in a multiple state characterized by layers of multiplicity and plurality not of singularity (Baudrillard, 1983). Such an image of multiple worlds that includes both actual and virtual realities is described in the recent movie Inception. It shows the coexistence of reality, virtual reality and another virtual reality inside the virtual reality in a stream of consciousness. It is also supported by a recent astrobiological research reported by NASA (National Aeronautics and Space Administration). An entirely new life form is reported to be discovered on our planet that "doesn't share the biological building blocks of anything currently living" on Earth: A microbe that lives on arsenic instead of iodine (NASA, 2010).

In a multi-society, different parts or part and the whole are related with each other and attempt to reformulate the world. Throughout such complex and dynamic process, a totally new world can emerge. It is shown in Michel Callon and John Law's big science project on space exploration. What they found is local networks that are embedded in a broader network (Callon and et. al., 1988). Likewise, a convergence system where incessant reconstruction is going on through a series of unbounded interactions tends to gain an amalgamative property due to their intra-systemic and inter-systemic intercourses.

3. A-Linearity

When the factors that structure the system provide the additional effect more than the sum of individual effects, the system is said to possess non-linear property. Like a strange attractor at a junction point, when a system is hard to predict the trajectory of its movement, it is said to be a non-linear complexity system (Capra, 1996). In mechanical world-view which is represented by the clock having the cog wheel with second, minute, and the hour hand, a linear logic or solution can be applied. However, the theorists of complexity system put consistent arguments that natural society or individual society gradually become the non-linear. Despite this, nowadays, more than the linear simple system and curve-linear complexity, the disconnection, leaping, ramification, confluence and reversion enter into a-linear meta-complexity system. It is witnessed that individuals' hypersensitive behaviors of multitudes are predominated with inclining, twisting, splitting, and splashing which cannot even be measured by high-dimensional functional equations (Hardt and Negri, 2004).

4. Co-Production

The theory of autopoiesis is derived by Humberto Maturana and Francisco Varela's: a study of the self-referential organization of living system that maintains itself through dynamic process of reflexive control. In their conceptualization, they emphasize the difference between organization and structure. Whereas living systems' structure implies the actual relation of physical components, the structure denotes the mode of relation that attributes a certain living system to a specific category. Therefore, organization as an abstractive description of relation has no relation with its actual components (Maturana and Varela, 1980).

Yet, if the theory of autopoiesis is prolonged with the non-human world, convergent system as a coproduction world must be postulated. Here, everything would be combined with everything else and make universal relations, universal collaborations and universal empathy possible. It helps to reproduce entire world including the human sphere, biosphere, ecosphere and any other spheres as well. This view that can be traced back to the emerging stage of radical constructivism is sharply contrasted to that of technological determinism. Regardless of the primacy debate on technology and society, the co-productionist view emphasizing socio-technical ensembles are gaining influence these days (Bijker, 1993). They also put audacious opinion about non-inhuman issues as being clearly proposed by actor-network theorists (Latour, 1991).

5. Complexity System vs. Convergence System

The transition of the super complexity system to supra-complexity system is considered as crucial evidence indicating the shift from differentiation civilization to convergence civilization. Through the process of 'convergentification,' the super complexity system moves beyond its basic properties to convergence system (Figure 12-1). In the convergence system, alliance structure is constituted through free association of individual elements. The alliance of convergence system can be said to be a series of diagrams or rules indicating the relations of everything, both human and non-human. This equalizes the relationship between subsystem, system and environment and re-conceptualizes the mutual recognition and collaboration under a new perspective. It also indicates that the order or dynamics of the system is neither planned nor predetermined by any external factor (Latour, 1997).

Figure 12-1 **Types of System Model**

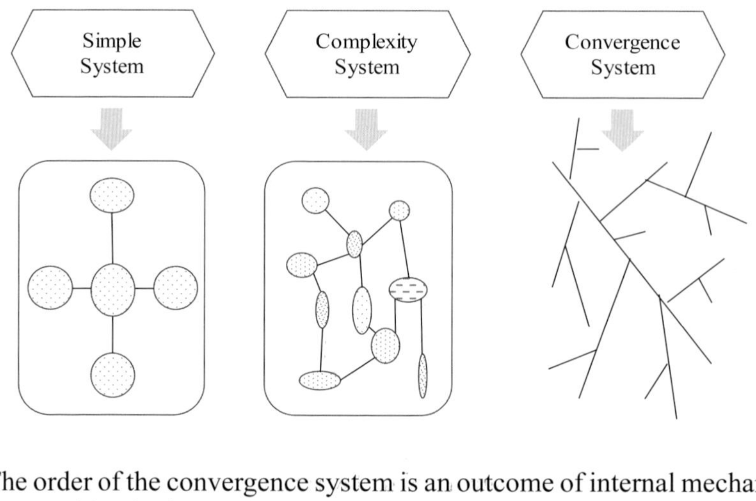

The order of the convergence system is an outcome of internal mechanism represented by the interactions of its constituents. Therefore, in the concept, idea, and theory of convergence system, the relationship rather than structure is of greater significance. The network of the convergence system is nothing else than the set of lines that exhibit connective elements of the system. Henceforth, convergence system is neither exhaustive nor systematic irrespective of its coverage. The convergence system can be likened to the thread of Ariadne which presupposes the prospective expansion from local to global or human to non-human realms. It does not remain as a system circumscribed within a fixed boundary. As a boundless existence, the convergent system can extend itself to convergence galaxy encompassing the whole universe. Given the conception, differences between complexity system and convergence system can be identified as follows (Table 12-1).

Table 12-1 **Comparing Complexity System and Convergence System**

Type	Complexity System	Convergence System
Degree of Complexity	Complex	Hyper-Complex
Focal Point	Node	Link
Key Concept	Structure	Relation
Metaphor	Tree	Rhizome
Coverage	Biosphere / Pseudo Biosphere	Total Universe
Theoretical Basis	Complexity Theory	Actor Network Theory
Division of System-Environment	Yes	No
Mode of Statement	Explanation	Description
Working Principle	Causality	Agencemen (Arrangement)
Goals	Harmonic Order	Hybrid Order
Zeitgeist	Modern	Non-Modern

IV. Discussion

Convergent civilization is the result of multi-dimensional transactions of techno-scape (development of digital technology), econo-scape (establishment of flexible regime of accumulation), politico-scape (reformulation of power structure), socio-scape (global extension of personal interdependence), culture-scape (spread of multiculturalism) and idea-scape (diffusion of postmodernism).

Again, it should be noted that convergence is not just a process of aggregation. It is an articulation process comprised of continuous series of diversification and confluence. Though the convergent society can be considered as a huge complexity system, it tends to incorporate such properties as hyper-openness, multiplicity, a-linearity, co-production and it reaches the state of convergence system substantially differentiated from conventional complexity system. The convergence system also takes into account the relationships between human and the non-human such as cyborgs, which were merely a topic of discussions in the past. Thus, the convergence system is expected to instigate a new worldview as being described by such dictum as "Nothing is free from convergence."

The human society has been developing from pre-industrial stage, through industrial stage and up to current post-industrial stage, i.e., the stage of information society. Then, how can we define the substance of the post-information society endowed with a new Zeitgeist of non-modernism? In regards to this, George Gilder suggests "Telecosm (Gilder, 2000)," Castells suggests a "Network Society (Castell, 2009)," Rolf Jensen and Gim Dator suggests a "Dream Society (Jensen, 1999; Dator, 2011[2007])," Daniel Pink suggests a "Conceptual Age (Pink, 2006)" and Jeremy Rifkin suggests an "Empathic Civilization (Rifkin, 2009)." "Convergent Civilization" is my answer to the question.

In light of convergent civilization paradigm, the information society (or digital society, cyber society and the like) cannot be considered as an independent civilization unit as it does not possess longevity. Instead, information society is considered as a momentary phase briefly marking the period of transition from high industrial civilization to convergence civilization stage. Thus, it would be regarded as a step before convergence civilization or a civilization of transient category soon to arrive at best. Information society, in other words, is the transition in between the industrial civilization and the convergence civilization to come.

References

Agre, E. Philip. 1997. "Surveillance and Capture: Two Models of Privacy." *The Information Society* 10: 101-127.

Altman, Drew, John Benson, Marcus Rosenbaum, Minah Kim, Mollyann Brodie, Rebecca Flournoy and Robert Blendon. 2001. "Whom to Protect and How? *Brookings Review* 19(1): 44-49.

Amin, Ash. ed. 1994. *Post-Fordism: A Reader*. Blackwell.

ARPI. 2012. *The Risk Policy Model, 2102 Edition*. Australian Risk Policy Institute.

Attali, Jacques. 1998. *Dictionnaire du XXIe siècle*. Fayard.

Auh, Taik-Sup. 2000. "Language Divide and Knowledge Gap in Cyberspace: Beyond Digital Divide." Retrieved from: http://www.unesco.or.kr/cyberlang/auhtaeksup.htm

Auletta, Ken. 2009. *Googled: The End of the World As We Know It*. Penguin.

Barabási, Albert-Lászió. 2002. *Linked: The New Science of Networks*. Perseus Publishing.

Barthes, Roland. 1973. *Mythologies*. Paladin.

Baudrillard, Jean. 1983. *Simulations*. Simiotext.

Bauman, Zygmunt. 2001. "The Great War of Recognition." *Theory, Culture & Society* 18(2/3): 137-150.

Bauman, Zygmunt, and David Lyon. 2013. *Liquid Surveillance: A Conversation*. John Wiley & Sons.

Beck, Ulrich and Elisabeth Beck-Gernsheim. 2002. *Individualization: Institutionalized Individualism and its Social and Political Consequences*. Sage.

Beck, Ulrich. 1992. *Risk Society: Toward a New Modernity*. Sage.

Beck, Ulrich. 2002. "The Terrorist Threat: World Risk Society Revisited." *Theory, Culture & Society* 19(4): 39-55.

Bell, Daniel. 1973. *The Coming of Postindustrial Society: A Venture in Social Forecasting*. Basic Books.

Bell, Gordon, and Jim Gemmell. 2009. *Total Recall: How the E-memory Revolution Will Change Everything*. Penguin.
Bendix, Reinhard. 1960. *Max Weber: An Intellectual Portrait*. Doubleday.
Beniger, R. James. 1986. *The Control Revolution: Technological and Economic Origins of the Information Society*. Harvard University Press.
Bentham, Jeremy. 1791. *Jeremy Bentham: Collected Work*, edited by J. Bowring, Athlone Press.
Berger, Peter. 1967. *The Sacred Canopy: Elements of a Sociological Theory of Religion*. Doubleday.
Berger, Peter and Hansfried Kellner. 1964. "Marriage and the Construction of Reality: An Exercise in the Microsociology of Knowledge." *Diogenes*. 12(46): 1-23.
Berger, Peter and Thomas Luckmann. 1991. *The Social Construction of Reality: A Treatise in the Sociology of Knowledge*. Penguin.
Berlin, Isaiah. 2002. *Liberty: Incorporating Four Essays on Liberty*. Oxford University Press.
Bjiker, E. Wiebe. 1993. "Do Not Dispair: There is Life after Constructivism." *Science, Technology & Human Values* 18: 113-138.
Bjiker, E. Wiebe. 1995. *Bicycles, Bikelites, and Bulbs: Toward a Theory of Sociotechnical Change*. MIT Press.
Bijker, Wiebe E., Thomas P. Hughes and Trevor J. Pinch. eds. 1987. *The Social Construction of Technological Systems: New Directions in the Sociology and History of Technology*. MIT press.
Blaut, M. James. 2000. *Eight Eurocentric Historians*. Guilford Press.
Blumer, Herbert. 1954. "What is Wrong with Social Theory." *American Sociological Review* 18: 3-10.
Boehlefeld, S. Polancic. 1996. "Doing the Right Thing: Ethical Cyberspace Research." *The Information Society* 12(2): 141-152.
Bogard, Willam. 1996. *The Simulation of Surveillance: Hypercontrol in Telematic Societies*. Cambridge University Press
Boudrillard, Jean. 2004. "This is the Fourth World War: The Der Spiegel Interview with Jean Baudrillard." *International journal of Baudrillard Stidies* 1(1). Retrieved from: https://www2.ubishops.ca/baudrillardstudies/vol1_1/spiegel.htm
Bourdieu, Pierre. 1984[1979]. *Distinction: A Social Critique of the Judgement of Taste*. Harvard University Press.
Bourdieu, Pierre and Loic Wacquant. 1992. *An Invitation to Reflexive Sociology*. University of Chicago Press.
Brasher, Brenda. 2001. *Give Me That Online Religion*. Jossey-Bass.
Braudel, Fernand. 1960. "History and the Social Sciences: Long Duration." *American Behavioral Scientist* 3(6): 3-13.
Brooks, David. 2000. *BOBOS in Paradise: The New Upper Class and How They Got There*. Simon & Schuster.

Brynjolfsson, Erik, and Andrew McAfee. 2014. *The Second Machine Age: Work, Progress, and Prosperity in a Time of Brilliant Technologies*. W. W. Norton & Company.

Burnham, David. 1983. *The Rise of Computer State*. Random House.

Burton, Suzan. 2007. *Terrorism and Homeland Security, 2nd. Edition*. Thompson Higher Education.

Callon, Michel, Arie Rip and John Law. eds. 1988. *Mapping the Dynamics of Science and Technology*. Macmillan.

Campbell, Jennifer, Paul Trapnell, Steven Heine, Ilana Katz, Loraine Lavallee and Darrin Lehman. 1996. "Self-Concept Clarity: Measurement, Personality Correlates and Cultural Boundaries." *Journal of Personality and Social psychology* 70(1): 141-156.

Capra, Fritjof. 1996. *The Web of Life*. Brockman.

Carpenter, Edmund. 1982. "The New Languages." In *Inter/Media*, edited by G. Gumpert and R. Cathcart. Oxford University Press.

Castells, Manuel. 1989. *The Information City*. Blackwell.

______. 1996. *The Rise of the Network Society*. Blackwell.

______. 1997. *The Power of Identity*. Oxford: Blackwell.

______. 1998. *End of Millenium*. Oxford: Blackwell.

______. 2009. *Communication Power*. Oxford University Press.

Castells, Manuel. ed. 2009. *The Network Society: A Cross-Cultural Perspective*. Edward Elga.

Castells, Manuel, Mireia Fernández-Ardèvol, Jack Linchuan Qiu and Araba Sey. 2006. *Mobile Communication and Society: A Global Perspective*. MIT Press.

Christakis, Nicholas and James Fowler. 2009. *Connected: The Surprising Power of Our Social Networks and How They Shape Our Lives*. Little, Brown and Company.

Clarke, Roger. 1994. "The Digital Persona and Its Application to Data Surveillance." *The Information Society* 10(2): 77-92.

Coalition for Abolition of Electronic National ID Card. 1997. *Electronic ID Card and the Coming of Electronic Surveillance Society*.

Cohen, Jean and Andrew Arato. 1992. *Civil Society and Political Theory*. MIT Press

Collins, Randal. 2000. "Situational Stratification: A Micro-Macro Theory of Inequality." *Sociological Theory* 18(1): 17-43.

Compaine, Benjamin. 1986. "Information Gaps: Myth or Reality?" *Telecommunications Policy* 10(1): 5-12.

Compaine, Benjamin. ed. 2001. *The Digital Divide: Facing a Crisis or Creating a Myth?* MIT Press.

Cooley, C. Horton. 1992. *Social Organization: A Study of the Larger Mind*. Transaction Books.

Cox, Harvey. 1977. *Turning East: The Promise and Peril of the New Orientalism*. Simon and Schuster.

Crook, Stephen, Jan Pakulski and Macolm Waters. 1992. *Postmodernization: Change in Advanced Society*. Sage.

Croteau, D. and W. Hoynes. 2000. *Industries, Images and Audiences*, Fine Forge Press.

Dator, A. James. 2011[2001]. "From Information Society to Dream Society." Retrieved from: http://adamas76.springnote.com/pages/58765?print=1

Deleuze, Gilles and Felix Gattari. 1999. *Anti-Oedipus: Introduction to Schizoanalysis*. Routledge.

Denney, David. 2005. *Risk and Society*. Sage.

Department of Domestic Affairs, Republic of Korea. 1996. *Proposal for Electronic National Identification Card*

______. 1997. *Congress Report for the Explanation of the Revised Electronic National Identification Card Proposal*

Derrida, Jacques. 1978. *Writing and Difference*. Routledge & Kegan Paul.

Dibbell, Julian. 1998. "A Rape in Cyberspace." In Composing *Cyberspace: Identity, Community, and Knowledge in the Electronic Age*, edited by R. Holeton. McGraw Hill: 83-98.

Diener, Ed. 2000. "Subjective Well-Being: The Science of Happiness and a Proposal for a National Index." *American Psychologist* 55(1): 34-43.

Doty, Philip. 2001. "Digital Privacy: Toward a New Politics and Discursive Practice." *Annual Review of Information Science and Technology* 35: 115-245.

Durkheim, Émile. 1947. *The Elementary Forms of Religious Life*, translated by J. W. Swain. Free Press.

Durkheim, Émile. 1947[1893]. *The Division of Labor in Society*, translated by G. Simpson. Free Press.

Edgell, Stephen. 1993. *Class*. Routledge.

Eldridge, John. 1999. *Risk, Society and the Media: Now you See it, Now you Don't*. Longman.

Elias, Norbert. 2000[1939]. *The Civilization Process: Sociogenetic and Psychogenetic Investigations*. Blackwell.

Elliott, Anthony. 2001. *Concepts of the Self*. Polity.

Ellison, Nicole, Charles Steinfield and Cliff Lampe. 2007. "The Benefits of Facebook "Friends": Social Capital and College Students' Use of Online Social Network Sites." *Journal of Computer Mediated Communication* 12(4): 1143-1168.

Ellul, Jacques. 2018[1964]. *The Technological System*. Wipf and Stock Publishers.

Erikson, H. Erik. 1968. *Identity, Youth, and Crisis*. W. W. Norton & Co.

Etzioni, Amitai. 1999. *The Poverty of Privacy*. Basic Books.

Faubion, D. James. 1999. *Aesthetics, Method, and Epistemology: Essential Works of Foucault, 1954-1984*, Vol II. New Press.

Flaherty, David. 1989. *Protecting Privacy in Surveillance Societies: The Federal Republic of Germany, Sweden, France, Canada and the United States*. Random House.

Forrester, W. Jay. 1968. *Principles of Systems*. Productivity Press.

Forster, Tom, and Perry Morrison. 1994. *Computer Ethics: Cautionary Tales and Ethical Dilemmas in Computing*, 2nd. Ed. MIT Press.

Foucault, Michel. 1975. *Discipline and Punishment: The Birth of the Prison*. Allen Lane.

Freud, Sigmund. 2002[1930]. *Civilization and Its Discontents*. Penguin.

Fromm, Erich. 1976. *To Have or to Be: A New Blueprint for Mankind*. Harper & Row.

Fuglsang, Lars. 2001. "Three Perspectives in STS in the Policy Context." In *Visions of STS*, edited by S. Cutcliffe and C. Mitcham. State University of New York Press.

Ganascia, G. Jean. 2010. "The Generalized Sousveillance Society." *Social Science Information* 49(3): 489-507.

Gandy, H. Oscar. 1993. *The Panoptic Sort: A Political Economy of Personal Information*. Westview.

Gans, Herbert. 1974. *Popular Culture and High Culture: An Analysis and Evaluation Of Taste*. Basic books.

Gibson, William. 1984. *Neuromancer*. Mass Market.

Giddens, Anthony. 1991. *Modernity and Self Identity: Self and Society in the Late Modern Age*. Blackwell.

______. 1999. *Runaway World: How Globalization is Reshaping our Lives*. Profile Books.

Gilder, George. 2000. *Telecosm: How Infinite Bandwidth will Revolutionize our World*. Free Press.

Gilkey, Langdon. 1959. *Maker of Heaven and Earth: The Christian Doctrine of Creation in the Light of Modern Knowledge*. Doubleday.

Gillmor, Dan. 2004. *We the Media*. O'Reilly Media.

Goffman, Erving. 1959. *The Presentation of Self in Everyday Life*. Doubleday Anchor.

Granovetter, G. Mark. 1973. "The Strength of Weak Ties." *American Journal of Sociology* 78: 1360-1380.

Green, Stephen. 1999. "A Plague on the Panopticon: Surveillance and Power in the Global Information Economy." *Information Communication & Society* 2(1): 26-44.

Gurrin, Cathal, Alan Smeaton and Aiden Doherty. 2014. "LifeLogging: Personal Big Data." Foundations and Trends in Information Retrieval 8-1: 1-107. Retrieved from: http://doras.dcu.ie/19998/1/FnTIR_lifelogging_journal.pdf

Guyer, Paul. ed. 1992. *The Cambridge Companion to Kant*. Cambridge University Press.

Habermas, Jürgen. 1981. *Theorie des kommunikativen Handelns : Handlungsrationalitaet und gesellschaftliche Rationalisierung*. Suhrkamp.

______. 1989. *Vorstudien und Ergaenzungen zur Theorie des kommunikativen Han-*

delns. Suhrkamp.

______. 1996. *Der Philosphische Diskurs der Moderne*. Suhrkamp.

Haggerty, Kevin and Richard Ericson. 2000. "The Surveillant Assemblage." *British Journal of Sociology* 51(4): 605-622.

Han, Byung-Chul. 2012. *Transparentzgesellschaft*. Matthers & Seitz Berlin Cerlagsgesellschaft mbH.

Hankuk-Ilbo. 1997. "Hidden Camera in the Lady's Room in a Large Department Store." (07/19/1997). (Korean).

Hara, Junske. and Kazuo Seiyama. 1999. *Social Stratification: Inequality in Affluence*. Tokyo University Press.

Hardt, Michael, and Antonio Negri. 2004. *Multitude: War and Democracy in the Age of Empire*. Penguin.

Harvey, David. 1989. *The Condition of Post modernity: An Enquiry into the Origins of Cultural Change*. Basil Blackwell.

Hawkins, J. David. 2000. "Privacy is Under Siege at Work, at Home and Online." *U.S. News & World Report* 10/02/2000 129(13): 62-68.

Helliwelll, John and Robert Putnam. 2004. "The Social Context of Well-Being." *Philos Trans R Soc Lond B Bil Sci* 359(1449): 1435-1446.

Highsmith, Patricia. 1970. *Ripley Under Ground*. Heinemann.

Hobbes, Thomas. 1642. *De Cive(On the Citizen)*. Retrieved from: http://en.wikipedia.org/wiki/De_Cive

Hochschild, R. Arlie. 1983. *The Managed Heart*. University of California Press.

Hong, Sung-Min and Joo-Hong Min. 2001. "Weakening Middle Class during IMF Period." *Sourcebook of Hyndai Institute for Economic Research*.

Honneth, Axel. 2001. "Recognition or Redistribution?: Changing Perspectives on the Moral Order of Society." *Theory, Culture & Society* 18(2/3): 43-55.

Huntington, P. Samuel. 1996. *The Clash of Civilizations and the Remaking of World Order*. Simon & Schuster.

Husserl, Edmund. 1954. *Gesammelte Werke, Husserliana*. Martinu Njihoff.

Husserl, Edmund. 1965[1910]. "Philosophy as Rigorous Science." In *Phenomenology and the Crisis of Philosophy*, translated and edited by Q. Lauer. Harper & Row.

Hwang, Joo-Seong. 2009. *General Report on Digital Convergence-Based Future Society*. Korea Information Society Development Institute. (Korean).

Illouz, Eva. 2006. *Cold Intimacies: The Making of Emotional Capitalism*. Polity.

Inglehart, Ronald. 1990. *Culture Shift in Advanced Industrial Society*. Princeton University.

Jenkins, Henry. 2006. *Convergence Culture: Where Old and New Media Collide*. NYU Press.

Jenkins, Richard. 2014. *Social Identity*, Fourth Edition. Routledge.

Jensen, V. Roderick. 1999. *The Dream Society: How the Coming Shift from Information to Imagination will Transfer Your Business?* McGraw-Hill.

John, P. Oliver, and Sanjay Srivastava. 1999. "The Big Five Trait Taxonomy: History, Measurement and Theoretical Perspectives." in *Handbook of Personality: Theory and Research*, 2nd. Ed, edited by L. Pervin. Guilford Press.

Jones, Steve. 1995. *Cybersociety: Computer-Mediated Communication and Community*. Sage.

______. 1997. *Virtual Culture: Identity and Communication in Cybersociety*. Sage.

JoongAng Daily. 2003. "Viewpoint: We Must Computerize Education." (06/12/2003). (Korean).

Jordan, Tim. 1999. *Cyberpower: The Culture and Politics of Cyberspace of the Internet*. Routledge.

Kahneman, Daniel, Edward Diener and Norbert Schwarz. Eds. 1999. "Well-being: The Foundations of Hedonic Psychology." Russell Sage Foundation.

Kant, Immanuel. 1991. "Perpetual Peace: A Philosophical Sketch." In *Kant's Political Writings*, 2nd. Ed, edited by H. Reiss. Cambridge University Press.

Kellner, Dougals. 2004. Baudrillard, Globalization and Terrorism: Some Comments on Recent Adventures of the Image and Spectacle on the Occasion of Baudrillard's 75th Birthday. Retrieved from: http://www. gseis.ucla.edu/faculty/kellner.

Kilger, Max. 1994. "The Digital Individual." *The Information Society* 10(2): 93-99.

Kim, Eung-Chul. 2000. "Religious Practices and Missionary Activities on Internet." Paper Presented at the 2nd Symposium of The Korean Society for Buddhist Studies. Chonnam National University. October 14. 2000. (Korean).

Kim, Hwan-Suk. 2006. *Problems in Sociology of Science and Technology*. Munjee Books. (Korean).

Kim, Kee-Joong. 1997. "Problems of Electronic National ID Card and the Possibility of Electronic Surveillance Society." *Journal of Cybercommunication Studies* 1: 88-110. (Korean).

Kim, Jong-Kil. 2013. *Peeping Tom Society*. Jipmoonding. (Korean).

Kim, Jong-Kil and Mun-Cho Kim. 2007. *Understanding Digital Korea*. Jipmoondang. (Korean).

Kim, Mun-Cho. 1999. *Science Technology and the Future of Korea*. Korea University Press. (Korean).

______. 2001. "Youths in the Information Age." *Social Study* 2(2): 13-36. (Korean).

______. 2008. *Future of Information Society and Searching for a New Paradigm of Media Policy*. Korea Information Society Development Institute. (Korean).

______. 2013. *The Coming of Convergence Civilization: From the Age of Analysis to the Age of Synthesis*. Nanam Publishing. (Korean).

Kim, Mun-Cho and Jong-Kil Kim. 2006. *Social Conflict and Conflict Management in the Technological Era*. The Korean Federation of Science and Technological Studies. (Korean).

Kim, Min-Hwan. 2002. *History of Journalism in Korea*. Nanam. (Korean).

Kim, Nam-Og. 2011. *A Sociological Study of Body in the High-tech Age*. Ph.D. Dis-

sertation, Department of Sociology. Korea University. (Korean).
Kingston, W. Paul. 2000. *The Classless Society*. Stanford University Press.
Kitchin, Rob. 1998. *Cyberspace: The World in the Wires*. John Wiley.
Kling, Rob. ed. 1996. *Computerization and Controversy: Value Conflicts and Social Choices*, 2nd. Ed. Academic Press.
Kling, Rob. 2000. "Learning about Information Technologies and Social Change: The Contribution of Social Informatics." *The Information Society* 16(3): 217-232.
Kling, Rob, Mark Ackerman and Jonathan Allen. 1995. "Information Entrepreneurialism, Information Technologies, and the Continuing Vulnerability of Privacy." *Computerization and Controversy*, 2nd. Ed. Academic Press, Inc.
Kling, Rob and Roberta Lamb, 2000. "IT and Organizational Change in Digital Economies: A Sociotechnical Approach." In *Understanding the Digital Economy*, edited by B. Kahnin. MIT Press.
Knights, David and Hugh Wilmott. 1988. *New Technology and the Labour Process*. Palgrave.
Koh, Young-Sam. 1997. "Electronic National ID Card and Routinization of the Privacy Invasion." *Korean Economy and Society* 35: 163-184.
Kourvetaris, George A. 1996. *Political Sociology: Structure and Process*. Allyn & Bacon.
Kroger, Jane. 1989. *Identity in Adolescence: The Balance Between Self and Other*. Routledge
Lash, Scott and John Urry. 1994. *Economics of Signs and Space*. Sage.
Latour, Bruno. 1991. *Nous n'avons jamais ete modernes*. La Decouverte.
______. 1997. "On Actor-Network Theory: A Few Clarifications plus More Than a Few Complications." Retrieved from: http://www.cours.fsu.ulaval.ca/edc-65804/latour-clarifications.pdf
______. 2005. *Reassembling the Social: An Introduction to Actor-Network-Theory*. Oxford University Press.
Lewenstein, Bruce. ed. 1992. *When Science Meets the Public*. Committee on Public Understanding.
Loader, D. Brian. ed. 1997. *The Governance of Cyberspace: Politics, Technology and Global Restructuring*. Routledge.
Luhmann, Niklas. 1995. *Systems Theory*. Stanford University Press.
Luhmann, Niklas. 1995[1984]. *Social Systems*. Stanford University Press.
Luhmann, Niklas. 1993[1991]. *Risk: A Sociological Theory*. Aldine De Gruyter.
Lupton, Deborah. 2016. *The Quantified Self*. Polity.
Lyon, David. 1988. *The Information Society: Issues and Illusions*. Polity.
______. 1994. *The Electronic Eye: The Rise of Surveillance Society*, University of Minnesota Press.
______. 1995. The Roots of the Information Society Idea." In *Information Technology and Society: A Reader*, edited by N. Heap. Sage: 52-73

______. 2001. Surveillance Society: Monitoring Everyday Life. Open University Press.

______. 2003. Surveillance after September 11, Blackwell Publishers.

Mackinnon, Richard Clark. 1995. "Searching for the Leviathan in Usenet." In *Cybersociety*, edited by S. Jones. Sage.

McAdam, Douglas, Linda Sterns, David Uglow and James Rule. 1984. *The Politics of Privacy: Planning for Personal Data System as Powerful Technologies*. Mentor.

Mann, Steve, Jason Nolan and Barry Wellman. 2003. "Sousveillance: Inventing and Using Wearable Computing Devices for Data Collection in Surveillance Environments." *Surveillance & Society* 1(3): 331-355.

Marcuse, Herbert. 1987. *Eros and Civilization: A Philosophical Inquiry into Freud*. Routledge.

Marx, T. Gary. 1985. "I'll Be Watching You: Reflection on the New Surveillance." *Dissent* 32(1): 26-34.

______. 1996. "The Case of the Omniscient Organization." In *Computerization and Controversy: Value Conflicts and Social Choices*, edited by R. Kling. Academic Press: 316-321.

Marx, Karl. 1967[1867]. *Capital, Vol. 1*. International Publishers.

______. 2007[1859]. *A Contribution to the Critique of Political Economy*. Kessinger Publishing.

Marx, Karl. and Friedrich Engels. 1954[1848]. *The Communist Manifesto*. Gateway.

Masuda, Yoneji. 1980. *The Information Society as Post Industrial Society*. Institute for the Information Society.

Maturana, Humberto and Francisco Varela. 1980. *Autopoiesis and Cognition: The Realization of the Living*. D. Reidel.

Maturana, Humberto. 1988. "Ontology of Observing : The Biological Foundations of Self-Consciousness and the Physical Domain of Existence." Retrieved from: http://www. inteco.cl/biology/ontology.

Maturo, Antonio. 2004. "Network Governance as a Response to Risk Society Dilemmas: A Proposal from the Sociology of Health." *Topoi* 23: 195-202.

Mayer, Verena. 2008. *Edmund Husserl: Logische Untersuchungen*. Akademie Verlag.

McGrath, E. Aliste. 1998. *The Foundation of Dialogue in Science & Religion*. Blackwell.

______. 1999. *Science & Religion: An Introduction*. Oxford: Blackwell.

McLuhan, Marshall. 1994. *Understanding Media: The Extension of Man*. McGraw-Hill.

McLuhan, Marshall. 1963. *The Gutenberg Galaxy*. RKP.

McLuhan, Marshall, and Quentin Fiore. 1968. *Medium is Message: An Inventory of Effects*. Penguin.

Merleau-Ponty, Mourice. 1962[1945]. *Phenomenology of Perception*, translated by

M. C. Smith. Humanities Press.
Michael, Donald. 1972. "Enriched or Impoverished? Master or Servant?," *Information Technology: Some Critical Implication for Decision Makers*. The Conference Board.
Michael, Mike. 2002. "Comprehension, Apprehension, Prehension: Heterogeneity and the Public Understanding of Science," *Science, Technology & Human Values* 27(3): 357-378.
Mills, Charles W. 1956. *Power Elite*. Oxford Press.
Morgan, L. Henry. 1877. *Ancient Society*. MacMillan.
Morrows, A. Raymond. 2009. "Norbert Elias and Figuration Sociology: The Comeback of the Century." *Contemporary Sociology: Journal of Reviews* 38: 215-219.
Mosco, Vincent and Janet Wasco. eds. 1995. *The Political Economy of Information*. University of Wisconsin Press.
Mueller, Walt. 1998. *Understanding Today's Youth Culture*. Tyndale House Publishers. Inc.
NASA. 2010. "Discovery of 'Arsenic-Bug' Expands Definition of Life." *NASA Science News* (December 2, 2010).
Norris, Pippa. 2001. *Digital Divide: Civic Engagement, Information Poverty, and the Internet Worldwide*. Cambridge University Press.
O'Hara, Kieron., Mischa, M. Tuffield and Nigel Shadbolt. 2008. "Lifelogging: Privacy and Empowerment with Memories for Life." IDIS I: 155-172.
O'Dea, F. Thomas. 1966. *The Sociology of Religion*. Prentice-Hall.
OECD. 2000.*The Digital Divide: Enhancing Access to ICTs*. OECD Publications Service.
______. 2001. *Understanding the Digital Divide*. OECD Publications Service.
______. 2003. *Emerging Systematic Risks in the 21th Century*. OECD Publications Service.
Offe, Claus. 2010. "Was (falls überhapt etwas) können wir uns heute unter politischem 'Fortschritt' vorstellen?" *Westend Neue Zeitschrift für Sozialforschung* 7(2): 3-13.
Pagels, R. Heinz. 1984. *The Cosmic Code: Quantum Physics and the Language of Nature*. Penguin.
Park, Hyung-Jun. 2003. "Analysis of Class Structure and Policy Strategy for Social Equality in the Information Age." Institute for IT Strategy, *Proceedings for Future Strategy Forum*. (Korean).
Park, Su-Ho. 2000. "Buddhist Religious Life in Cyberspace." *The Buddhist Review* 2(Winter): 299-319.
Pecora, Vincent P. 2002. "The Culture of Surveillance." *Qualitative Sociology* 25(3): 345-58.
Pink, H. Daniel. 2006. *A Whole New Mind: Why Right-Brains Will Rule the Future*. Berkeley Publishing.

Pongs, Armin. 1999. *In welcher Gesellschaft leben wir eigentlich?* Band 1: Dilemma Verlag.

Poster, Mark. 1990. *The Mode of Information: Postmodernism and Social Context*. University of Chicago Press.

______. 1995. *The Second Media Age*. Polity Press.

Postman, Neil. 1985. *Amusing Ourselves to Death: Public Discourse in the Age of Show Business*. Penguin.

Prince, Dale J. 2014. "The Quantified Self: Operationalising the Quotidien." Electronic Resources in Medical Libraries 11(2): 91-99.

Prior, Markus. 2007. *Post-Broadcast Democracy*. Cambridge University Press.

Progress Network. 1997. "Electronic ID Card and the Coming of Electronic Surveillance Society." A Sourcebook.

Putnam, D. Robert. 2000. *Bowling Alone: The Collapse and Revival of American Community*. Simon & Schuster.

Rao, Madanmohan. 2001. "Struggling with the Digital Divide: Internet Infrastructure, Content, and Culture." Retrieved from: http://www.isoc.org/oti/articles/1000/rao.html

Redden, Jim. 2000. *Snitch Culture: How Citizens are Turned into the Eyes and Ears of the State*. Feral House.

Reid, M. Elizabeth. 1991. "Electropolis: Communication and Community on Internet Relay Chat." *Electronically Distributed Version of Honors Thesis for the Department of History*, University of Melbourne.

Rheingold, Howard. 1993a. *The Virtual Community: Homesteading on the Electronic Frontier*. A William Patrick Book.

______. 1993b. "A Slice of Life in My Virtual Community." In *Global Networks*, edited by L. M. Harasim. MIT Press: 57-80.

Rifkin, Jeremy. 2000. *The Age of Access: The New Culture of Hypercapitalism, Where All of Life Is a Paid-for Experience*. Putnam.

______. 2009. *The Empathic Civilization: The Race to Global Consciousness in a World in Crisis*. Jeremy P. Tarcher.

Robins, Kevin and Frank Webster. 1999. *Times of Technoculture*. Routledge.

Roderick, Rick. 1986. *Habermas and the Foundation of Critical Theory*. Macmillan.

Rowe, Gene and Lynn Frewer. 2005. "A Typology of Public Engagement Mechanism." *Science, Technology & Human Values* 30(2): 251-290.

Rushkoff, Douglas. 1996. *Playing the Future: How Kid's Culture Can Teach Us to Thrive in an age of Chaos*. HaperCollins.

Ryu, Seoung-Ho. 1999. "Net Generation in the Network Age." *Education Arena 21*, April: 38-41 (Korean).

______. 2012. *Are You Social?* Samsung Economic Research Institute (Korean).

Sachs, Hiram. 1995. "Computer Networks and The Formation of Public Opinion: An Ethnographic Study." *Media, Culture and Society* 17: 81-99.

Said, W. Edward. 1985. *Orientalism Reconsidered*. RKP.

Salvaggio, Jerry and Jennings Bryant. eds. 1989. *Media Use in the Information Age: Emerging Patterns of Adoption and Consumer Use*. Lawrence Erlbaum Associates.

Schiller, Herbert. 1984. *Information and The Crisis Economy*. Ablex Publishing Corporation.

______. 1996. *Information Inequality: The Deeping Social Crisis in America*. Routledge.

Schroeder, Ralph. ed. 2002. *The Social Life of Avartars*. Springer.

Schutz, Alfred. 1970. *On Phenomenology and Social Relations*, Introduced by H. Wagner. University of Chicago Press.

Schwartz, Barry. 2004. *The Paradox of Choice: Why Many is Less?* Harper Collins.

Sciolino, Elaine. 2005. August 1, "Europe Confronts Changing Face of Terrorism." *The New York Times*: A1(L).

Selke, Stefan. 2014. *Lifelogging*. Econ.

Sennett, Richard. 1998. *The Corrosion of Character*. W. W. Norton & Company.

Shin, Kwang-Yeong, Don-Mun Cho and Eun Cho. 2003. *Understanding Korean Class Structure*. Hanul. (Korean).

Shirky, C. 2008. *Here Comes Everybody: The Power of Organizing Without Organizations*. Penguin Press.

Slevin, James. 2000. *The Internet and Society*. Polity Press.

Slouka, Mark. 1995. *War of the Worlds: Cyberspace and the Assault on Reality*. Basic Books.

Smith, A. Marc. 1999. *Communities in Cyberspace*. Routledge.

Snow, P. Charles. 2012[1959]. *The Two Cultures*. Cambridge University Press.

Sorokin, Pitirim. 1959[1927]. *Social and Cultural Mobility*. Free Press.

Soukup. Petr. 1999. "On-Line Religion: A New Context for Religious Practice." *America* 180-16 (May 8): 8-10.

Spencer, Harbert. 1885[1874]. *The Principles of Sociology*. Appleton-Century-Crofts.

Steinfield, Charles, Nicole Ellison and Cliff Lampe. 2008. "Social Capital, Self-Esteem, and Use of Online Social Network Sites: A Longitudinal Analysis." *Journal of Applied Developmental Psychology* 29(6): 434-445.

Stephenson, Wen. 1995. "The Message is the Medium: A Reply to Sven Birkerts and *The Gutenberg Elegies*." *Chicago Review* 41(4): 116-130.

Stern, Paul C. and Harvey Fineberg, eds. 1996. *Understanding RISK: Informing Decisions in a Democratic Society*. National Academy Press.

Stone, Carole. 2001. *Networking: The Art of Making Friends*. Vermilion.

Swan, Melanie. 2015. "Connected Car: Quantified Self Becomes Quantified Car." *Sensor and Actuator Networks* 4-1: 2-29.

Swise, Peter. "Markets, Self-Regulation, and Government Enforcement in the Protection of Personal Information." *Working Paper Series*, Moritz College of Law if the Ohio State University (August 15, 1997). Retrived from: http://papers.ssrn.com/sol3/papers.cfm?abstract_id=11472

Tapscott, Don. 1998. *The Rise of the Net Generation: Growing up Digital*. McGraw Hill.

Taylor, Charles. 1992. *Multiculturalism and the Politics of Recognition*. Princeton University Press.

The Royal Society. 1985. *The Public Understanding of Science*.

Thomas, R. 1995. "Access and Inequality." In *Information Technology and Society: A Reader*, edited by N. Heap, R. Thomas, G. Einon, R. Mason and H. Mackay. Sage Publications: 90-100.

Thompson, J. Jarvis. 1990. *The Realm of Rights*. Harvard University Press.

Tichenor, P.J. , C.N. Olien and C.N. Donohue, 1970. "Mass Media Flow and Differential Growth in Knowledge." *Public Opinion Quarterly* 34: 197-209.

Toffler, Alvin. 1980. *The Third Wave*. Morrow.

Tönnis, Ferdinand. 1988. *Community & Society*. Transaction Books.

Touraine, Alain. 1988. *Return of the Actor: Social Theory in Postindustrial Society*. University of Minnesota Press.

Turkle, Sherry. 1995. *Life on the Screen: Identity in the Age of the Internet*. Simon & Schuster.

______. 2011. *Alone Together: Why We Expect More from Technology and Less from Each Other*. Basic Books.

______. ed. 2007. *Evocative Objects: Things we Think with*. MIT Press.

Turner, Bryan S. 1984. *The Body and Society: Explorations in Social Theory*. Basil Blackwell Publishing.

Turn, Rein. 1977. "Privacy protection in Information Systems." In *Advances in Computers* 16, edited by M.C. Yovits: 221-335.

U.S. Department of Commerce. 1995. "Falling Through the Net: A Survey of the 'Have Nots' in Rural and Urban America." Retrieved from: http://www.digitaldivide.gov/, July.

______. 1998. "Falling Through the Net II: New Data on the Digital Divide." Retrieved from: http://www.ntia.doc.gov/ntiahome/digitaldivide

______. 1999. "Falling Through the Net III: Defining the Digital Divide." Retrieved from: http://www.ntia.doc.gov/ntiahome/digitaldivide

______. 2000. "Falling Through the Net III: Toward Digital Inclusion." Retrieved from: http://www.ntia.doc.gov/ntiahome/digitaldivide

Valenzuela, Sebastián, Namsu Park and Kerk Kee. 2009. "Is There Social Capital in a Social Network Site? Facebook Use and College Students' Life Satisfaction, Trust, and Participation." *Journal of Computer-Mediated Communication* 14(4): 875-901.

Van Dijck, José. 2004. "FCJ-012 Composing the Self: Of Diaries and Lifelogs." *The Fibreculture Journal* 03.

______. 2013. *The Culture of Connectivity: A Critical History of Social Media*. Oxford University Press.

Virno, Paolo. 2003. *A Grammar of the Multitude*. MIT Press.

Wagner, Helmut. 1983. *Alfred Schutz: An Intellectual Biography*. University of Chicago Press.

Wajcman, Judy. 1991. *Feminism Confronts Technology*. Penn State Press.

Wallerstein, M. Immanuel. 1991. *Unthinking Social Science: The Limits of Nineteenth-Century Paradigms*. Temple University Press.

Walters, J. Gregory. 2001. *Human Rights in an Information Age: A Philosophical Analysis*. University of Toronto Press.

Weber, Max. 1946[1919]. *From Max Weber: Essays in Sociology*, translated and edited by H. Girth and C.W. Mills. Oxford University Press: 129-156.

Weber, Max. 1959[1920]. *The Protestant Ethic and the Spirit of Capitalism*. Charles. Scribner's sons.

Weber, Max. 1968[1921]. *Economy and Society*. Bedminister Press.

Webster, Frank. 1995. *Theories of the Information Society*. Routledge.

Webster, Frank. and Kevin Robins. 1986. *Information Technology: A Luddite Analysis*. Ablex Publishing.

Weeden, A. Kim. 1999. *From Borders to Barriers: Strategies of Occupational Closure and the Structure of Occupational Rewards*. Ph.D. Dissertation, Department of Sociology. Stanford University.

Weisband, P. Suzanne and Bruce. A. Reinig. 1995. "Managing User Perceptions of Email Privacy" *Communication of the ACM* 38(12): 40-47.

Wellman, Barry, Janet Salaff, Dimitrina Dimitrova, Laura Garton, Milena Gulia, and Caroline Haythornthwaite. 1996. "Computer Networks as Social Networks." *Annual Review of Sociology* 22: 211-238.

Wheeless, R. Lawrence. 1978. "A Follow-up Study of the Relationship Among Trust, Disclosure, and Interpersonal Solidarity." *Human Communication Research* 4(2): 143-157.

Whitaker, Reg. 1999. *The End of Privacy*. Newpress.

Williams, Dmitri. 2006. "On and Off the 'Net': Scales for Social Capital in an Online Era." *Journal of Computer-Mediated Communication* 11(2): 593-628.

Wokler, Robert. 1995. *Rousseau*, Oxford University Press.

Wolf, Gary. 2009. "Know thyself: Tracking Every Facet of Life, from Sleep to Mood to Pain," 24/7/365. *Wired Magazine*, June, 2009.

World Bank. 2001. "World Bank Calls for a Narrowing of the 'Knowledge Gap' between Rich and Poor." *World Bank Group News Release* no. 99.

Wynne, Brian. 1991. "Knowledge in Context." *Science, Technology & Human Values* 16(1): 111-121.

______. 2006. "Public Engagement as a Means of Restoring Public Trust in Science: Hitting the Notes, but Missing the Music?" *Community Genetics* 9(3): 211-220.

Yoon, Do-Hyun. 2000. *Farewell to Class?* Hanul. (Korean).

Yun, Young-Min. 2000. *Politics in Cyberspace*. Hanyang University Press. (Korean).

Index